MALAWI IN MAPS

MALAWI IN MAPS

edited by
Swanzie Agnew, M.A.,
Professor in Geography, University of Malawi
and
Michael Stubbs, M.A., D.Phil.,
Associate Professor in Geography,
Lehman College of the City University of New York, USA;
formerly Senior Lecturer in Geography,
University of Malawi

UNIVERSITY OF LONDON PRESS LTD

ISBN 0 340 11768 0

University of London Press Ltd
St Paul's House, Warwick Lane, London EC4P 4AH

Printed and bound in the United Kingdom by
Hazell Watson & Viney Ltd, Aylesbury, Bucks

CONTENTS

LIST OF CONTRIBUTORS

SWANZIE AGNEW *Professor in Geography, University of Malawi*

J AMER *formerly Geography Master, Blantyre Secondary School*

C A BAKER, MBE *Principal, Institute of Public Administration, University of Malawi*

R W BUCKINGHAM *Secretary, Tobacco Control Commission of Malawi*

DIRECTOR OF FORESTRY AND GAME *Ministry of Agriculture and Natural Resources, Malawi*

J HALL *Ministry of Agriculture, Malawi*

G JACKSON *Senior Lecturer in Botany, University of Ibadan, Nigeria*

STELLA LINEHAM *Officer in charge of Rainfall Services, Department of Meteorological Services, Rhodesia*

LINLEY LISTER *Lecturer in Geology, University of Rhodesia*

R A MINCHELL *Director of Surveys, Malawi*

B PACHAI *Professor in History, University of Malawi*

J G PIKE *Food and Agriculture Organization (Project Manager, UNDP/SF/FAO Botswana Project) and formerly Principal Hydrologist, Malawi Government*

R H SCHMIDT *Assistant Professor in Geography, University of Texas at El Paso and formerly Lecturer in Geography, University of Malawi*

J F SHRODER *Associate Professor in Geography, University of Nebraska at Omaha and formerly Lecturer in Geography, University of Malawi*

A R STOBBS *Principal Scientific Officer, Land Resources Division, Directorate of Overseas Surveys, Tolworth, UK*

MICHAEL STUBBS *Visiting Associate Professor in Geography, Northwestern University and formerly Senior Lecturer in Geography, University of Malawi*

J D TORRANCE *Assistant Director, Department of Meteorological Services, Rhodesia*

A YOUNG *Lecturer in Environmental Sciences, University of East Anglia, UK*

ACKNOWLEDGMENTS

The editors and the publisher wish to thank the following for permission to reproduce copyright material:

The Government of Malawi for the basis of Maps, 2, 3, 4, 5, 7, 17, 35, 38, 39, 40, 56.

Thomas Nelson and Sons Ltd for a map extract on p. 23 taken from *Principles of physical geology* by Arthur Holmes; North Holland Publishing Company for a map extract on p. 21 taken from *Geochronology of equatorial Africa* by L Cahen and N J Snelling; Oxford University Press for three climatic tables on p. 30 and 139 taken from *Malawi: a geographical study* by J G Pike and G T Rimmington; and Pall Mall Press Ltd for the basis of Map 15 taken from *Political and economic geography of Malawi* by J G Pike.

NOMENCLATURE

Place-names which were inaccurately reproduced during the colonial period are being replaced by correct versions. All those for which definitive forms had been decided upon by the beginning of 1971 are shown in their revised form in this work. Those amended after the preparation of the maps could not be altered.

INTRODUCTION

Under the British administration, which was established in 1891, statistical information on the physical environment of the country that is now Malawi was systematically collected and utilized by the various government departments. However, it was not until after the Second World War, when reliable maps based upon aerial surveys began to be produced, that spatial relationships could be accurately mapped.

The 1966 Population Census was the first census to be carried out with a comprehensive demarcation of enumeration areas, and the final report, which appeared in 1968, included a brief summary of the data obtained in terms of the total population; geographic distribution and density; age and sex; racial and ethnic composition; languages spoken; economic characteristics; and population outside Malawi.

Since most of this material, particularly the demographic, economic and social aspects of the population structure now appears in map form for the first time, *Malawi in Maps* assumes the significance of a national atlas, at least in content if not in presentation. Its preparation was inspired by its very successful fore-runner, *Sierra Leone in Maps*, by Professor J I Clarke (University of London Press Ltd).

The amount of detail shown on the maps varies according to the data which were available, but it is hoped that the series will provide a useful background for the understanding of the rapidly changing geography of Malawi.

In the text metric measures have been given wherever possible followed by imperial measures in parentheses, but where in the text or on the maps equivalent measures would lead to complications, a conversion figure is given as a footnote to each table. Malawi currency was decimalized in 1970, and conversion from sterling to Malawian currency at the rate pertaining on 15th February 1971 is as follows:

£1 sterling is equivalent to 2 Kwachas
100 Tambala equal 1 Kwacha

The production of *Malawi in Maps* was made possible thanks to the help generously given by many organizations and people.

The editors are especially grateful for the advice, information and material which was supplied to them by the Secretary for Agriculture and by many of the officers of his Ministry, the Ministries of Education, Health and Community Development, Information and Tourism, Natural Resources, Trade and Industry, Transport and Communications, and the Town Planning Department of the Ministry of Works and Supplies, the Geological Survey Department, the Survey Department, the Meteorological Services of the Department of Civil Aviation, and the Physical Planning Division of the Office of the President and Cabinet.

They are also indebted to the Electricity Supply Commission of Malawi, the Farmers' Marketing Board and Malawi Railways Ltd for a great deal of very useful factual information.

Their thanks are due to the following: Mr J G Pike and to the Society of Malawi for permission to use the material contained in the paper on the *Hydrology of Lake Malawi* in the society's *Journal*, Vol. XXI, No. 2, July 1968, in the chapter on Hydrology in *Malawi in Maps*; and the Tea Association (Central Africa) Ltd for providing the information which appears in the chapter on tea.

The editors gratefully acknowledge the help they received from the following: Mr J Hall whose knowledge of Malawi and of the material available in maps was invaluable to them in the preliminary stages of planning; Mr Minchell, Director of Surveys, who had prepared and made available a base map on the scale of 2½ million on which distributions were plotted and for his permission to use information from maps published by the Department of Surveys; and Mr J Carver who very kindly supplied information on the Capital City Development Plan.

They also wish to express their indebtedness to Mr J Lupoka and Mr B Makwiti, draughtsmen in the Department of Geography at the University of Malawi, for their untiring help and devoted effort in the preparation of the maps for publication. A year before the work was completed, Mr Makwiti was called away to undertake further studies in the United Kingdom and, thereafter, Mr Lupoka assumed full responsibility for the preparation of the maps.

The editors wish to thank their fellow contributors for the preparation of texts and maps and for their forbearance at the delay in publication. Finally they would like to record their appreciation of the financial assistance given them by the Research Committee of the University of Malawi towards the costs incurred in the preparation of *Malawi in Maps*.

SWANZIE AGNEW
MICHAEL STUBBS

KEY TO INFORMATION AREAS

Material has been presented in this work either in relation to the official administrative sub-divisions of the country, or to unofficial divisions specially defined for the purpose of presenting data in relation to functional sub-divisions, and often coinciding with the fields of influence of urban centres of various defined categories. This was accomplished by aggregating data available only for the smallest data collection units, those defined for the purposes of the 1966 census: villages, urban areas, trading centres, missions and government stations. The relationships between official and unofficial sub-divisions will be discussed with respect to three spatial orders: first (national), second (regional) and third (sub-regional). Data has not been presented for smaller spatial sub-divisions, except in the aggregate situation mentioned above.

First order
Both official and unofficial data collection sub-divisions coincide at this, the national, level, and no further discussion is required.

Second order
The official administrative sub-divisions at this level are three ADMINISTRATIVE REGIONS, with headquarters at Mzuzu (Northern), Lilongwe (Central), and Blantyre (Southern). They consist of groups of administrative districts and their boundaries coincide with the aggregate district boundaries. The composition of each is as follows: *Northern*—Chitipa, Karonga, Nkhata Bay, Rumphi and Mzimba (five); *Central*—Kasungu, Ntchisi, Dowa, Lilongwe, Mchinji, Dedza, Ncheu, Salima and Nkhota Kota (nine); and *Southern*—Mangoche, Kasupe, Zomba, Chiradzulu, Blantyre, Thyolo, Mulanje, Chikwawa and Nsanje (nine). There are 23 administrative districts in the country. In the text the administrative regions are shown with an initial capital letter to distinguish them from the similarly named unofficial sub-divisions, which will be discussed next, and which are always shown with a small initial letter.

Seven unofficial data collection regions have been used, definition being based upon the configuration of the urban system of the country, which suggests a division of the Northern administrative Region into two sections, centred upon Karonga and Mzuzu respectively, between which is considerable transportation closure. These two unofficial regions have been designated the northern and north-central regions respectively. In order that data available for administrative districts might be presented for these unofficial regions, their boundaries coincide with aggregates of administrative districts. The Northern Region includes Chitipa and Karonga, and the north-central region includes Rumphi, Nkhata Bay, and Mzimba. For similar reasons the Central administrative Region was divided between the central lakeshore region, consisting of Nkhota Kota and Salima administrative districts, and the Central Region, which included Kasungu, Ntchisi, Dowa, Dedza, Lilongwe and Mchinji. Apart from Kachindomoto C.A. in Dedza District, which is located on the lakeshore lowlands, the whole of the region lies on the western plateau of the country. The remaining administrative district in the Central administrative Region, Ncheu, was placed in the south-central unofficial data collection region, together with Mangoche and Kasupe Districts of the Southern administrative Region. The remaining districts in this administrative region constituted the southern data collection region, with the exception of Chikwawa and Nsanje Districts which constituted the Lower Shire data collection region. Almost all of the boundaries coincide with major topographic boundaries which present also areas of closure of regional transportation networks and spheres of influence of second order urban centres. Only in the case of the south-central region is the delimitation somewhat artificial, in that this region has no well-developed regional centre as yet, and has some continuity of transportation with the Southern Region, the spheres of influence of Blantyre and Zomba extending northwards of their respective administrative district boundaries. Although they have some deficiencies, therefore, presentation of material for these seven unofficial regions permits more precise inter-regional comparison than does presentation in relation to the three larger, official, administrative regions.

Third order
The official sub-divisions at this level are chiefs' and sub-chiefs' areas, which include within them for data collection and presentation purposes, all smaller units, whether villages under headmen and group village headmen on non-alienated land, or urban centres, except for those incorporated, and trading centres, estates, missions and government stations, all on alienated land. The incorporated urban centres are the City of Blantyre, Municipality of Lilongwe, and Townships of Zomba, Mzuzu, Salima, Dedza, Mangoche, and Balaka.

The unofficial data collection and presentation sub-divisions at this level consist of thirty-six (third order) urban centres, including those incorporated and listed above, and their respective fields of transportation accessibility, whose boundaries are defined by transportation cost indifference between adjacent centres. Such boundaries were determined empirically, and all lower order units within them assigned to the respective third order urban centre. In the case of some of the presentation of demographic data the non-incorporated third order centres themselves (without their hinterlands, and as designated in the 1966 census, which defined them either as urban areas or as trading centres) were separately shown in addition to the chiefs' and sub-chiefs' areas within which they were located. In other presentations the data is presented for the third order urban centre and its hinterland as a single unit. The centres were themselves defined according to their central place functions.

Some of the chiefs' and sub-chiefs' areas had such small populations that individual presentation of material for them was impossible at the scale used, and so in a few areas several were aggregated. Chiefs' and sub-chiefs' areas and urban areas of third order are listed numerically for each administrative district, grouped numbers indicating the aggregations discussed above. The key to the numbered references is on pp. 46, 48 and 49.

In order to further clarify the distribution of population and social and economic indicators, those parts of the country unoccupied at the time of the 1966 census, defined specifically as those being located farther than one kilometre from the nearest officially recognized village, have been separately annotated on this and most other maps in this work. Some of these areas are, of course, utilized for grazing, occasional shifting agriculture, berry collecting, hunting, fishing, fuel collection and recreational purposes, and also contribute to the well-being of the country by acting as water conservation areas.

MICHAEL STUBBS

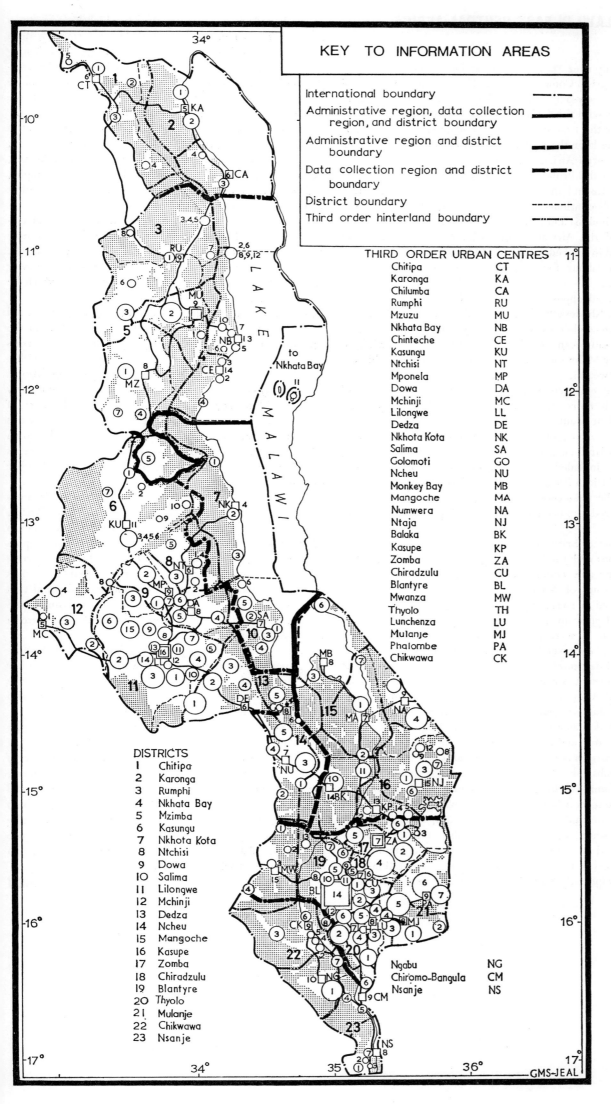

KEY TO INFORMATION AREAS

International boundary	—·—
Administrative region, data collection region, and district boundary	——
Administrative region and district boundary	——
Data collection region and district boundary	—·—
District boundary	- - -
Third order hinterland boundary	—··—

THIRD ORDER URBAN CENTRES

Chitipa	CT
Karonga	KA
Chilumba	CA
Rumphi	RU
Mzuzu	MU
Nkhata Bay	NB
Chinteche	CE
Kasungu	KU
Ntchisi	NT
Mponela	MP
Dowa	DA
Mchinji	MC
Lilongwe	LL
Dedza	DE
Nkhota Kota	NK
Salima	SA
Golomoti	GO
Ncheu	NU
Monkey Bay	MB
Mangoche	MA
Numwera	NA
Ntaja	NJ
Balaka	BK
Kasupe	KP
Zomba	ZA
Chiradzulu	CU
Blantyre	BL
Mwanza	MW
Thyolo	TH
Lunchenza	LU
Mulanje	MJ
Phalombe	PA
Chikwawa	CK
Ngabu	NG
Chiromo-Bangula	CM
Nsanje	NS

DISTRICTS

1 Chitipa
2 Karonga
3 Rumphi
4 Nkhata Bay
5 Mzimba
6 Kasungu
7 Nkhota Kota
8 Ntchisi
9 Dowa
10 Salima
11 Lilongwe
12 Mchinji
13 Dedza
14 Ncheu
15 Mangoche
16 Kasupe
17 Zomba
18 Chiradzulu
19 Blantyre
20 Thyolo
21 Mulanje
22 Chikwawa
23 Nsanje

GMS-JEAL

1 MALAWI IN EAST CENTRAL AFRICA

On 6th July 1964 Malawi became an independent state within the British Commonwealth. This marked the end of seventy-three years of British administration which began in May 1891 with the declaration that 'the Nyasaland Districts are under the Protectorate of Her Majesty the Queen'. A short time later the Nyasaland Districts were renamed the British Central African Protectorate.

In 1907 the Protectorate was gazetted as the Nyasaland Protectorate and an Executive Council was set up. Direct British rule continued until August 1953, when the Federation of Rhodesia and Nyasaland came into being against the wishes of the African people who believed the role of Nyasaland in the Federation would be to provide a reservoir of cheap labour for the white enterprises of the two Rhodesias.

Continued opposition by the Africans in Nyasaland and Northern Rhodesia finally brought the Federation to an end on 31st December 1963, and in July 1964 the protectorate of Nyasaland became the independent state of Malawi. Two years later Malawi was declared to be a Republic within the Commonwealth.

Malawi emerged from the turbulent experience of Federation more nearly a nation-state than many other independent countries in Africa. One of the reasons for this was that the core of the culturally homogeneous peoples, known as far back as the sixteenth century as the Amaravi, had been included within the boundaries of the British Central African Protectorate. This cluster of peoples, at the time of the 1966 census, numbered more than one million six hundred thousand out of a total population of four million.

As a former British territory Malawi has maintained close associations with the United Kingdom and some of the other Commonwealth countries. The currency, issued by the Reserve Bank of Malawi, is linked to sterling and was decimalized in 1971. English is the language used in parliament and government offices, and is also the medium of instruction in secondary schools and further education, including the University of Malawi which opened in 1965.

Malawi lies some 560 km. (350 miles) west of the Indian Ocean where it is marginal to the East African region with its coastal Arab culture and abuts upon the economic and cultural sphere of Southern Africa. The Yao people who are now settled in an area stretching from Mangoche (formerly Fort Johnston) and Dedza to Blantyre entered Malawi from the East African region where they had been trade associates of the Arabs. The Yao now form the southernmost outpost of the Islamic world in Africa. Ngoni warrior pastoralists, driven from their home areas by the wars and disturbances which accompanied the rise of the Zulu, entered Malawi from the south, and from the south also came the missionaries and white settlers who penetrated up the Zambezi and Shire Rivers in the wake of Livingstone's explorations.

Topographically Malawi is dominated by the final section of the East African rift valley system which here fractures the high plateau of south central Africa forming a deep trough. Lake Malawi, which is 570 km. (355 miles) long and 16 to 80 km. (10 to 50 miles) wide, occupies two-thirds of the fault trough. The lake is drained by the Shire River which, following the line of the rift, joins the Zambezi some 400 km. (250 miles) from the lake outlet.

Malawi is a long and narrow country which measures 852 km. (530 miles) in length and never more than 160 km. (100 miles) in breadth. In shape it is comparable to Dahomey, Togo and Gambia but having a very diversified topography, Malawi possesses a wider resource base than the other attenuated countries.

Malawi resembles Uganda in having a wide range of elevation and relief which gives rise to agricultural diversity ranging through tropical, sub-tropical and temperate crops. Also like Uganda, Malawi has considerable water and power resources in her major rivers and the four lakes which lie wholly or in part within her boundaries.

With a land area of 94 396 sq. km. (36 481 sq. miles) and an overall average population density of 70 persons to the sq. km. (111 p. to the sq. mile) at the time of the 1966 census, Malawi ranks as one of the smaller countries within the Commonwealth with a medium density of population.

A railway connects Malawi with Beira and a new railway line opened in 1970 connects Malawi with the port of Nacala, 1126 km. (700 miles) north of Beira. Malawi is fortunate in having access to the sea so close to her own borders but she is, nevertheless, dependent on agreements with Moçambique for transit facilities for a large part of her external trade.

For historical reasons Malawi obtains many of her imports from or through Rhodesia and the Republic of South Africa. Moreover, many Malawians work in Rhodesia and South Africa where there are at present more employment opportunities than in their own country. According to information given to the enumerators of the 1966 population census of Malawi, 266 000 relatives of the enumerated population were working or looking for work abroad at the time of the census. It is probable that a large majority of these were in Rhodesia or South Africa.

In view of Malawi's geographical position and the historical growth of the communications systems that link her with the outside world, it has followed naturally that she has developed close ties and economic relations with Moçambique, Rhodesia and South Africa.

However, with the move of the capital and of the international airport to Lilongwe in the Central Region, the completion of the lakeside road, the rapid development of road communications throughout the length of the country, the opening of new industrial plants in all the Regions, and the improvements in agriculture and stock-breeding which are taking place and leading to larger surpluses becoming available for export, it is likely that greatly increased trade and commercial relations with countries lying to the north and west of Malawi will follow.

SWANZIE AGNEW

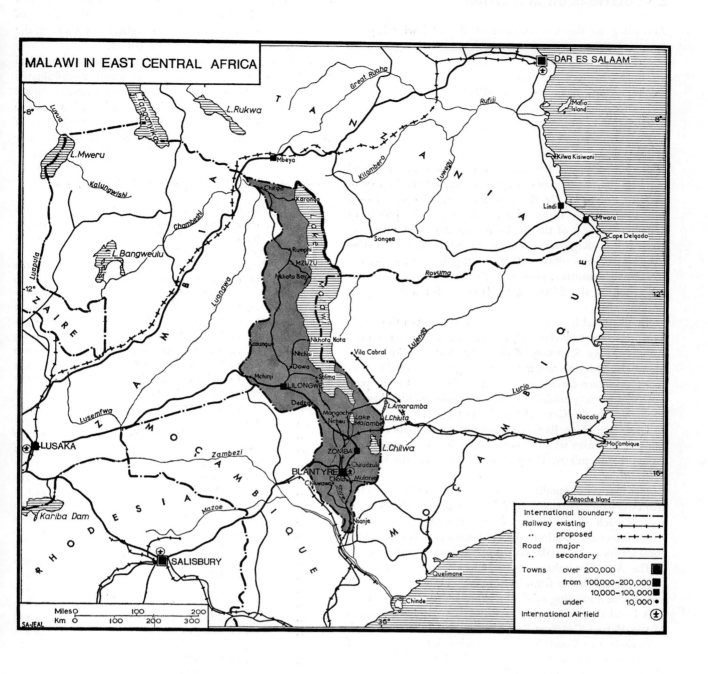

MALAWI IN EAST CENTRAL AFRICA

International boundary
Railway existing
  "   proposed
Road major
  "   secondary
Towns over 200,000
       from 100,000-200,000
       10,000-100,000
       under 10,000
International Airfield

15

2   POLITICAL ORGANIZATION

According to the Constitution of the Malawi Congress Party a six-tier system operates in the political organization of the country.

1 The President of the Party
2 The National Executive Committee
3 The Regional Committee
4 The District Committee
5 The Area Committee
6 The Local Committee

The President of the Party is nominated at an annual convention of the Malawi Congress Party, save in the case of the first President, Dr H Kamuzu Banda, who was elected Life President in 1960. The President has the power to appoint members of the National Executive Committee as well as the Regional Committee; while the Executive Committee loses office with the out-going President, the Regional Committee, chosen by the President from names submitted by the Districts, holds office for a three year period.

The National Executive Committee consists of the President, the Secretary-General, the Treasurer-General and the Administrative Secretary of the Party and ten Committee Members. Three members representing the National Executive Committee conducted district conferences for the purpose of selecting candidates for nomination as members of Parliament in the General Elections of 1971.

There are three Regional Committees in Malawi, each under a chairman who heads the six office-bearers and four committee members. The present chairmen are the Regional Ministers.

The District Committees consist of ten members elected from the executive officials of the area and Local Committees of each of the twenty-four Districts. The District Committees are required to meet once a month to consider local affairs and to make recommendations upon them.

The Area Committees meet once a fortnight and comprise officials drawn from local branches. They are elected annually at a meeting of the local branches in that area.

A Local Committee may be formed by any ten members of the Malawi Congress Party who wish to form a branch with their own Committee. Application for recognition of the local branch must be made to the National Executive Committee and registration follows with the payment of a small fee towards party funds. A local branch must meet at least once a week to consider pertinent matters and any recommendations made are submitted to the Area Committee.

Candidates for the Parliament of 1971 were selected at District Conferences at which full representation of local interests was ensured. Each District Conference was supervised by three members representing the National Executive Committee who called upon officials of the Malawi Congress Party, League of Malawi Women and League of Malawi Youth at District and Area levels to select candidates for the parliamentary elections. Other delegates to the conference were drawn from the District Councils, Town Councils, the Chiefs and Sub-chiefs of the Districts concerned.

The Districts, according to the number of registered voters, are allotted from one to five constituencies. The District Conferences of 1971 submitted names to the President for his final selection. Not more than five names were forwarded for each constituency. Delegates to the conference were free to choose persons from outside the constituency concerned if necessary.

Delegates to the twenty-four District Conferences in 1971 numbered 4850; the smallest number of 79 members represented Karonga District and the largest number of 369 delegates represented Dedza District. These delegates selected candidates for sixty constituencies, the largest of which, Mulanje West, had 69 821 registered voters and the smallest, Mchinji South, had 5000 voters.

Since the Malawi Congress Party is the only political party in the country, the parliamentary candidate nominated by the President from the short list for each constituency is returned unopposed, the ordinary people having had the opportunity of expressing their acceptance or rejection of any candidate at the District Conferences convened earlier on. Three general elections have been held since 1961.

Number of Registered Voters for General Election of 1961

Constituency	No.		
,,	No. 1	Chitipa North	16 007
,,	No. 2	Chitipa South	10 443
,,	No. 3	Karonga North	26 072
,,	No. 4	Karonga South	28 852
,,	No. 5	Rumphi West	12 540
,,	No. 6	Rumphi East	14 769
,,	No. 7	Mzimba North	8 211
,,	No. 8	Mzimba North-East	9 057
,,	No. 9	Mzimba Central	27 111
,,	No. 10	Mzimba South	11 645
,,	No. 11	Mzimba South-East	8 043
,,	No. 12	Nkhata Bay North	43 554
,,	No. 13	Nkhata Bay South	21 112
,,	No. 14	Kasungu North	14 338
,,	No. 15	Kasungu West	24 362
,,	No. 16	Kasungu East	11 204
,,	No. 17	Nkhota Kota North	10 257
,,	No. 18	Nkhota Kota South	25 464
,,	No. 19	Ntchisi	61 007
,,	No. 20	Dowa West	51 759
,,	No. 21	Dowa East	44 651
,,	No. 22	Salima North	24 877
,,	No. 23	Salima South	24 876
,,	No. 24	Mchinji North	15 000
,,	No. 25	Mchinji Central	15 756
,,	No. 26	Mchinji South	5 000
,,	No. 27	Lilongwe North	30 160
,,	No. 28	Lilongwe West	47 622
,,	No. 29	Lilongwe Town	59 227
,,	No. 30	Lilongwe East	14 902
,,	No. 31	Lilongwe South	70 462
,,	No. 32	Dedza North	65 225
,,	No. 33	Dedza West	62 145
,,	No. 34	Dedza Central	17 252
,,	No. 35	Dedza East	24 014
,,	No. 36	Ncheu North	16 797
,,	No. 37	Ncheu Central	50 625
,,	No. 38	Ncheu South	17 425
,,	No. 39	Mangoche West	43 840
,,	No. 40	Mangoche East	63 426
,,	No. 41	Kasupe West	42 263
,,	No. 42	Kasupe East	62 428
,,	No. 43	Zomba West	38 623
,,	No. 44	Zomba South	41 124
,,	No. 45	Zomba East	51 036
,,	No. 46	Chiradzulu	65 408
,,	No. 47	Blantyre City East	17 268
,,	No. 48	Blantyre City West	25 267
,,	No. 49	Blantyre Rural	50 613
,,	No. 50	Neno	9 125
,,	No. 51	Mwanza	11 425
,,	No. 52	Thyolo North	51 713
,,	No. 53	Thyolo South	57 633
,,	No. 54	Mulanje North	65 355
,,	No. 55	Mulanje West	69 821
,,	No. 56	Mulanje South	60 603
,,	No. 57	Chikwawa North	36 892
,,	No. 58	Chikwawa South	39 597
,,	No. 59	Nsanje North	28 497
,,	No. 60	Nsanje South	28 240

B PACHAI

POLITICAL ORGANIZATION
1971

Chitipa
North

Karonga
North

Chitipa
South

Karonga
South

Rumphi
East

Rumphi
West

Mzimba
North

Mzimba
North East

Nkhata
Bay
North

Mzimba
Central

Nkhata Bay
South

Mzimba
South

Mzimba
South
East

Kasungu
North

Nkhota Kota
North

Kasungu
East

Nkhota kota
South

Kasungu
West

Ntchisi

Mchinji
North

Dowa
West

Dowa
East

Salima
North

Mchinji
Central

Lilongwe
West

Lilongwe
North

Salima
South

Mchinji South

Lilongwe
Town

Lilongwe
East

Dedza
North

Lilongwe
South

Dedza
West

Dedza
Central

Dedza
East

Mangoche
West

Mangoche
East

Ncheu
North

Ncheu
Central

Kasupe
West

Kasupe
East

Ncheu
South

Neno

Zomba
West

Zomba
East

Zomba
South

Blantyre
Urban

Mwanza

Blantyre
West

Blantyre
City

Chiradzulu
East

Mulanje
North

Chikwawa
North

Thyolo
North

Mulanje
West

Mulanje
South

Thyolo
South

Chikwawa
South

Nsanje
North

Nsanje
South

ZAMBIA

TANZANIA

Lake Malawi

MOÇAMBIQUE

MOÇAMBIQUE

International boundary.........................
Constituency boundary ....

0   50   100 Miles
0   50   100   150 km

bwm

3 SURVEYS AND MAPPING

The first topographical map of Malawi was produced by the military at the turn of the century. Its scale was 1/1 million and it was compiled from a 1/250 000 series which consisted of plane table productions. For many years these maps together with sketch maps drawn by District Commissioners provided the only topographic data available in Malawi.

In 1949 two important survey events occurred. The Directorate of Overseas Surveys, a United Kingdom organization designed to provide basic mapping in developing countries within the Commonwealth, began operations in Malawi, and a Department of Surveys was also set up in Malawi.

The Directorate of Overseas Surveys confined their activities to trigonometrical and topographical surveys and mapping while the Malawian Department of Surveys concentrated upon cadastral work which had previously been done under licence by surveyors attached to the Lands Section of the Secretariat. Systematic survey in Malawi can thus be said to date from 1949. Since then very great progress has been made in all fields, and Malawi is now as well mapped as most other countries in Africa.

Before any systematic survey or mapping can be undertaken it is necessary to have a base upon which to control survey work. This is built up by means of a triangulation network consisting of a series of points accurately fixed in both horizontal and vertical planes and indicated on the ground by concrete survey pillars.

Malawi has full coverage at primary and secondary level of trigonometrical control and some 400 stations are distributed throughout the country. Although these form the basis for all survey and mapping, it is still necessary to have tertiary systems with stations at less than 24 km. (15 miles) apart (which is the distribution for secondaries) in areas of rapid development. This is a continuous process which occupies one branch of the Department of Surveys.

In addition to the triangulation network, continuous progress is made with the provision of bench marks by geodetic levelling and each year township reference mark systems are introduced for precision and large-scale work.

Topographical heighting and control for mapping of the standard 1/50 000 and smaller-scale series was completed in 1969 and future topographical control requirements will be either for small-scale revision or for new large-scale mapping.

Modern map production is based upon aerial surveys.

Once the ground control has been supplied, map compilation is done by reference to aerial photographs, and the Department of Surveys maintains a comprehensive library of aerial photographs which now cover the whole of Malawi at a scale of 1/40 000 or larger.

The standard national series of maps of Malawi is on the scale of 1/50 000. This series is made up of 160 sheets of which the last 22 sheets covering the northern part of Malawi was printed in 1971.

Other maps which are available are the single sheet publications of the whole of Malawi on scales of $1/2\frac{1}{2}$ million and 1/1 million, and the 1/250 000 layered sheets of which ten sheets are required to cover the country. Maps of the whole or parts of the municipalities or townships of Blantyre, Mangoche, Lilongwe, Mzuzu, Salima and Zomba have been produced on scales of 1/5000 and 1/2500. Large-scale mapping is also being undertaken in some special development areas.

Since its inception, one of the primary functions of the Department of Surveys has been the surveying of land for cadastral purposes. This involves the subdivision of estates which are to be taken over by government for settlement schemes and other purposes; the surveying of land for leases and the recording of all information in this connection; the laying out of plots and roads for private, commercial and industrial purposes; and the preparation of plans for trading centres and town development.

The ultimate aim is to tie all cadastral surveys into the national triangulation network, but this is possible only in those areas where a sufficiently dense tertiary control exists which is, at present, the case in the main towns and townships and in certain areas of the Southern and Central Regions only. Outside these areas cadastral surveys are based on local non-integrated systems which is far from satisfactory because, if all the property beacons of isolated surveys were lost or removed, it would be virtually impossible to replace them in their original positions.

As the country develops so the demand for larger scale and more detailed maps increases. In order to keep pace with the demand, the Department of Surveys extended its activities in 1969 to provide a map revision and reproduction unit with photogrammetric equipment, a process camera and enlarger, and plate-making and printing sections. Malawi is therefore now able to undertake all the intricate processes involved in the production and revision of maps.

R A MINCHELL

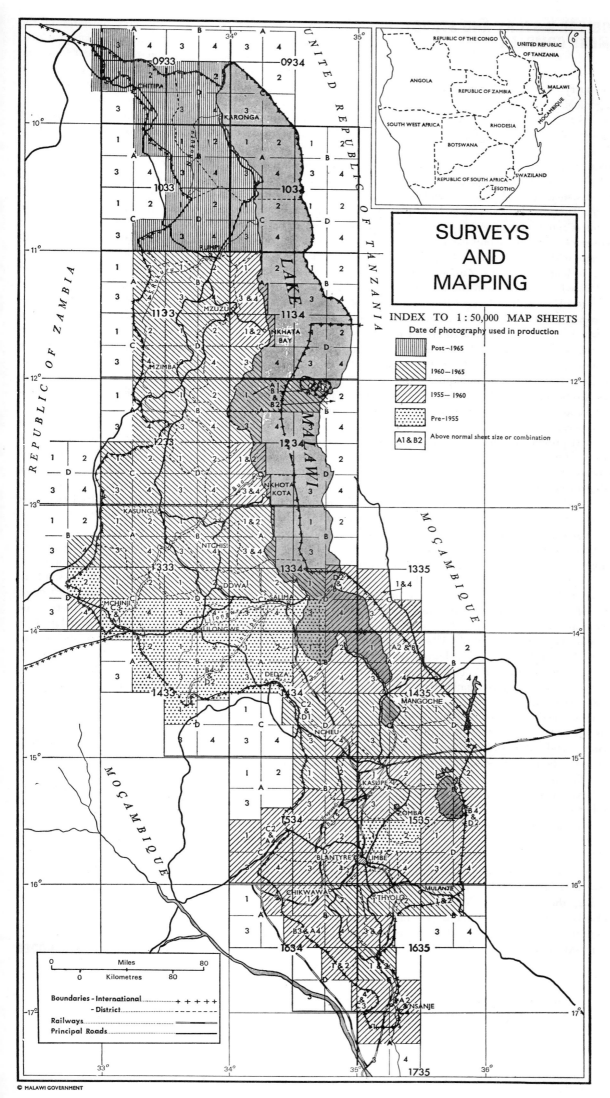

SURVEYS
AND
MAPPING

INDEX TO 1:50,000 MAP SHEETS
Date of photography used in production

▦	Post–1965
▨	1960–1965
▨	1955–1960
⠿	Pre-1955
A1 & B2	Above normal sheet size or combination

Miles
0   80
Kilometres
0   80

Boundaries – International .... + + + + +
            – District ....
Railways ....
Principal Roads ....

© MALAWI GOVERNMENT

4 GEOLOGICAL HISTORY AND STRUCTURE OF BASEMENT COMPLEX

All of the country of Malawi has now been mapped by government geologists at a scale of 1/25 000 for publication at 1/100 000. As a result of this work a clear picture of the complex geology of Malawi is beginning to emerge. It is now possible to fit the geological history of the country into a regional framework.

Much of Malawi is made up of igneous and metamorphic rocks of the Basement Complex of Precambrian to early Palaeozoic age. These rocks make up a large part of the *Malawi Province* (Cannon and others, 1969) which is considered a convenient descriptive unit based on some related geological events within the Basement Complex of Africa. This province is bounded by the Zambezi valley on the south, Lake Malawi on the east and the Luangwa valley in Zambia on the north-west. The Malawi Province is part of three large orogenic belts which occur in and surrounding Malawi and which have differing structural and metamorphic characteristics (see inset map). However, the province derives its name and configuration from the largest and youngest of these belts, the Moçambiquian. The Malawi Province may also be subdivided into northern and southern sub-provinces because of lithological, structural and metamorphic differences.

The very oldest pre-metamorphic rocks of the Basement Complex are unknown. However, Bloomfield (1968, pp. 46–55) postulated that the metamorphic rocks in the southern sub-province were derived from marine geosynclinal sediments with some igneous rock. This assumption was based partly on the occurrence of intercalated marbles which may have originally been marine limestone and partly on the fact that the chemical composition of the metamorphic rock approximates to that of some modern marine sediments with igneous material. Because of lack of evidence it is impossible at this time to suggest what the pre-metamorphic rocks of the northern subprovince might have been (Cannon, personal communication).

Over 1800 million years ago the Rusizi-Ubendian orogeny (see inset map) deformed and metamorphosed the original rocks in the northern sub-province (Cannon and others, 1969) along a zone of diastrophism running from the Congo, Ruwanda and Burundi, north-west–south-east through southern Tanzania and northern Zambia into northern Malawi. This zone may have extended at that time south through Malawi and Moçambique into the Limpopo (Messina) orogenic belt of Rhodesia and northern South Africa. Thus the original rocks in the southern sub-province of Malawi may have also been metamorphosed by this orogeny but most evidence in the south has been destroyed by later orogenesis (Cannon, personal communication).

The Irumide orogeny then occurred between 1600 and 900 million years ago and caused deformation, intrusion and metamorphism in a belt extending east to east-north-east through Zambia, the northern sub-province of Malawi (Cannon and others, 1969), and Tanzania (see inset map). The Nyika granite was intruded at this time in a small area in the northern sub-province.

The mudstones, sandstones and conglomerates of the Mafingi group, which occur in the northern sub-province, were deposited on a shallow-water marine shelf following the intrusion of the Nyika granite. Formerly the rocks of the Mafingi group were thought to have been intruded by the Nyika granite and were therefore older (Bloomfield, 1968, p. 101). However, new evidence (Fitches, 1967) shows that the Mafingi was deposited on, and is therefore younger than, the Nyika granite.

The Dzalanyama granite, which occurs around the junction of the borders between Malawi, Zambia, and Moçambique, may be contemporaneous with the Nyika but this is only a speculation based on the similarity of lithology and mode of occurrence of the two granites. The Dzalanyama granite intruded the sandstones and partly calcareous mudstones of the Mchinji group which were deposited in a marine shallow-water shelf environment, like the Mafingi with which it has been sometimes correlated. The absence of any radiometric or other reliable age data in the area makes the chronological placement of the Dzalanyama granite and Mchinji group highly tentative. However, if the Dzalanyama granite is contemporaneous with the Nyika granite then the Mchinji group would have to have been deposited sometime after the end of the Rusizi-Ubendian orogeny and before the intrusion of the granites during the Irumide orogeny.

The Moçambiquian orogeny took place between about 750 and 500 million years ago. The earlier part of this orogeny is termed the *Katangan episode* and the later part is the *Damaran episode*. This orogeny occurred in a vast area encompassing most of Moçambique, eastern Tanzania and Kenya, part of Zambia, and nearly all of Malawi (see inset map). The area of this orogeny is divided into provinces, which include the previously mentioned Malawi Province.

During the time of the Moçambiquian orogeny most of the Basement Complex became regionally metamorphosed and migmatized to a greater or lesser extent. In the southern sub-province, where plastic deformation and high-grade metamorphism were common, large areas of biotite and hornblende gneisses and charnockitic granulites and gneisses were produced. Isoclinal folding in some areas was accompanied by the formation of metasomatic perthite gneisses and granulites. Some infracrustal ring complexes were also intruded at this time. The Mchinji sedimentary rocks underwent some slight metamorphism which altered them to low-grade metamorphic rocks. The final event in the Moçambiquian orogeny in the southern sub-province was the emplacement during the early Palaeozoic of the granites, syenites and associated minor intrusion of the Lake Malawi Granitic Province.

During the Moçambiquian orogeny in the northern sub-province, phyllonites produced within older gneisses indicate that much of the deformation there was of the brittle type. Syenites and nepheline syenites were intruded in a few places at this time. In addition, the Mafingi sedimentary rocks, like the Mchinji, underwent some slight metamorphic alteration to low-grade metamorphic rocks.

J F SHRODER

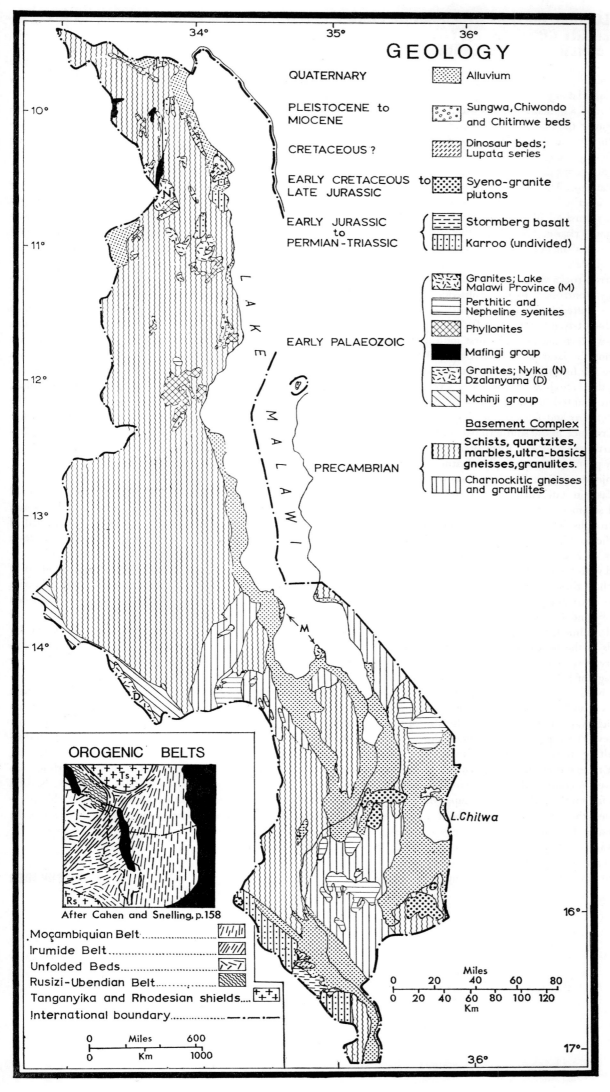

GEOLOGY

QUATERNARY	Alluvium
PLEISTOCENE to MIOCENE	Sungwa, Chiwondo and Chitimwe beds
CRETACEOUS ?	Dinosaur beds; Lupata series
EARLY CRETACEOUS to LATE JURASSIC	Syeno-granite plutons
EARLY JURASSIC to PERMIAN-TRIASSIC	Stormberg basalt Karroo (undivided)
EARLY PALAEOZOIC	Granites; Lake Malawi Province (M) Perthitic and Nepheline syenites Phyllonites Mafingi group Granites; Nyika (N) Dzalanyama (D) Mchinji group

Basement Complex

PRECAMBRIAN	Schists, quartzites, marbles, ultra-basics gneisses, granulites. Charnockitic gneisses and granulites

L.Chilwa

OROGENIC BELTS

After Cahen and Snelling, p.158

Moçambiquian Belt
Irumide Belt
Unfolded Beds
Rusizi-Ubendian Belt
Tanganyika and Rhodesian shields
International boundary

Miles
0   600
Km
0   1000

Miles
0   20   40   60   80
0   20   40   60   80   100 120
Km

LAKE MALAWI

5 GEOLOGICAL HISTORY OF ROCKS OF POST-BASEMENT COMPLEX, RIFT-FAULTING, AND MINERAL OCCURRENCES

Geological history and rifting

The terrestrial sedimentation and vulcanism of the Karroo system began in the Permian and ended in the Early Jurassic. The Nachipere series of clastic terrestrial sedimentary rocks, formerly thought to be Devonian in age (Bloomfield, 1966), is now considered to be Karroo (Cannon, personal communication). The sedimentary rocks of the Karroo consist of interbedded mudstones, sandstones, marls, and some coal seams, all of which were deposited during the Permian and Triassic. Stormberg vulcanicity in the Early Jurassic resulted in dolerite intrusions and basalt flows in the south of Malawi.

The Karroo rocks were probably deposited in a series of tectonically controlled basins. Subsequently these rocks were down-faulted into a series of north–south and north-west–south-east-trending normal fault troughs in northern and south-western Malawi. The first indications of faulting occur during the later part of Karroo deposition and could possibly be the first fractures associated with rift-faulting.

During the Late Jurassic and Early Cretaceous, alkaline magmatism resulted in the intrusion of carbonatites, granites, and feldspar and feldspathoidal syenites of the Chilwa Alkaline Province in the southern part of the country. Most of the intrusions took the form of ring complexes which now form prominent topographic features such as Zomba and Mulanje Mountains. The intrusions were associated in a complex fashion with rifting which probably allowed some terrestrial sedimentation into north-west–south-east-trending fault troughs. This resulted in the fossiliferous Dinosaur beds of the north and possibly in the calcareous pebbly sandstones of a unit in the south which is provisionally correlated with the Lupata series of the Zambezi valley. The age of both of these units is questionable.

Possible down-warping or fault-trough sedimentation in the Tertiary and Quaternary resulted in the deposition of the varied sediments of the Sungwa, Chiwondo and Chitimwe beds of the northern lakeshore area. This deposition probably represents the first lacustrine sedimentation of the earliest stage of Lake Malawi. At this time the lake surface may have been 229 to 305 m. (750 to 1000 ft) above its present level and was possibly confined to an area in the north which was about one quarter the size of the present lake (Dixey, 1926, p. 132). Continued down-faulting and possible tilting allowed the lake to advance to the south and lowered it to an elevation of about 198 m. (650 ft) above its present level. A continuation of this trend caused the lake to extend as far south as the present Cape Maclear Peninsula and dropped the water surface to about 122 m. (400 ft) above present lake level. The Dwangwa gravels, which occur in various places around the shores of Lake Malawi, may then have been produced as a beach deposit.

At some time during the Pleistocene, the Songwe vol-canics were produced by a small extrusion of lava in the extreme north.

Rift-faulting continued during the latter part of the Quaternary and resulted in sedimentation in the Shire River valley and around the shores of Lakes Malawi, Malombe, Chilwa, and Chiuta. Lake Malawi at this time was about 46 m. (150 ft) above its present level and occupied nearly the same location as the present lake but was slightly larger. Down-faulting and/or down-cutting of the Shire River valley allowed the lake to fall in successive stages with concomitant sedimentation to its present level.

The Rift Valley in Malawi is but a small part of a much larger feature which extends in a discontinuous fashion through Africa from the Zambezi to the Red Sea. In Moçambique and Malawi the southern Rift is a single linear zone of lakes and valleys created, as mentioned previously, by down-faulting of large sections of the earth's crust during the late Mesozoic and Cenozoic. North of Malawi the Rift bifurcates and passes through East Africa as a double zone of down-faulting. The western Rift dies out north of Uganda but the eastern or Gregory Rift continues through Ethiopia and into the Red Sea (see inset map). There it splits again into one branch which passes up the Red Sea and Dead Sea to die out in Syria and another branch which passes out through the Gulf of Aden and into the great world-girdling, undersea rift zones known as the oceanic ridges. Thus the African Rift joins with and is a part of a world-wide feature which is probably third in topographic and geological importance after the continents and ocean basins.

Mineral occurrences

Known exploitable mineral resources in Malawi are limited but exploration continues. The carbonatite complexes may be the most valuable in terms of future potential. All of these deposits contain rare earth elements (possible use in alloys and space-age industries), apatite (source of phosphate), barite (source of barium), strontianite (source of strontium), and pyrochlore (source of niobium). Bauxite (aluminium ore) on Mulanje Mountain may be mined when cheap power becomes available. Pyrite and pyrrhotite (source of sulphur) near Lilongwe could be mined. Low quality coal occurs in the north but is uneconomic to mine at present. Kyanite (used in refractories) is being mined near Ncheu and numerous deposits of nepheline syenite in conjunction with kaolin and sand deposits could provide a base for a ceramics and glass industry. Gem-quality corundum and scattered deposits of semi-precious stones may allow development of a limited jewel production. Rutile and ilmenite (titanium ore), magnetite and hematite (iron ore), corundum (an abrasive) and graphite (source of carbon) also occur as possible marginally exploitable resources. Natural building materials such as sources of cement (marble limestone, and aggregates) and brick clays occur throughout the country although the cement carbonates are scarce in the north.

J F SHRODER

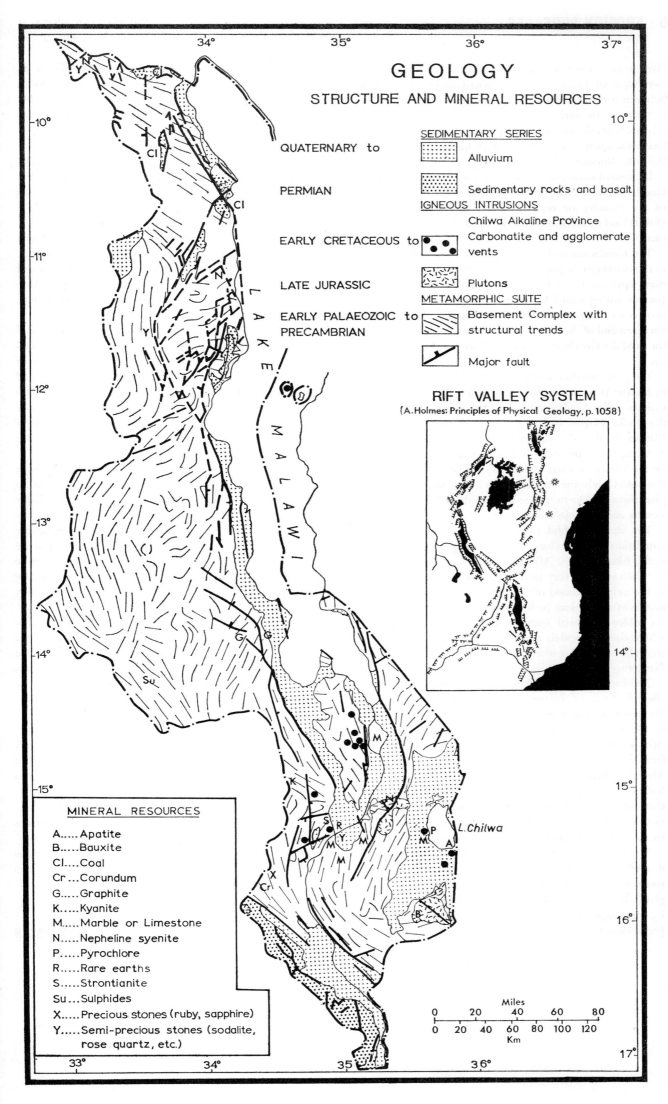

GEOLOGY
STRUCTURE AND MINERAL RESOURCES

QUATERNARY to

PERMIAN

EARLY CRETACEOUS to

LATE JURASSIC

EARLY PALAEOZOIC to
PRECAMBRIAN

SEDIMENTARY SERIES

Alluvium

Sedimentary rocks and basalt

IGNEOUS INTRUSIONS
Chilwa Alkaline Province
Carbonatite and agglomerate
vents

Plutons
METAMORPHIC SUITE
Basement Complex with
structural trends

Major fault

RIFT VALLEY SYSTEM
(A.Holmes: Principles of Physical Geology, p. 1058)

LAKE MALAWI

L.Chilwa

MINERAL RESOURCES

A.....Apatite
B.....Bauxite
Cl....Coal
Cr...Corundum
G.....Graphite
K.....Kyanite
M.....Marble or Limestone
N.....Nepheline syenite
P.....Pyrochlore
R.....Rare earths
S.....Strontianite
Su...Sulphides
X.....Precious stones (ruby, sapphire)
Y.....Semi-precious stones (sodalite,
        rose quartz, etc.)

Miles
0   20   40   60   80
0   20 40 60 80 100 120
Km

6 EROSION SURFACES

Five principal erosion surfaces occur in Malawi. The Gondwana of Jurassic age; the post-Gondwana developed between early and mid-Cretaceous times; the African, late Cretaceous to early Miocene; the post-African, which evolved from the late Miocene through to the Pliocene; and finally the Quaternary surface which has been evolving from the end-Pliocene to the present day.

Because of their considerable age the Gondwana and post-Gondwana surfaces are either limited to the highest regions of the country or occur, though rarely, as resurrected (fossil) land surfaces at the basal contacts of Cretaceous sediments.

The Gondwana surface is displayed on the Nyika Plateau in the Northern Region. The surface rises to heights of more than 2438 m. (8000 ft) on the peaks, and exhibits post-Jurassic tilting which has caused the general altitude of the surface to increase northwards across the plateau. At the northern end of the Vipya Plateau a few isolated peaks carry traces of the Gondwana surface at altitudes of 2134 m. (7000 ft).

The post-Gondwana erosion cycle is far more widespread in Malawi than is the older Gondwana. It occurs as broad, shallow valley-heads eroded into the Gondwana surface on the Nyika Plateau and as a dissected plain on the Vipya Plateau at altitudes increasing northwards from 1524 to 2134 m. (5000 to 7000 ft). The summit levels of inselbergs on the Lilongwe Plain and the Kirk Plateau are assigned to the post-Gondwana erosion cycle as are also the high-level planations at 1830 m. (6000 ft) altitude and above on Dedza, Zomba and Mulanje Mountains.

The steep youthful valleys which cut into these post-Gondwana levels belong to the younger African erosion cycle. Elsewhere the African land surface occurs as a senile, flat plain which is very well seen on the Lilongwe Plain; but in the neighbourhood of the post-Gondwana inselbergs the nature of the African pediplain depends upon the spacing of the older erosional features, being characteristically flat where they are widely scattered, as in the Dedza area and irregular where the older residuals form clusters as around Blantyre.

The formation of the Rift Valley during the Pleistocene affected the lie of the practically horizontal African surface. The entire axial area along the line of the rift was up-warped in the earth movements prior to fracturing, so that the African and post-African land surfaces became tilted away from the line of the trough. Thus the present altitude of the African surface is at a maximum along the crest of the Rift Valley scarp and drops with increasing distance away from that line, as in the Lilongwe Plain where from approximately 1372 m. (4500 ft) near Ntchisi the elevation falls to 1067 m. (3500 ft) near the Bua River.

Along the edge of the uptilted rift scarp post-African dissection is marked but incision decreases with distance westwards. Thus the middle reaches of the larger rivers are gently let down into the African pediplain giving a composite topography without the usual nick point to indicate the presence of two erosion cycles. A more markedly composite topography is represented in the Mzimba Plain where, at approximately 1340 m. (4400 ft) altitude, both African and post-African erosion cycles are present.

The frontier between Malawi and Zambia follows an insignificant watershed developed upon a typically smooth African surface which separates the drainage basin of Lake Malawi from that of the Luangwa trough. Along this indeterminate divide the post-African cycle has not yet encroached upon the older pediplain.

To the south-east of Lilongwe in areas such as the Kirk Plateau, the main bevel is principally of African age but the landscape is complicated by residuals of post-Gondwana provenance, while at lower levels the post-African cycle is progressively encroaching on these older surfaces.

Bordering Lake Malawi the Kandali ridge in the Nkata Bay area shows a high level planation at more than 914 m. (3000 ft). This can be attributed to the post-African cycle and is one of the few examples where the older and higher African surface, so often in association with the post-African cycle, is absent.

Along the Rift scarp zone, faulting has been complex and fault splinters bearing the African erosion cycle occur, dissected to a varying degree by the later cycle. To the north of Blantyre within the Rift Valley, the chief airport is placed upon such a smooth fault splinter. In the Ncheu-Balaka-Bilila area a series of fault steps occurs at progressively lower levels towards the floor of the trough, each showing a smooth African surface impinged upon by the ramifying dissection of the post-African cycle.

The Quaternary cycle is represented in Malawi by both erosional features and lowland deposition. Pleistocene to Recent deposits form littoral plains margining the major lakes. Attack by the recently initiated Quaternary cycle extends up the Shire Valley from the Zambezi River, having progressed farther in the Lower Shire Rift Valley than in the upper reaches. Between these two sections of the river occurs the succession of cataracts where the Shire is directly superimposed upon the basement rocks and cuts its way through a succession of rock barriers.

Quaternary erosion is active along the Rift Valley escarpment and the rim may be notched by the active thrust of the new cycle. In the case of the larger rivers such as the Bua and the South Rukuru, the Quaternary cycle has already breached the escarpment edge and has penetrated beyond the rim impinging upon the post-African cycle to give a valley-in-valley form.

Along the lakeshore littoral, phases within the Quaternary cycle can be examined where deepening of the rift trough has led to a fall in lake level leading to a scouring of the deposits of an earlier infill in those subsidiary basins lying parallel to the main rift trough.

The landscapes of Malawi date therefore from the late Mesozoic period to the present. These ancient surfaces evolved slowly through 130 million years until earth movements associated with rift faulting brought radical changes that have affected the relationship between the land surfaces and have changed their relative altitudes.

LINLEY LISTER

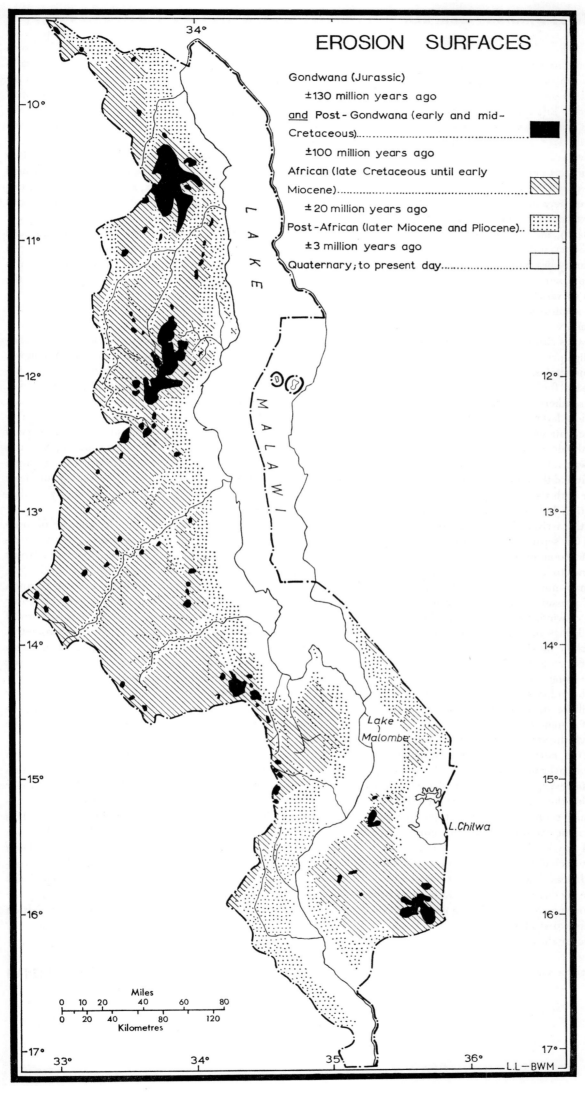

EROSION SURFACES

Gondwana (Jurassic)
±130 million years ago
<u>and</u> Post-Gondwana (early and mid-
Cretaceous).. ■
±100 million years ago
African (late Cretaceous until early
Miocene)..
±20 million years ago
Post-African (later Miocene and Pliocene)..
±3 million years ago
Quaternary; to present day........................

LAKE

MALAWI

Lake
Malombe

L.Chilwa

Miles
0 10 20   40   60   80
0 20 40   80   120
Kilometres

L.L—BWM

7 CLIMATE 1: WIND AND WEATHER

Malawi is a long, narrow country stretching some 885 km. (550 miles) from $9\frac{1}{2}°$ to 17°S, but only 160 km. (100 miles) wide at its broadest part. Lake Malawi, occupying a part of the Great Rift system, borders the country on the east from the northern frontier to about as far south as Mangoche. The lake has an elevation of about 472 m. (1550 ft) above sea level and is flanked for much of its length by mountains and escarpments which rise in places to over 2438 m. (8000 ft). The southern part of Malawi is less rugged but even here marked contrasts are to be found between the extremes of Mount Mulanje, which rises to 3013 m. (9884 ft), and the Shire valley which drops to less than 70 m. (200 ft) on the Moçambique border. Thus, while the whole country lies within the tropics, altitude tempers the temperatures normally expected in these latitudes. The topography is so varied and the range of altitude so great that climatic conditions are complex with many gradations between dry and wet and between hot and cold.

Since Malawi is situated on the equatorward side of the sub-tropical high pressure belt, the prevailing winds, unless deflected by mountains, are mainly from the south-east, less so from the east, for about six months of the year which make up the southern winter. These winds are characterized by a shallow layer of moist air overlaid by much drier air and produce fair-weather cloud which varies in amount according to the depth of the moist layer.

After the September equinox the winds tend to become more northerly and the temperatures and water vapour content of the air both rise. Showers and thunderstorms occur from time to time but rain and thunderstorms only become general with the arrival of the Inter-tropical Convergence Zone. The ITCZ separates the South-east Trades and the North-east Monsoon of the Indian Ocean and, in mid-summer, it tends to lie across the Central Region of Malawi, although it may move north or south depending on the movement of pressure systems farther to the south. Any strengthening of winds towards the ITCZ increases the convergence and brings an increase in cloudiness and rainfall. A tropical cyclone moving down the Moçambique Channel usually distorts or displaces the ITCZ, often drawing very much moister Congo air from across Zambia into Malawi. Although such cyclones rapidly lose their gale force, the winds may still be strong over the lake, and heavy rain is still the rule for some days.

About March the strengthening of the South-east Trades drives the ITCZ northwards thereby bringing the rainy season to an end over most of the countries in the Zambezi catchment. However, in the case of Malawi, the escarpments bordering the lake and therefore directly exposed to the strengthening south-east winds continue to receive rain due to orographic causes and, in the northern parts of Malawi, April may be the month of heaviest rainfall.

Gradually rain conditions disperse and weather reverts to fair again in all areas. The dry season is marked by increasing haziness of the air due to extensive grass burning in Malawi and in neighbouring countries. The smoke haze is persistent and reaches its worst about October, but temporary improvements occur during periods of inflow of clean maritime air.

Throughout the year there are other transient weather features that are superimposed on the seasonal trends described above. The movements of high and low pressure systems along the South African coasts are felt as far north as Malawi. Falling pressure over Natal or southern Moçambique tends to cause winds over Malawi to back towards the north-east. Rising pressure over Natal has the inverse effect of bringing winds round to the south-east or south, and cool maritime air may then enter the Zambezi valley and fan outwards along the tributaries. Over Malawi such invasions of maritime air arrive as south to south-east winds which cause the *chiperoni* conditions over all rising ground and windward-facing escarpments, and also cause the strong *mwera* winds over the lake. These phenomena are described more fully in the section on winds. Such conditions may last only one day, or perhaps two or three days at a time, and such spells may occur almost weekly or only once or twice a month. There is no doubt that such cool spells do much to ameliorate the sticky heat which can be very trying in the lower-lying areas at certain times of year.

Winds

In January the main impression is one of the high frequency of light winds (see Rainfall map). Only Mzimba, Lilongwe, Blantyre (Chileka) Airport, and Nsanje have winds exceeding 13 knots and then only on about 1% of occasions. While easterly directions are common, the most significant feature is the occurrence at all stations from Karonga to Blantyre of north-westerly winds, a result of the presence of the Inter-tropical Convergence Zone at about 15°S at this time of the year. The wind directions shown for Blantyre Airport are to some extent local, the prevailing southerly winds being deflected around the Thyolo (formerly Cholo)-Blantyre massif.

During July there are much greater frequencies of moderate and strong winds, and winds of over 13 knots are recorded at all stations, especially Mzimba. Blantyre Airport again experiences the local south-west winds, and Lilongwe north-east winds, but otherwise winds in the east to south quadrant predominate. On Lake Malawi the periodic strong south-westerly winds are known as *mwera*. Whilst born of the same circumstances as *chiperoni*, namely barometric pressure rising rapidly over southern Moçambique, *mwera* winds over the lake are associated with fine weather, apart from possible rain or storms at the outset, in contrast to the persistent low cloud and drizzle of *chiperoni* weather over rising ground. Speeds may be high, of the order of 25–30 knots over the lake, often much stronger than may be expected from observations taken on the lake shore.

One other wind régime needs to be mentioned. As in neighbouring countries, northerly components in the surface winds become increasingly evident during the latter half of the dry season, i.e. the hot season, and north-easterly winds are strongest in October and November. This is especially true of the lake itself where shores which are normal to the wind direction and/or have the longest fetch across water experience the strongest winds. It is also probable that the steepness of the lakeshore escarpments affects wind strengths considerably. Deep Bay and Nkata Bay are noted for their strong winds but the effects are also felt on occasions as far south as Salima.

STELLA LINEHAM

WIND AND WEATHER

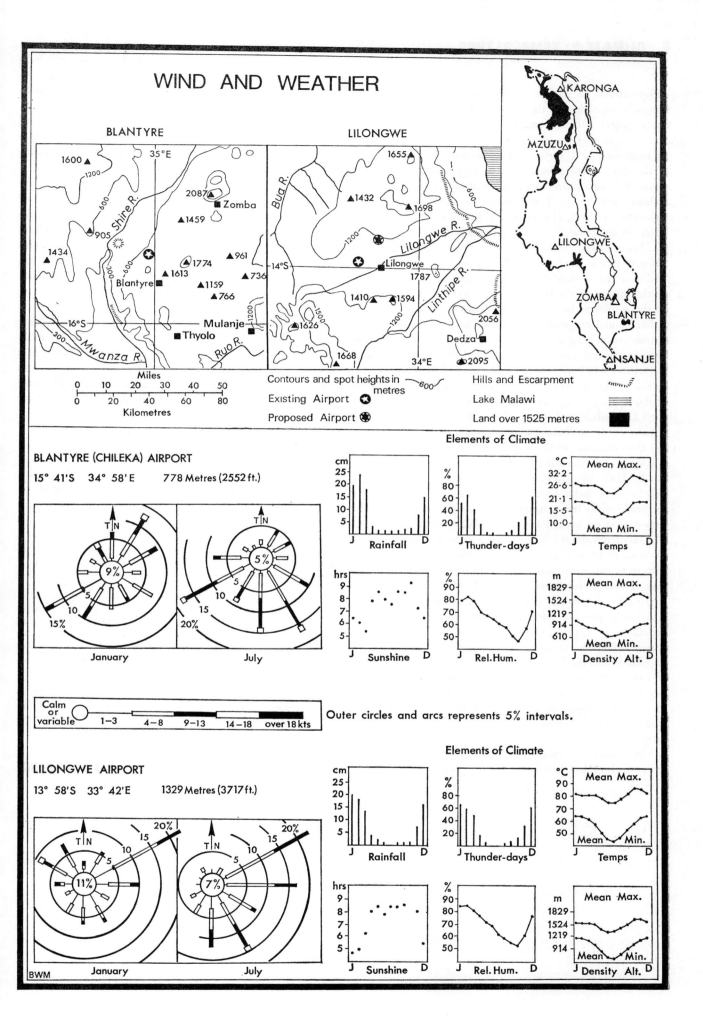

BLANTYRE

LILONGWE

Miles
0 10 20 30 40 50

Kilometres
0 20 40 60 80

Contours and spot heights in metres ~600~
Existing Airport ✪
Proposed Airport ✪

Hills and Escarpment
Lake Malawi
Land over 1525 metres

Elements of Climate

BLANTYRE (CHILEKA) AIRPORT

15° 41'S   34° 58'E   778 Metres (2552 ft.)

January

July

Rainfall
Thunder-days
Temps   Mean Max. Mean Min.
Sunshine
Rel. Hum.
Density Alt.   Mean Max. Mean Min.

Calm or variable   1–3   4–8   9–13   14–18   over 18 kts

Outer circles and arcs represents 5% intervals.

Elements of Climate

LILONGWE AIRPORT

13° 58'S   33° 42'E   1329 Metres (3717 ft.)

January

July

Rainfall
Thunder-days
Temps   Mean Max. Mean Min.
Sunshine
Rel. Hum.
Density Alt.   Mean Max. Mean Min.

BWM

8 CLIMATE 2: TEMPERATURE

Temperatures in Malawi are greatly influenced by the rugged topography and though there is a general decrease in temperatures with increasing altitude of about 0·55°C for every 100 metres at night and in the early morning, increasing to about 0·92°C for every 100 metres during the hot part of the day, other effects such as higher cloudiness over mountains cause more localized variations. In addition Lake Malawi exercises profound effects on almost all weather elements – rainfall, cloudiness and sunshine, wind and, not least, on temperature. Maximum temperatures run about 5°C lower in the vicinity of the lake than at equivalent altitudes near the Zambian border. When temperatures are 'reduced' to a standard level, the isotherms run north–south, parallel to the lake, and only in the Southern Region do the isotherms become oriented east to west.

The annual range of temperature is about 12°C at most stations, increasing to about 15°C in the extreme south. The lowest temperatures occur in June and July, and the highest in October and November. The coming of the rains and the increased cloudiness cause a drop in maximum temperature of about 3°C, though minimum temperatures go on rising until December or January. Thereafter temperature levels remain steady until the end of the rains in March or April, and then decrease to the winter minimum.

Changes in temperature between one day and another are usually fairly small and the monthly average exceeds 2°C only in the period September to November. However, there are occasionally large changes from one day to another. The largest rises on record are about 8°C, whereas the largest falls vary from about 8°C for places north of 14°S, increasing southwards to as much as 17°C at Blantyre Airport. One pattern of successive day to day changes occurs commonly, that of several small rises followed by one or two much larger falls, due to the arrival of cool south-easterly winds.

Altitude plays a dominating role in the temperature distribution. The lower Shire valley has the highest temperatures while the mountain areas (Mulanje, Shire and Kirk Highlands, and the Vipya and Nyika plateaux) are all regions of low maximum temperatures. Where these mountains face directly into wind as, for example, Mount Mulanje and the Thyolo Highlands and parts of the Vipya and Nyika plateaux, temperatures will be moderated further by the orographic cloud.

Minimum temperatures, in addition to the altitude control, are also subject to purely local exposure influences, the most important one being the slope of the ground in controlling air drainage at night. Often this factor will outweigh altitude effects and, because these effects are so localized, it is not possible to map minimum temperature to the same degree of accuracy as maximum temperature. In general the temperature range is least in the mountains and on steep upper slopes and greatest along the major river valleys into which colder air can be pooled without draining away.

Lake Malawi acts as a temperature reservoir, with comparatively little temperature variation, and it is of sufficient size to set up marked land and lake breezes. Thus cool air from the lake tends to move over the heated land during the day, but at night cold air from the land drains towards the lake. The onset of the lake breeze halts the normal diurnal rise of temperature and the maximum temperature is several degrees lower than would otherwise be the case.

The following table for three stations shows the average number of days when the maximum temperature occurs in certain ranges. Blantyre Airport illustrates conditions at a land station in the south of the country, while Nkhota Kota and Karonga refer to lake shore stations and also illustrate how the cooler spells associated with the south-easterly air streams do not always reach the north end of the lake.

MAXIMUM TEMPERATURES
(Average number of days falling within five ranges)

Range	J	A	S	O	N	D	J	F	M	A	M	J
BLANTYRE AIRPORT												
35·0–39·9°C	—	—	—	2	3	—	—	—	—	—	—	—
30·0–34·9°C	—	2	11	22	16	11	7	4	3	5	2	—
25·0–29·9°C	9	17	16	6	9	18	22	22	26	22	17	9
20·0–24·9°C	20	11	3	1	2	2	2	2	2	3	11	18
15·0–19·9°C	2	1	—	—	—	—	—	—	—	—	1	3
KARONGA												
35·0–39·9°C	—	—	—	1	2	—	—	—	—	—	—	—
30·0–34·9°C	—	1	14	29	24	19	13	11	7	5	1	—
25·0–29·9°C	30	29	16	1	4	12	18	17	24	25	29	29
20·0–24·9°C	1	1	—	—	—	—	—	—	—	—	1	1
NKHOTA KOTA												
35·0–39·9°C	—	—	—	—	3	1	—	—	—	—	—	—
30·0–34·9°C	—	1	11	26	22	13	5	2	3	2	—	—
25·0–29·9°C	20	25	18	5	5	16	25	25	28	28	28	20
20·0–24·9°C	11	5	1	—	—	1	1	1	—	—	3	10

Source: Meteorological Services, Salisbury.

J D TORRANCE

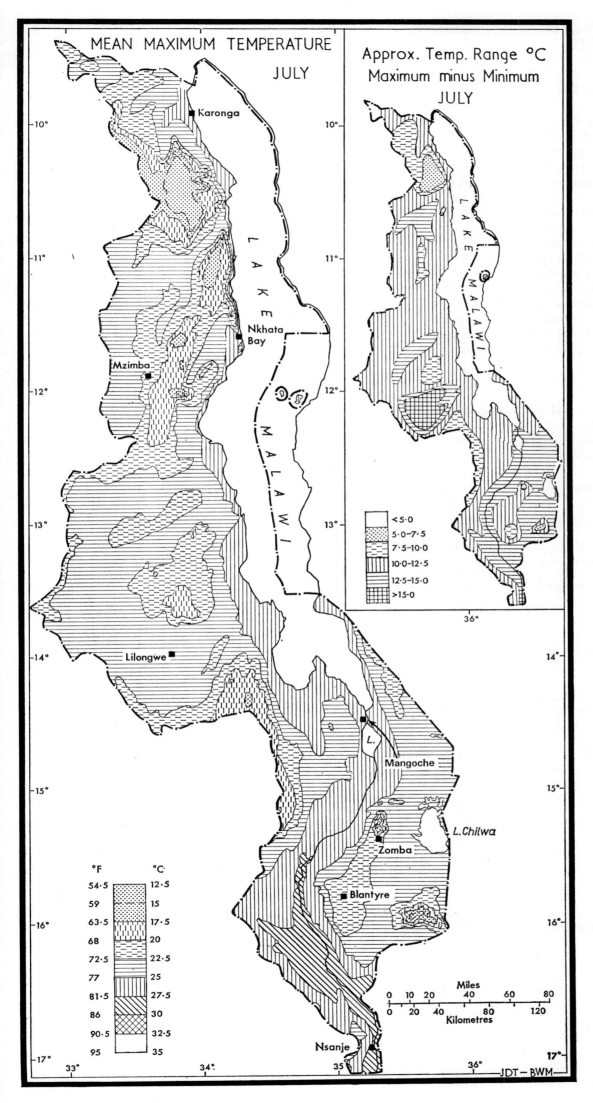

MEAN MAXIMUM TEMPERATURE
JULY

Approx. Temp. Range °C
Maximum minus Minimum
JULY

Karonga

Nkhata
Bay

Mzimba

LAKE MALAWI

LAKE MALAWI

	<5.0
	5.0-7.5
	7.5-10.0
	10.0-12.5
	12.5-15.0
	>15.0

Lilongwe

Mangoche

L.

L.Chilwa

Zomba

Blantyre

°F		°C
54.5		12.5
59		15
63.5		17.5
68		20
72.5		22.5
77		25
81.5		27.5
86		30
90.5		32.5
95		35

Miles
0 10 20   40   60   80

0   20   40   80   120
Kilometres

Nsanje

JDT—BWM

9 CLIMATE 3: HUMIDITY, SUNSHINE, CLOUDINESS

Relative humidity

A natural consequence of the large diurnal variation in temperature is that relative humidity also shows a large variation during the day, being highest when temperature is lowest, and lowest when temperature is highest. At dawn, values of over 90% are common at most stations in many months of the year while, by afternoon, the relative humidity has fallen to 40–60%, depending on the season. The lowest humidities occur in October, immediately preceding the arrival of the rains.

Two maps are presented, to match the temperature maps, i.e. January and July, representing typical wet season and dry season months. It will be seen that the diurnal ranges are least over Lake Malawi and its immediate vicinity and in the mountainous areas bordering the north of the lake. The greatest range occurs along the Zambian border. These facts result in the humidity gradient (from high to low) reversing during the day, more obviously so during the dry months.

Sunshine

In general substantial amounts of sunshine are recorded even during the rainy season. Accumulations of hours of sunshine over six monthly periods covering the rainy season and the dry season, although differing in level, show similar patterns.

Maximum sunshine occurs over the southern portion of Lake Malawi and its western shore; the northern portion of the lake appears to be much cloudier, presumably an effect of consistently higher humidities and proximity of mountains; and the lowest sunshine values occur over the mountainous areas, such as Mount Mulanje, Shire and Kirk Highlands, and by inference the Vipya and Nyika plateaux.

Maximum sunshine occurs over the lake, since during the day the lake is cooler than the land, and convection cloud therefore forms over the land, leaving the lake almost, or relatively, unclouded. Apart from the rainy season, when the air is moist enough for large amounts of cloud, over both land and lake, the biggest sunshine losses occur during *chiperoni* spells.

Cloudiness

Under the influence of rising pressure along the Moçambique coast, cool moist maritime air enters Malawi from the south-east. Orographic cloud (and precipitation) occurs on all windward-facing slopes, and these conditions may last two or three days at a time. The areas most often affected are Mount Mulanje and the Shire Highlands and to some extent the Kirk Highlands. Really strong winds extend the effect up the lake also, with the lake and mountains tending to constrain the winds to a south-south-easterly direction, and the effects become most pronounced where the wind is most directly on-shore, i.e. the Dowa Highlands beyond Salima, the Vipya escarpments south-west of Nkhata Bay, and the Nyika escarpments near Livingstonia. Places such as Likoma Island and Karonga in the lee of the Portuguese Highlands and the Nyika Plateau respectively experience much more broken or short-lived cloud.

J D TORRANCE

TABLE 1: RELATIVE HUMIDITY AT SELECTED STATIONS IN MALAWI (%)

Station	Jan.	Feb.	Mar.	Apr.	May	Jun.	Jul.	Aug.	Sep.	Oct.	Nov.	Dec.	Mean
Makanga	77	81	78	79	78	76	76	65	61	69	76	77	72
Bvumbwe	83	88	86	85	80	80	70	69	65	62	69	84	77
Chileka	79	80	80	75	70	69	63	57	52	50	60	74	67
Zomba	82	82	86	80	77	76	70	60	61	52	64	82	73
Lilongwe	83	86	82	77	72	67	61	58	54	50	62	77	69
Mzimba	82	83	82	80	74	72	68	65	60	52	64	76	71
Chitipa	80	83	82	80	74	70	64	61	52	47	54	74	68

Source: Pike and Rimmington, *Malawi: A geographical study*, Oxford University Press, 1965, p. 65

DURATION OF SUNSHINE IN MALAWI (HOURS)

Station	Jan.	Feb.	Mar.	Apr.	May	Jun.	Jul.	Aug.	Sep.	Oct.	Nov.	Dec.	Mean
Makanga	6·4	6·6	8·2	8·6	8·4	6·9	7·7	7·8	7·9	8·8	8·3	7·0	7·7
Bvumbwe	5·5	5·7	6·7	7·4	7·9	6·3	7·4	7·6	7·8	8·4	7·5	4·9	7·0
Chileka	6·0	6·0	6·1	7·7	8·0	7·1	7·3	7·9	8·2	8·6	7·3	6·2	7·2
Monkey Bay	5·4	5·9	7·5	8·9	9·3	8·7	8·2	9·2	9·3	9·8	9·5	7·9	8·3
Lilongwe	4·6	4·9	6·1	8·0	8·4	7·7	8·3	8·3	8·5	9·9	7·9	5·4	7·3
Mzimba	4·1	4·0	5·3	7·4	8·5	8·6	9·0	9·4	9·7	10·3	8·5	5·4	7·5
Fort Hill	5·0	3·9	4·7	7·4	9·5	9·2	9·3	8·7	9·9	9·1	7·5	4·6	7·4

Source: Pike and Rimmington, *Malawi: A geographical study*, Oxford University Press, 1965, p. 62

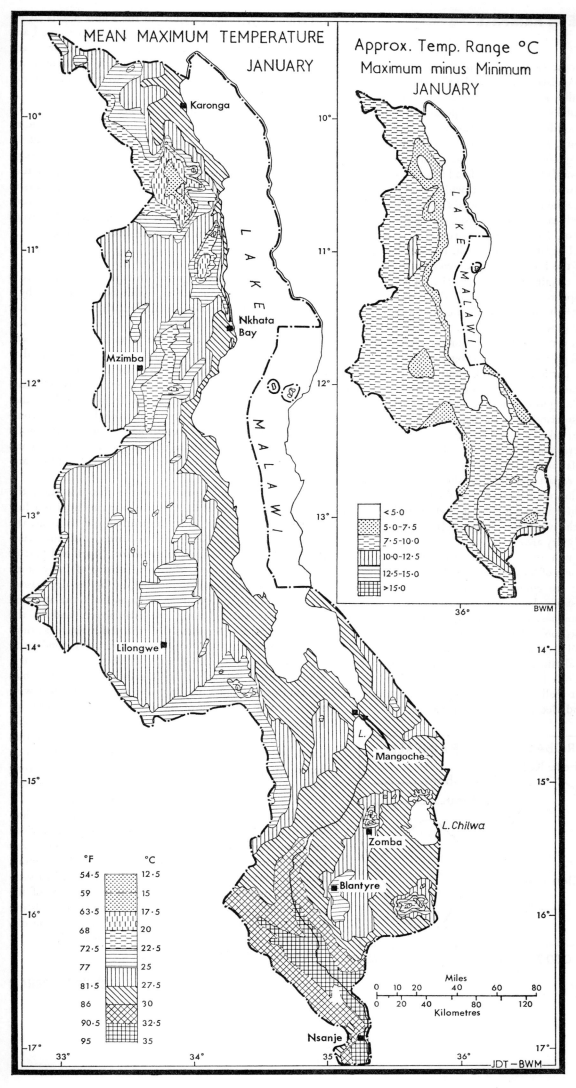

MEAN MAXIMUM TEMPERATURE
JANUARY

Karonga

Nkhata
Bay

Mzimba

Lilongwe

Mangoche

L. Chilwa

Zomba

Blantyre

Nsanje

°F		°C
54·5		12·5
59		15
63·5		17·5
68		20
72·5		22·5
77		25
81·5		27·5
86		30
90·5		32·5
95		35

Approx. Temp. Range °C
Maximum minus Minimum
JANUARY

	< 5·0
	5·0-7·5
	7·5-10·0
	10·0-12·5
	12·5-15·0
	>15·0

BWM

L A K E   M A L A W I

Miles
0 10 20   40   60   80
0 20 40   80   120
Kilometres

JDT—BWM

10 CLIMATE 4: RAINFALL

Malawi occupies the southern end of the Great Rift Valley of Africa, between latitudes 9½° and 17° South. The southern end of the valley is open to maritime climatic influences crossing the coastal plain of Moçambique and the effects are funnelled northwards, the lake acting as a supplementary source of moisture. Prevailing winds are easterly to southeasterly, blowing outwards from the Indian Ocean high pressure cell towards the equator. In addition to the Southeast Trades the two other airstreams which can bring moisture to Malawi are the recurved 'Congo air' from the Atlantic and the North-east Monsoon from the Indian Ocean. Rainfall is seasonal, November to March in the south, but lasting into April or later in the north. It is associated with the presence of the Inter-tropical Convergence Zone, the boundary between air of Northern Hemisphere and of Southern Hemisphere origin. Much of the heaviest rainfall is associated with the freshening of the South-east Trades, driving back the northerly airstreams.

As Malawi is a very mountainous country the distribution of rainfall is strongly influenced by orography. The Southern Highlands, and particularly their south-east (windward) slopes, have some two or three times the amount of rain received in adjoining low-lying areas. Elsewhere the wettest conditions are associated with the Vipya and Nyika Plateaux and also with the lake shore where the coastal trend is set against the direction of the prevailing wind, as in the Chinteche area. Rainfall along sections of the lakeshore parallel to the wind is lower, particularly in the sheltered area south of Karonga. Other low rainfall areas are in the sheltered valleys, notably of the Shire and Kasitu and around the southern end of the lake, but the word 'low' is used relatively, for Malawi has no extremely dry areas.

Most falls of rain are the result of convective activity, coming in the form of local showers and thunderstorms. In most areas they are commonest in the afternoon, when heating is greatest over land. Along the lake shore, however, storms are commonest in the early hours of the morning when the land has cooled but convection is taking place over the now relatively warmer waters of the lake. Rain occurs in spells of several raindays (that is, days on which some rain is recorded) followed by spells of several dry days. In the wetter areas wet spells increase in length at the expense of the dry ones, and vice versa in the drier areas.

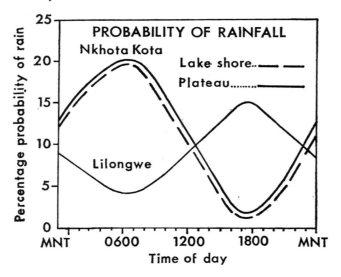

Periodically, rising pressure to the south results in incursions of cool moist air, bringing orographic cloud and rain or drizzle known as *chiperoni*. This can occur at any time of year but the effect is particularly apparent when contrasted with the otherwise fine weather of the dry season.

Occasional torrential downpours are associated with the movement inland of tropical cyclones from the Indian Ocean. The high winds characteristic of these storms at sea quickly moderate after the coast is crossed, and the passage of the cyclone is marked by a trail of rain damage rather than wind damage. The heaviest fall recorded in 24 hours in Malawi was 570 mm. (22·45 in.) at Nkhota Kota on 20th February 1957, while at Zomba 711 mm. (28·01 in.) were recorded in 33 hours on 13th–14th December 1946.

Variability

Annual rainfall totals vary greatly from year to year. There is a tendency for a number of wet years to be followed by a number of years of poor rainfall, but there is no regular cycle. The coefficient of variability shown on the map is the standard deviation expressed as a percentage of the mean. Normally the lower the rainfall the greater the variability and the higher the rainfall the less the variability (that is, the greater the reliability). The lake shore stations in Malawi show, unexpectedly, some departure from this rule in that their coefficient of variability is relatively high when compared with less wet areas away from the lake. This appears to be due to occasional outstandingly heavy downpours which serve to increase both the mean rainfall and the variability.

The rainfall graphs shown on the map illustrate the seasonal distribution of rainfall, the year running from July to June. In most areas, and particularly the drier areas, the season extends from November to March, with the maximum in January. The post-rainy season (April and part of May) is characterized by showers, usually of fairly small amounts, and little rain is recorded during the dry season. There are some interesting variations from the standard pattern, particularly along the lake shore, and in the mountains of the Southern Region. Lake shore stations show a secondary maximum in January, corresponding to the main maximum elsewhere. After decrease in February, rainfall increases sharply to the main maximum in March as the south-east winds, blowing over the lake, freshen with the northwards retreat of the Inter-tropical Convergence Zone. It is interesting to compare the distribution of rainfall for Likoma Island (in the lee of the Moçambique coast) which shows a decrease in March, with Chinteche (in an exposed position on the lake shore) which shows a strong March maximum, and Mzimba (on approximately the same latitude) which conforms to the standard pattern.

In the mountains of the Southern Region, and particularly in the Mulanje area, there is no truly dry season since maritime air from the coast may bring some rain at any time of year. On the windward slopes of Mulanje Mountain the March maximum again appears (see Lujeri graph) associated with freshening south-easters and the retreat of the Inter-tropical Convergence Zone. As the source of moisture is this time the sea, not the lake, and the area is some distance from the sea, the effect is less well marked.

A rainfall table is shown on p. 139.

STELLA LINEHAM

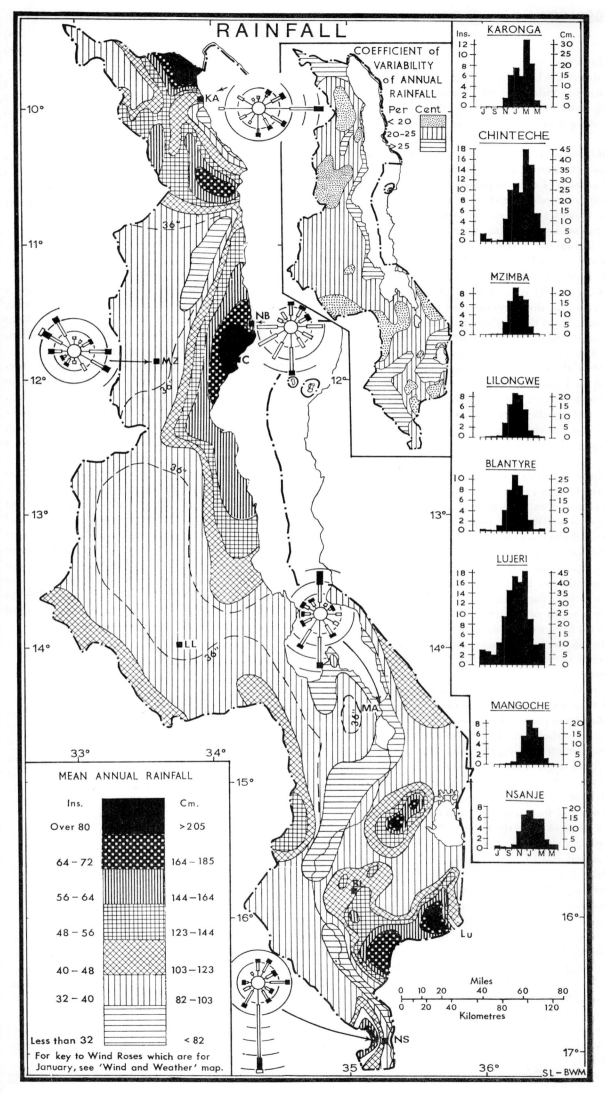

RAINFALL

COEFFICIENT of
VARIABILITY
of ANNUAL
RAINFALL
Per Cent
< 20
20-25
>25

KARONGA
CHINTECHE
MZIMBA
LILONGWE
BLANTYRE
LUJERI
MANGOCHE
NSANJE

MEAN ANNUAL RAINFALL

Ins.		Cm.
Over 80		>205
64 – 72		164 – 185
56 – 64		144 – 164
48 – 56		123 – 144
40 – 48		103 – 123
32 – 40		82 – 103
Less than 32		< 82

For key to Wind Roses which are for
January, see 'Wind and Weather' map.

Miles
0 10 20   40   60   80
0 20 40   80   120
Kilometres

SL – BWM

11 HYDROLOGY

Lake Malawi

The total area of the Lake Malawi catchment is 96 918 sq. km. (28 678 sq. miles) of which about 29 604 sq. km. (11 430 sq. miles) are occupied by the waters of Lake Malawi, making it the third largest of the Central African lakes.

South of latitude 11°S on the eastern side of Lake Malawi the catchment is narrow, not more than 40 km. (25 miles) wide, and consists of short impermanent rivers which contribute little to the inflow into the lake. North of this line the catchment widens to include the Ruhuhu River which drains 15 540 sq. km. (6000 sq. miles) of Karoo sediments contained within the Livingstone Mountains. From the north-western corner of the Ruhuhu basin the watershed follows the Kipengere Range and then turns westward along the 2134 m. (7000 ft) summit ridge of the Poroto Mountains. Thereafter the divide crosses the Bundali Range to the Mbozi plateau. From the headwaters of the Songwe River, which separates Malawi from Tanzania, the watershed follows the Malawi-Zambia border to a point near Fort Jameson. Here the divide swings south-east and then eastwards along the Dzalanyama Range to the Kirk Range in the neighbourhood of Dedza and thence to the southern limit of the lake near Mangoche. Between Dedza and Mangoche the divide separates the short parallel rivers draining towards the lake from those flowing southwards into the Shire River rift.

The mean annual rainfall over the Lake Malawi catchment excluding the lake, is 1179 mm. (46·4 in.) with a recorded maximum of 2946 mm. (116 in.) at Kyela and minimum of 686 mm. (27 in.) at Rumphi (formerly Rumpi). Less than 5% of the total catchment area receives less than 762 mm. (30 in.) of rainfall in an average year.

The Lake Malawi basin is asymmetrical. The eastern side has been downthrown by one main fault or series of faults whereas the western part of the downthrown block has been dropped in a series of western sloping steps by parallel faults. This tilt from west to east is reversed between Nkata Bay and Deep Bay and, on the west shore, the lake attains its greatest depth of 706 m. (2310 ft.). In its long axis the average depth of the lake is some 366 m. (1200 ft) in the north, deepening to over 610 m. (2000 ft) towards the centre and then becoming shallower to an average depth of 1030 m. (600 ft) in the southern section.

The seasonal variation in the level of Lake Malawi averages just over a metre (3 or 4 ft) but this has been as much as 2 m. (6 ft in a single year). Over long periods of years the cumulative rise or fall may be much greater and since 1896, when the lake levels began to be recorded, the level of the lake has fluctuated from 468 m. (1538 ft) to over 474 m. (1556 ft), a range of more than 6 m. (18 ft).

The long-term changes in the level of Lake Malawi are related to annual rainfall, run-off, evaporation and outflow from the lake. If the amount of water contributed by run-off from the land, i.e. by the rivers flowing into the lake, is greater than the amount of water lost by evaporation over the lake, then this surplus quantity or freewater can be stored in the lake or drawn off by the Shire River.

Each year the lake level falls during the dry season and rises again during the rainy season reaching its highest level about March when the rains are ending. This is the annual fluctuation. But over a period of years with good rainfall and run-off into the lake, the lake level may rise steadily from year to year until a maximum level is reached. Then, if the rainfall and run-off decrease over a number of years, the lake level will fall each year until the trend is again reversed by a new cycle of high annual rainfall.

Water balance of Lake Malawi

1	Lake area	28 678 sq. km. (11 430 sq. miles)
2	Catchment area	96 918 sq. km. (37 420 sq. miles)
3	Ratio item 2 to item 1	3·3
4	Rainfall, land	1179 mm. (46·4 in.)
5	Rainfall, lake	1359 mm. (53·5 in.)
6	Mean air temp.	25·7°C (74·6°F)
7	Evaporation	1945 mm. (76·6 in.)
8	Outflow	343 mm. (13·5 in.)
9	Run-off	259 mm. (10·2 in.)
10	Run-off, per cent rain	22%
11	Mean free water	+ 295 mm. (+ 11·6 in.)

Note: 1 in. = 20·54 mm.

The Shire River

The outlet of Lake Malawi to the Shire River is across a submerged sand bar 4 km. (2½ miles) north of Mangoche. Eight km. (five miles) south of Mangoche the Shire River enters the shallow waters of Lake Malombe which is 29 km. (18 miles) long and 14·5 km. (9 miles) wide.

The Shire River has three main sections. The upper section extends for 132 km. (82 miles) from the outlet to Matope and has an average gradient of 5·29 m. per km. (28 ft per mile); the middle section where the river plunges through cataracts of a total fall of 384 m. (1260 ft) in 80 km. (50 miles); and the lower section that comprises a wide alluvial valley stretching from the foot of the cataracts to the Zambezi River over a distance of 281 km. (174 miles) at an average gradient of 0·2 m. per km. (1·06 ft per mile).

A few tributaries of the Shire River are perennial and 80% of their annual flow occurs between November and April. The Ruo is the largest tributary draining a catchment area of 4921 sq. km. (1900 sq. miles) which includes most of the heavy rainfall area of Mulanje Mountain and the eastern Shire Highlands. Floods in the lower Shire valley are usually due to the River Ruo. Following cyclone 'Edith' in April 1956, the Ruo discharged a peak flood at the rate of 190 000 cusecs into the Shire at Chiromo. See the table on p. 139.

Lake Chilwa

This lake is saline, occupying a shallow basin of inland drainage of about 2590 sq. km. (1000 sq. miles). Margined by swamp, Lake Chilwa periodically dries up but in normal years of rainfall the open water varies in depth between 1·2 m. (4 ft) and 4·28 m. (16 ft) with a seasonal fluctuation in level from 0·6 to 2·19 m. (2 to 7·5 ft). Raised beaches are evidence of its progressive recession.

Lake Chiuta

It is separated from Lake Chilwa by a 15·24 m. (50 ft) sand-bar and is fed by small seasonal streams. The waters remain relatively fresh by reason of their effluence into Lake Amaramba during the dry season. Since Lake Amaramba has a wider drainage net than Lake Chiuta, it rises faster than the latter and when the waterlevel overtops that of Lake Chiuta reversal of flow takes place southwards to the upper lake. Back flow persists until March, then the process is reversed and water drains again from Lake Chiuta into Lake Amaramba.

Seasonal and periodic fluctuations in levels of lakes and seasonal and erratic flow in rivers are characteristic of the hydrology and drainage in Malawi.

J G PIKE

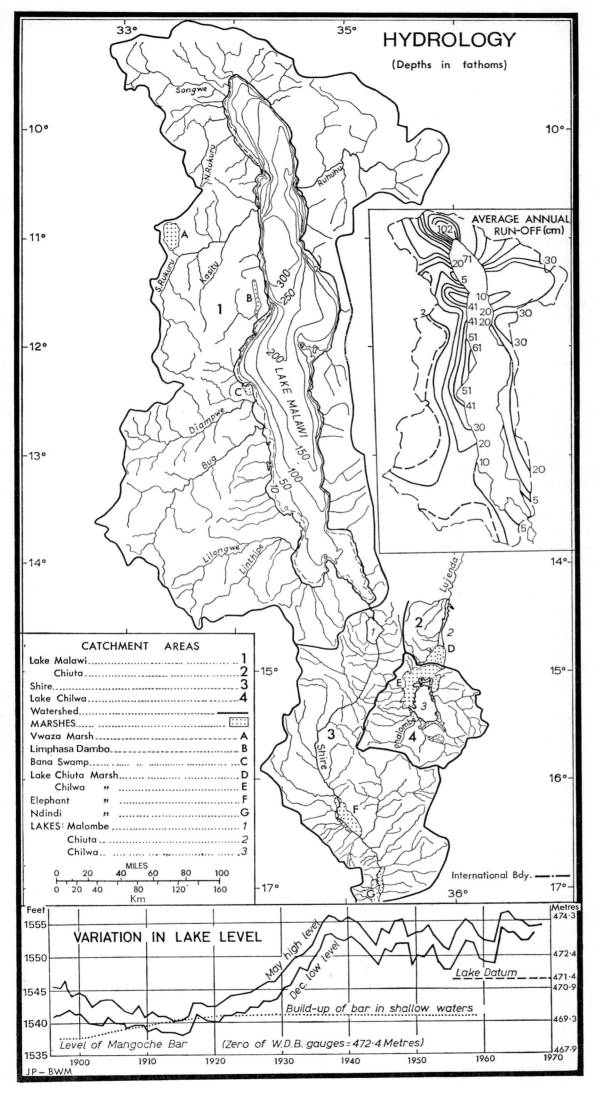

HYDROLOGY

(Depths in fathoms)

AVERAGE ANNUAL RUN-OFF (cm)

CATCHMENT AREAS

Lake Malawi..	1
Chiuta..	2
Shire...	3
Lake Chilwa......................................	4
Watershed...	————
MARSHES...	[⋯⋯]
Vwaza Marsh...................................	A
Limphasa Dambo.............................	B
Bana Swamp...................................	C
Lake Chiuta Marsh..........................	D
Chilwa „	E
Elephant „	F
Ndindi „	G
LAKES: Malombe.............................	1
Chiuta......................	2
Chilwa......................	3

MILES
0 20 40 60 80 100
0 20 40 80 120 160
Km

International Bdy. ———·—

VARIATION IN LAKE LEVEL

May high level

Dec. low level

Lake Datum

Build-up of bar in shallow waters

Level of Mangoche Bar   (Zero of W.D.B. gauges = 472·4 Metres)

Feet: 1555, 1550, 1545, 1540, 1535
Metres: 474·3, 472·4, 471·4, 470·9, 469·3, 467·9

1900 1910 1920 1930 1940 1950 1960 1970

JP — BWM

12 SOILS

There are four main soil groups, differing markedly from each other in the environmental conditions under which they have been developed, in processes of soil formation, and in profile characteristics and analytical properties. The *latosols* are red to yellow, leached, acid soils in which water movement within the profile is predominantly downwards; they occupy freely drained sites, mainly on the gently sloping plains but also in some more steeply dissected areas. The *calcimorphic* soils are grey to greyish brown with a weakly acid to weakly alkaline reaction in which water movement is upward during at least part of the year; they occur on nearly level depositional plains with imperfect site drainage. The *hydromorphic* soils are black, grey or mottled and are waterlogged for all or part of the year. The fourth group comprises *lithosols* which are shallow or stony soils and *regosols* which are immature soils developed from sands.

The soil classification system used in the map is based on that of the *C.C.T.A. Soils Map of Africa*, modified to accommodate local conditions. The main characteristics of each soil type are as follows:

1. Latosols

(a) The ferruginous soils are dark red to reddish brown, mainly clays or sandy clays with a strongly developed blocky structure and visible clay skins on structural surfaces. They are moderately weathered with clay minerals mainly but not entirely kaolinitic. Typical values are pH 5·0 to 6·0, with an exchangeable cation saturation of 50 to 80%. Development is mainly from rocks of basic to intermediate composition.

(b) The ferrisols are red clays with a deep, uniform profile. There is a strong structural aggregation, giving a crumbly consistency and free profile drainage despite the high clay content. The values are pH 4·0 to 5·0, saturation 15 to 40%, and topsoil organic matter content 2 to 4%. This class is developed in areas with a mean annual rainfall exceeding 1270 mm. (50 in.). (In applying to Malawi soils the definitions of the ferrisol class in the *Soil Map of Africa* a conflict exists between field and analytical characteristics. The red clays are classed as ferrisols on the basis of a moderately developed blocky structure and the presence of clay skins and weatherable minerals in depth; they are, however, more acid and have lower values of subsoil cation saturation than the soils classed, on the basis of profile characteristics, as ferrallitic soils.)

(c) The humic ferrisols are similar to the ferrisols but with a humic topsoil containing 5 to 10% organic matter.

(d) The ferrallitic soils are yellowish red to red with a moderately sandy topsoil overlying a compact, heavier textured subsoil. The subsoil structure is weakly developed, blocky or structureless with clay skins absent or weakly developed. Highly weathered with clay minerals predominantly kaolinitic the values register pH, 4 to 4·5 saturation 30 to 70%. This soil class is developed mainly from rocks of acid composition.

(e) The ferrallitic soils with laterite are similar to the preceding class but contain a horizon of hard iron concretions, partially or wholly cemented together. Laterite, besides occurring widely with this group of soils, outcrops also near valley floor margins amid other latosols.

(f) The humic ferrallitic soils are reddish to yellowish soils of moderate depth characterized by a humic topsoil with 5 to 10% organic matter in contrast to the 1 to 2% of other latosol classes. pH is 4·0 to 5·0 and cation saturation 5 to 20%. These are developed on high altitude plateaux above 1524 m. (5000 ft) and on Mulanje Mountain occur as yellow bauxitic soils.

2. Calcimorphic soils

(a) The calcimorphic alluvial soils are grey to dark brown soils formed from alluvium. They are variable in texture, sometimes showing depositional bedding and have commonly a higher silt content than the very much lower values found in the latosols. Calcium carbonate concretions may occur in depth. The pH registers 6·0 to 8·0 and base saturation 80 to 100%. Development is mainly on the depositional plains of the lake shore and the upper and lower Shire valley but calcimorphic soils are also found in certain river valleys, e.g. the North Rukuru.

(b) Vertisols or 'Black cotton' soils are dark brown to black. Locally called *makande* soils, they possess a strongly developed blocky structure, very friable when dry but sticky when wet. There is a thick horizon of calcium carbonate concretions in depth. The soil swells when wet and shrinks to form cracks when dry owing to the presence of montmorillonitic clay minerals. pH measures 7·0 to 8·5 and saturation 100%.

(c) Mopanosols, a name of local origin applied to soils occupied by the tree *Colophospermum mopane*. Dark greyish brown soils with poor structure, alkaline reaction, and sometimes abundant calcium carbonate concretions.

3. Hydromorphic soils

Usually clays with a strongly developed, very coarse blocky to prismatic structure; these soils which are seasonally waterlogged are called locally *dambo*, and are black grey or mottled in colour. The water-table lies close to the surface during the rains but falls to lower horizons in the dry season. The marsh soils constitute permanently waterlogged hydromorphic soils.

4. Skeletal soils

(a) The lithosols are stony and often shallow soils. A stone line, usually of quartz stones, is common. Such soils are developed mainly on steep slopes, and also over quartzites.

(b) Regosols. These are immature soils developed from sands of lucustrine origin and are very sandy, therefore structureless, with little profile development except for slight humus accumulation in the topsoils.

Soil associations and catenas

Where two of the above classes are both common they are shown on the map as a soil association. This is used principally for dissected areas in which lithosols occur in association with one of the latosol classes.

Soil catenas, that is, the systemic change in profile characteristics from interfluve crest to valley centre, are well developed in Malawi. On descending the catena the soil normally becomes paler or less red and a mottle appears in depth. A belt of sandy soils frequently occurs at valley floor margins with hydromorphic clays in valley centres.

A YOUNG

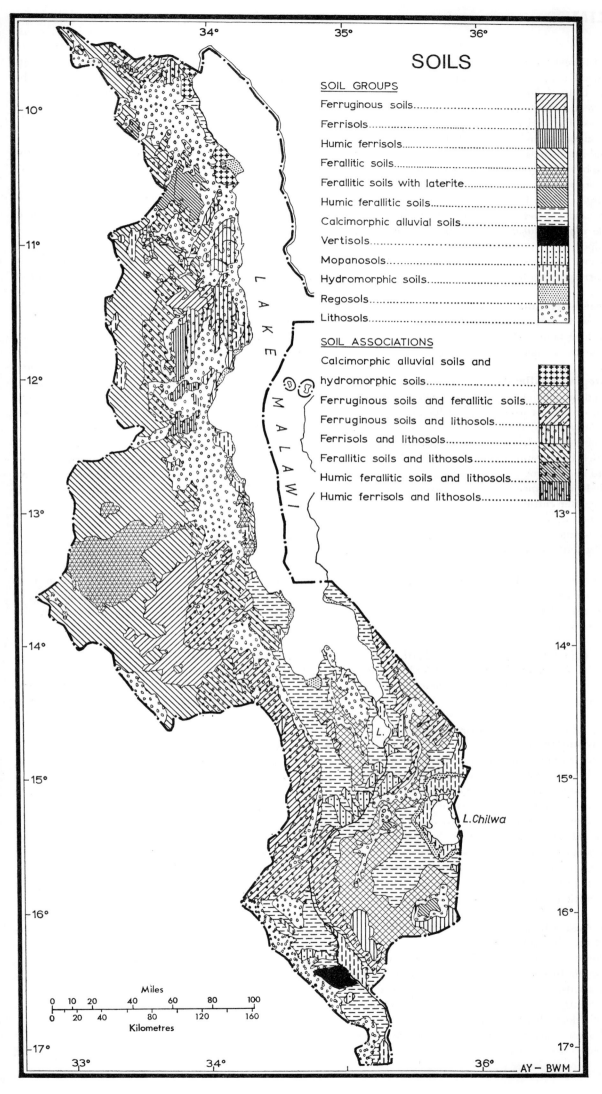

SOILS

SOIL GROUPS

Ferruginous soils

Ferrisols

Humic ferrisols

Ferallitic soils

Ferallitic soils with laterite

Humic ferallitic soils

Calcimorphic alluvial soils

Vertisols

Mopanosols

Hydromorphic soils

Regosols

Lithosols

SOIL ASSOCIATIONS

Calcimorphic alluvial soils and
hydromorphic soils

Ferruginous soils and ferallitic soils

Ferruginous soils and lithosols

Ferrisols and lithosols

Ferallitic soils and lithosols

Humic ferallitic soils and lithosols

Humic ferrisols and lithosols

LAKE MALAWI

L.

L.Chilwa

Miles

0 10 20   40   60   80   100

0   20   40   80   120   160

Kilometres

13 VEGETATION

1. Montane forests, scrubs and grasslands

The montane communities are those which occur above the low-montane belts of *Brachystegia spiciformis* woodland, at levels of between 1524 to 1828 m. (5000 to 6000 ft) above sea level. These highland areas usually present a picture of forest relics in valleys and in isolated stands, with rolling grasslands and scrub-lands between. The pattern appears to be controlled by annual grass fires and by the moisture of the lower-lying areas maintaining a greener and more fire-resistant margin to the forest relics. The forests vary in composition and include communities dominated by *Widdringtonia whytei* (Mulanje cedar) and *Juniperus procera* (African juniper).

The grasslands are divisible on the basis of altitude, soil depth and corresponding floristics.

1a. Moist semi-deciduous forest

A forest type with evergreen and semi-deciduous elements, found in the high rainfall enclave of the Nsanje Hills. The species include the unique *Burttdavya nyasica*.

2. Brachystegia woodlands

This woodland category covers those communities referred to as *miombo*, or savanna woodland, in which one or more species of *Brachystegia* is characteristic and *Jubernalia globiflora* is almost ubiquitous. There are many associations involved which have features in common, justifying their grouping into one category. The grass layer is depressed by the relatively light-crowned trees, which have the ability to coppice freely after cutting and also show the striking pre-rains flush. The various species of *Brachystegia* are dispersed by the explosive mechanism of the seed pod and often have a distinct distribution of species associated with habitat factors.

Topographically controlled communities which cannot be separated out from woodlands on the scale of the map, include the grasses of the *Hyparrhenia* spp. and *Arundinellae* swamp and swamp grasslands and riparian forests.

2a. Brachystegia-Evergreens closed woodlands

In the high rainfall areas of Nkhata Bay and Mulanje are tall semi-evergreen forests dominated by *Brachystegia spiciformis* associated with other genera.

3. *Combretum – Acacia – Piliostigma* broad-leaved, deciduous woodlands

These are the tall-grass-woodlands referred to as *chipeta* which are subject to fierce annual burns. Fire tolerance and features associated with this character are typical of the species involved. Unlike most trees of the *Brachystegia* woodlands, many of the broad-leaved woodland species are dispersed by animals. Selective felling has given rise to various communities with single species dominance, and cultivation and grazing have produced numerous scrub and thicket communities. Edaphic grasslands are similar in species composition to those of the *Brachystegia* group.

4. Woodlands scrubs and thickets of the rift escarpment and its foothills

The communities of the escarpments and foothills could be defined according to floristics as *Brachystegia* woodlands or *Lowland* woodlands. The terrain, especially of the escarpment, is sufficiently well defined to make it a valid category based upon physiography. Also floristically the understorey species are often characteristic, particularly the grasses. The escarpments also display clear-cut sequences in the distribution of *Brachystegia* spp. from the higher to the lower levels. On the low foothills standards such as *Adansonia digitata* (baobab) are characteristic, with an understorey of thicket growth. *Oxytenanthera abyssinica* (bamboo) thickets are frequent. The various vegetation types appear to be correlated with the water relations of the sites.

5. Woodlands, thickets, scrubs and parklands of low altitude

This physiographic division includes the flatter lands below approximately 488 m. (1600 ft). Soils and rainfall vary widely according to location, hence a wide floristic spectrum is encountered. Soils are influenced by drift and colluviation and are often rich in calcium. The most striking feature of the vegetation is the regular occurrence of standard and thicket types, a physiognomic type where tall mature trees such as *Adansonia*, *Pseudocadia*, and *Sterculia* spp. stand within a dense thicket understorey which includes *Commiphora* spp., *Bauhinia tomentosa* and *Popowia obovata*. These communities are likely to be man-induced since the standards are elsewhere found standing in cultivation parklands. Woodlands and induced thicket are formed by many of the *Mimosaceae* such as *Acacia polyacantha* var. *campylacantha*, *A. spirocarpa*, *A. nigrescens*, *Albizia harveyi* and *Dichrostachys cinerea* with *Acacia seyal* and *A. xanthophloea* in wet places. *Ricinodendron rautanenii* and *Terminalia sericea* form woodlands on sandy soils and in the Lower River *Pterocarpus antonesii*, *Fagara* spp., and *Grewia* spp. with *Acacia pennata* and the *Acanthaceae* form thickets and standards. Base-rich soils support *Euphorbia ingens* and *Commiphora* thicket whilst *Hyphaene ventricosa crinita* and *borassus aethiopum* palms give rise to characteristic communities where the water table is high.

6. Mopane woodlands

This woodland of *Colophospermum mopane* in almost pure stand is a floristic division of section 5, but because of its striking appearance and well marked distribution it is readily mappable, the occurrence being on topomorphic or lithomorphic base rich soils. It is close to a forest type with open glades.

7. Parklands on fertile alluvia

This is an edaphic division of section 5 developed upon the almost continuously cultivated alluvia, and is dominated by tall trees left standing in the cultivations, in particular by *Acacia albida* and *Cordyla africana*.

8. Terminalia woodlands

These are a further floristic division found on semi-swamps, sandy soils and sandbars. The species usually involved is *Terminalia sericea*. Near Lake Chilwa, on soils known as Kawinga grey sands, it forms open woodland with *Brachystegia boehmii*.

9. Swamp and swamp grasslands

These are edaphic communities under the control of a high water table which may give rise to permanent swamps or seasonally inundated grasslands. They are complex in species but well zoned according to the depth of the water and the seasonal fluctuations. Typical swamp species include *Typha australis*, *Vossia cuspidata*, *Pennisetum purpureum*, *Echinochloa pyramidalis* and *Cyperus papyrus*. The seasonal swamp areas are typified by *Hyparrhenia rufa*, *Setaria palustris*, *Panicum repens*, *Bothriochloa* spp., and *Cynodon* spp. and by *Chloris gayana* on the more base-rich swamps.

A key to the vegetation of Malawi is given on p. 140.

G JACKSON

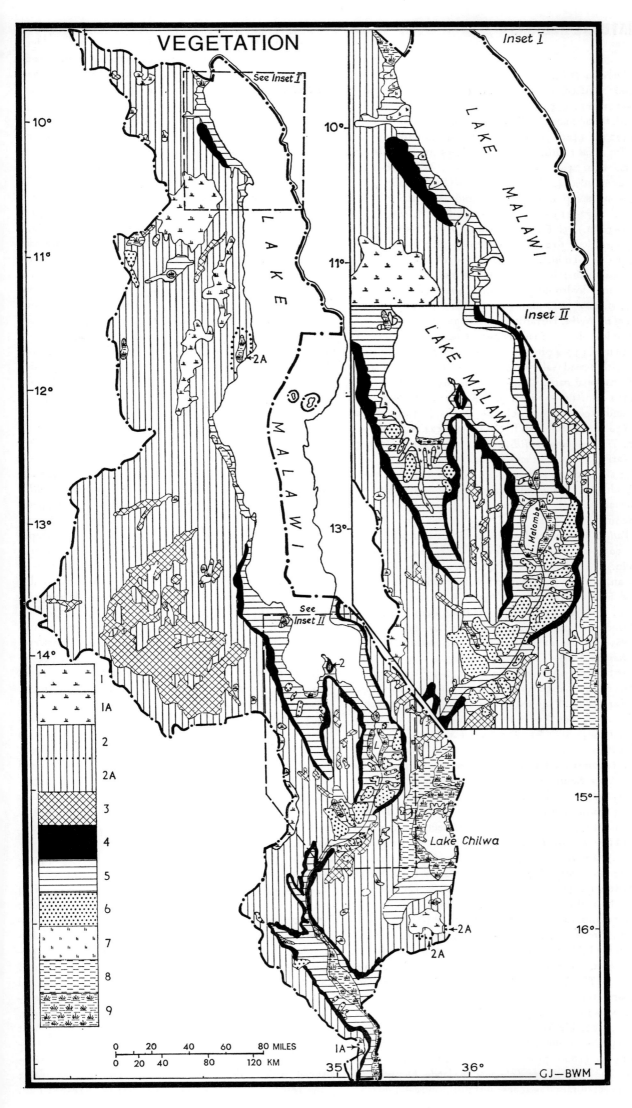

VEGETATION

Inset I

Inset II

LAKE MALAWI

LAKE MALAWI

LAKE MALAWI

See Inset I

See Inset II

L. Malombe

Lake Chilwa

2A

2A

2A

2A

2

1A

10°
11°
12°
13°
14°
15°
16°

10°
11°
13°
15°
16°

35°
36°

	1
	1A
	2
	2A
	3
	4
	5
	6
	7
	8
	9

0   20   40   60   80 MILES
0   20   40   80   120 KM

GJ—BWM

14 NATURAL REGIONS

1. *The Ruwenya Hills.* Stony hills; dissected plateaux and valley floor patches. 1219–1829 m. (4000–6000 ft); rainfall 889–101 mm. (35–40 in.). 2. *The Chitipa Plain.* Undulating with broad marshy valleys; poor sandy ferrallitic soils. 1219–1372 m. (400–4500 ft); rf. 889–1006 mm. (35–40 in.). 3. *The Misuku Hills.* Ridges and valleys and high plateau remnants. 610–2498 m. (2000–6200 ft); rf. 1270–1524 mm. (50–60 in.). 4. *The Plateaux and Hills of the Upper Lufira.* Stony steep hills; high altitude plateaux; fertile alluviums. 1372–2130 m. (4500–7000 ft); rf. 889–1270 mm. (35–50 in.). 5. *The Karonga Scarp Zone.* Dissected hill region; unsettled. 610–1158 m. (2000–3800 ft); rf. 889–1270 mm. (35–50 in.). 6. *The Karonga Lakeshore Plain.* Depositional plain; beaches, sandbars and marshes; calcimorphic and hydromorphic soils. 472–610 m. (1550–2000 ft); rf. 762–3048 mm. (30–120 in.). 7. *The plains and hills west of the Nyika.* Ferrallitic soils on gentle slopes; steep, stony residual hills. 1219–1829 m. (4000–6000 ft); rf. 889–1128 mm. (35–45 in.). 8. *The Nyika Plateau.* Undulating plateau with broad valleys and convex interfluves; scarp rimmed; national park. 1981–2591 m. (6500–8500 ft); rf. 1006–1524 mm. (40–60 in.). 9. *The Nyika Hills.* Deep dissection and steep slopes including Nyika Plateau scarps. 1067–2130 m. (3500–7000 ft); rf. 762–1524 mm. (30–60 in.). 10. *The Livingstonia Hills.* Slopes vary, gentle to very steep; Karroo sandstones and shales. 762–1372 m. (2500–4500 ft); rf. 1128–1778 mm. (45–70 in.). 11. *The Luwewe Plain.* Undulating plain with impeded drainage; scattered hills; ferrallitic soils. 1036–1122 m. (3400–3700 ft); rf. 635–762 mm. (25–30 in.). 12. *The Lower South Rukuru-Kasitu Valley.* Pediments lead from hills to broad infilled valleys. 1036–1250 m. (3400–4100 ft); rf. 635–762 mm. (25–30 in.). 13. *The North Vipya Plateau and Hills.* Undulating plateau, broad convexities and rocky residuals; maturely dissected hills. 1067–1981 m. (3500–6500 ft); rf. 1006–1778 mm. (40–70 in.). 14. *The Lakeshore Scarp Zone.* High steep dissected scarps; narrow raised beaches. 472–1524 m. (1550–5000 ft); rf. 1270–1778 mm. (50–70 in.). 15. *The Middle Kasitu Valley.* Gentle to moderate slopes; valley floor marshy with termite mounds. 1122–1219 m. (3700–4000 ft); rf. 762–1270 mm. (30–50 in.). 16. *The Upper South Rukuru Valley.* Plain with broad, swampy valleys; sandy ferrallitic soils. 1067–1372 m. (3500–4500 ft); rf. 635–889 mm. (25–35 in.). 17. *The Central Mzimba Hills.* Low, dissected hills with lithosols; partly forest reserve. 1341–1615 m. (4400–5300 ft); rf. 762–1006 mm. (30–40 in.). 18. *The Upper Kasitu Valley.* Vipya scarp; steep hill land pediments and open valleys. 1122–1829 m. (3700–6000 ft); rf. 762–1270 mm. (30–50 in.). 19. *The Vipya Plateau.* Senile summit topography; peripheral dissection; moderate slopes. 1219–1829 m. (4000–6000 ft); rf. 1270–1398 mm. (50–55 in.). 20. *The East Vipya Scarp Zone.* A steep dissected hill zone; deep gorges. 732–1372 m. (2400–4500 ft); rf. 1128–2286 mm. (45–90 in.). 21. *The Nkata Bay Lakeshore Lowlands.* Low altitude, dissected stony hills enclosing the Limpasa swamp. 472–700 m. (1550–2300 ft); rf. 1778–2286 mm. (70–90 in.). 22. *The Chimaliro Hills.* Massive ridge striking E.N.E. and passing into an undulating plateau. 1219–1829 m. (4000–6000 ft); rf. 889–1270 mm. (35–50 in.). 23. *The Kasungu Plain.* Gently undulating; poor soils, coarse sandy topsoil, compact subsoil, laterite, game reserve. 975–1311 m. (3200–4300 ft); rf. 762–1006 mm. (30–40 in.). 24. *The Nkhota Kota Scarp Zone.* Dissected zone with steep slopes and river gorges; largely uninhabited. 548–1615 m. (1800–5300 ft); rf. 889–1270 mm. (35–50 in.). 25. *The Nkhota Kota Lakeshore Lowlands.* Depositional plains; dissected raised beaches; ferrallitic and calcimorphic

soils. 472–548 m. (1550–1800 ft); rf. 1270–1524 mm. (50–60 in.). 26. *The Mchinji Hills.* Massive quartzitic ridge; hills with pediments; ferrallitic soils. 1150–1829 m. (3800–6000 ft); rf. 889–1006 mm. (35–40 in.). 27. *The Upper Bua Plain.* Gently undulating plain; poor ferrallitic soils. 1067–1158 m. (3500–3800 ft); rf. 889–1006 mm. (35–40 in.). 28. *The Lilongwe Plain.* Undulating with broad marshy valleys; ferruginous soils. 975–1341 m. (3200–4400 ft); rf. 762–889 mm. (30–35 in.). 29. *The Dowa Hills.* Moderate to high relief; ferruginous soils and lithosols. 640–1585 m. (2100–5200 ft); rf. 889–1128 mm. (35–45 in.). 30. *The Salima Lakeshore Plain.* Plain with hydromorphic and calcimorphic soils; low dissected hills with poor soils. 472–669 m. (1550–2200 ft); rf. 762–1270 mm. (30–50 in.). 31. *The Dzalanyama Range.* High, massive, structurally controlled ridges; lithosols; forest reserve. 1280–1646 m. (4200–5400 ft); rf. 889–1270 mm. (35–50 in.). 32. *The Dedza Hills.* Plateau surmounted by high hills; ferruginous and ferrallitic soils; forest reserve. 1280–2256 m. (4200–7400 ft); rf. 889–1270 mm. (35–50 in.). 33. *The Dedza Scarp Zone.* Heavily dissected with deep gorges; scarp foothills. 518–1463 m. (1700–4800 ft); rf. 889–1270 mm. (35–50 in.). 34. *The Ncheu Scarp Zone.* Dissected high plateau and escarpment; ferrallitic soils and lithosols. 914–1829 m. (3000–6000 ft); rf. 1006–1270 mm. (40–50 in.). 35. *The Ncheu Region.* Plains and foothills with moderate slopes; ferrallitic to ferruginous soils. 610–1524 m. (2000–5000 ft); rf. 762–1128 mm. (30–45 in.). 36. *The Bwanje Valley.* Heavily cultivated pediment; moderately cultivated depositional plains. 472–762 m. (1550–2500 ft); rf. 762–1006 mm. (30–40 in.). 37. *The Phirilongwe Hills.* Steep sided massif; dissected peripheral hills; fringing pediments. 610–1524 m. (2000–5000 ft); rf. 762–1128 mm. (30–45 in.). 38. *The Mangoche Lakeshore Region.* Depositional plains; hill masses with uncultivated pediments. 472–914 m. (1550–3000 ft); rf. 762–889 mm. (30–35 in.). 39. *The Namwera Region.* Moderately to heavily cultivated plains and rocky hills; ferrallitic to ferruginous soils. 914–1646 m. (3000–5400 ft); rf. 889–1270 mm. (35–50 in.). 40. *The Namizimu Escarpment.* Dissected escarpment and gorges; rocky steep sided massif; forest reserve. 610–1067 m. (2000–3500 ft); rf. 889–1270 mm. (35–50 in.). 41. *The Balaka Region.* Undulating plains and dissected stony hills; ferrallitic to ferruginous soils. 548–914 m. (1800–3000 ft); rf. 762–889 mm. (30–35 in.). 42. *The Upper Shire Valley.* Flat alluvial terraces; escarpment piedmont; swamp and mopane land. 457–610 m. (1500–2000 ft); rf. 762–889 mm. (30–35 in.). 43. *The Shire Highlands.* Dissected plains truncated by escarpments and surmounted by residual hills; heavily cultivated. 610–1981 m. (2000–6500 ft); rf. 1006–1778 mm. (40–70 in.). 44. *The Kawinga Plain.* Level to undulating plain; lakeside swamps; mainly ferrallitic soils. 610–914 m. (2000–3000 ft); rf. 762–1006 mm. (30–40 in.). 45. *The Chilwa-Phalombe Plain.* Heavily cultivated pediplains; sparsely to heavily cultivated depositional plains; marshes. 610–914 m. (2000–3000 ft); rf. 762–1006 mm. (30–40 in.). 46. *The Mulanje Massif.* High altitude dissected plateau; ferrallitic and bauxitic soils; forest reserve. 914–3048 m. (3000–10 000 ft); rf. 1006–3048 mm. (40–120 in.). 47. *The Upper Ruo Basin.* Undulating plain and pediment; ferrallitic soils to ferrisols. 457–914 m. (1500–3000 ft); rf. 1006–1778 mm. (40–70 in.). 48. *The Mwanza Escarpment.* Dissected escarpment and plateau remnants; ferrallitic and ferruginous soils. 610–1433 m. (2000–4700 ft); rf. 889–1397 mm. (35–55 in.). 49. *The Chikwawa-Thyolo Escarpment.* Dissected escarpment with fault step. 107–1244 m. (350–4700 ft); rf. 762–1524 mm. (30–60 in.). 50. *The Lower Shire Valley.* Depositional plains; floodplain marshes; basaltic clay plain; game reserve. 36–107 m. (120–350 ft); rf. 635–889 mm.

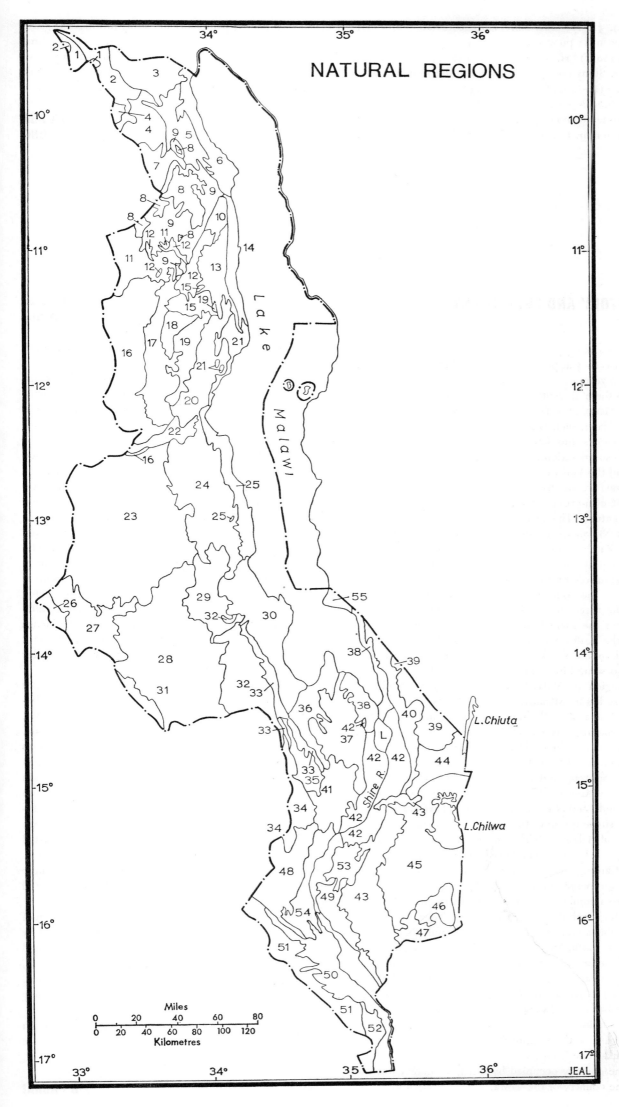

NATURAL REGIONS

Lake Malawi

L.Chiuta

L.Chilwa

Shire R.

Miles
0   20   40   60   80
0 20 40 60 80 100 120
Kilometres

JEAL

41

(25–35 in.). *51. The Lower Shire Hills.* Undulating uplands; steep rocky hills; poor lithosols; forest reserve. 107–376 m. (350–1300 ft); rf. 762–889 mm. (30–35 in.). *52. The Nsanje Hills.* Stony escarpment and foothills; game reserve. 91–914 m. (300–3000 ft); rf. 889–1524 mm. (35–60 in.). *53. The Chileka Region.* Plains; gentle to moderate slopes; ferrallitic to ferruginous soils. 610–914 m. (2000–3000 ft); rf. 889–1006 mm. (35–40 in.). *54. The Middle Shire Valley.* Depositional plains; pediplains and stony hill masses; game reserve. 457–1066 m. (1500–3500 ft); rf. 762–889 mm. (30–35 in.). *55. The Makanjila Peninsula.* Undulating plains; fringing sand dunes; alkaline alluviums and regosols. 472–610 m. (1550–2000 ft); rf. 889–1006 mm. (35–40 in.).

A R STOBBS
A YOUNG

15   HISTORY AND SETTLEMENT

The Bantu-speaking peoples of Malawi have been moving into the areas they at present occupy during at least the last six hundred years.

Prior to the nineteenth century the main settlement was that of the Maravi, the Tumbuka-Kamanga and the people of northern Malawi, such as the Ngonde. Since the nineteenth century, besides the later arrivals of these three main clusters, fresh migration brought to the country the Ngoni, the Yao and the Lomwe.

The Maravi are said to have set out from southern Katanga in different clan-groups at different times from about the fifteenth century. The main clans were the Phiri, Banda, Mwali and Nkhoma. The important halting places were at Choma in Zambia and at Kaphirintiwa in the Dzalanyama ranges of central Malawi. From here the main party led by the Kalonga moved on to Msinja and finally to a place called Malawi near the south-western lakeshore. From one or more of the three main halting places in Malawi splinter groups from the main host broke away. Undi settled at Mano on the headwaters of the Kapoche River; Kaphwiti on the banks of the Wankurumadzi River; Lundu at Mbewe-wa-Mitengo some fifteen miles south of Chikwawa. In the Central Region of Malawi the three important splinter groups were led by Mkanda, Culu and Mwase Kasungu.

At one time around the seventeenth century the Maravi political structure was a powerful one under the Kalonga whose influence extended from the Luangwa valley to the Indian Ocean. At a later date, however, the Maravi or Cewa community split up and came to be known by different names such as Cewa, Nyanja, Mang'anja, Ntumba, Mbo, Chipeta, Zimba and Nsenga, but the Cewa have always been the largest single group of the former Maravi host.

That part of Malawi which lies north of the Dwangwa River was occupied by the Tumbuka-Kamanga peoples. The Tumbuka-Kamanga were originally a closely related group, if not a single people but, like the Maravi, they later subdivided into a number of groups of which the most important were the Tumbuka, Kamanga, Henga, Tonga and Siska.

The Tumbuka first occupied the area bounded by the Bua River in the south, the Songwe River in the north, Lake Malawi in the east, and the Luangwa River in the west.

The Tonga, as a sub-section of the Tumbuka-Kamanga cluster, seem to have been an amalgam of at least four different groups—the Nyaliwanga, Kapunda Banda, Kabunduli and Mankhambira.

With regard to the relationship between the Tonga and the Tumbuka, one Tonga view is that Tonga was only the name of the country occupied by them, as Maravi was the name of the country of the Cewa.

Northernmost Malawi and parts of neighbouring Tanzania are inhabited by the Nyakusa-Ngonde, the Hehe-Bena, the Nyiha and the Tumbuka.

The nineteenth century arrivals were the Ngoni and the Yao.

The Jere clan of the Ngoni, led by Zwangendaba, crossed the Zambezi near Zumbo in 1835 and continued north-eastwards, stopping at Mkoko near present Petauke and at Mawiri near Loudon and then, passing near Lake Kazuni, reached Mapupu in Tanzania. At about the same time a second clan of the Ngoni, led by Ngwane Maseko, crossed the Zambezi farther downstream than Zwangendaba had made his crossing, and continued eastwards past Dzonze Hill in the Kirk Range, near the present Dedza, and round the south of Lake Malawi and then northwards to Songea.

When Zwangendaba died in 1848 the Northern Ngoni host broke up into a number of splinter groups. The Ntabeni group moved north to the shores of Lake Victoria. The Zulu Gama group joined the Ngwane Maseko group at Songea until a quarrel led to the Maseko group being driven southward until it reached Domwe under Chidiaonga around 1871. One Jere group moved into the Henga valley where in 1855 M'Mbelwa was installed paramount chief in succession to Zwangendaba. Another group under Ntuto or Mpezeni migrated into what is now Zambia.

The second migratory people of the nineteenth century were the Yao who claim that their original home was between the Lujenda and Ruvuma Rivers east of Lake Malawi. Between 1850 and 1870 the Yao were attacked by the Makua, the Lomwe, and the Ngoni. Consequently four Yao groups moved into what is now Malawi. They were the Achisi Yao and the Amasaninga Yao whose descendants now live in the Mangoche (Fort Johnston) area; the Amachinga Yao who settled in four parties in Mangoche, Domasi and Liwonde; and the Amangoche Yao, who constitute more than half of the present Yao population in Malawi, and are settled in the Dedza, Chiradzulu and Blantyre districts.

The last large group of Bantu-speaking people to enter Malawi were the Lomwe whose traditional home is stated to be Namuli Hill, east of Lake Chilwa.

Between about 1897 and 1907, following the extension of the Portuguese administration into the country occupied by the Lomwe, thousands of these people left their homeland for Malawi. Their numbers have been increasing ever since, particularly in the districts of Mulanje, Thyolo (Cholo), Chiradzulu and Zomba which are now the most densely populated areas of the country.

More recently the Sena people have been infiltrating from the Zambezi area into the Nsanje district of the lower Shire River.

B PACHAI

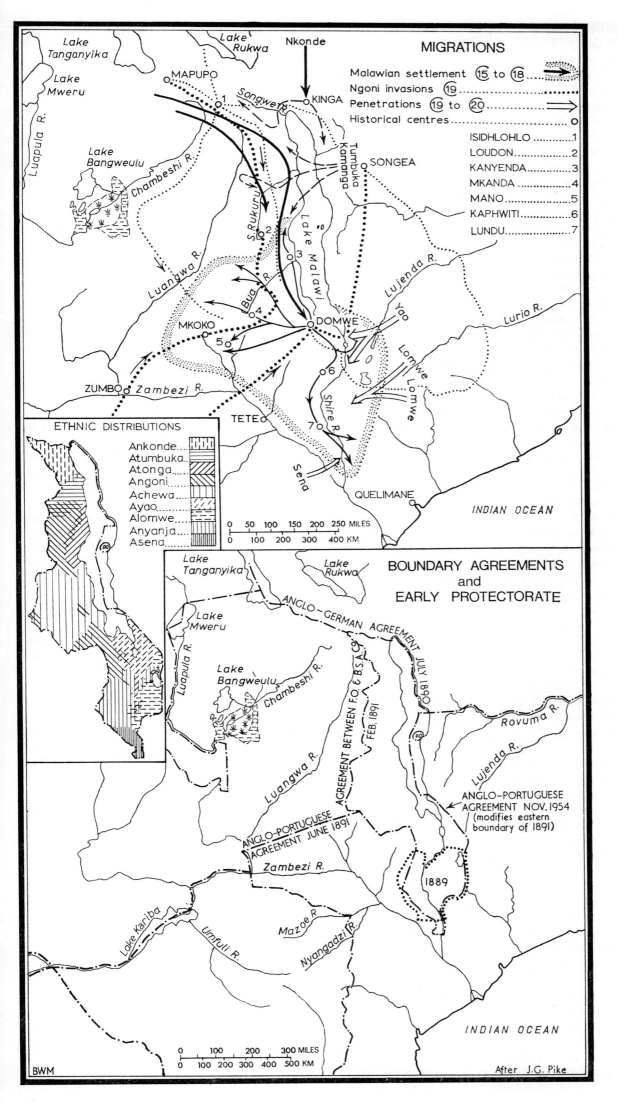

MIGRATIONS

Malawian settlement ⑮ to ⑱ ....
Ngoni invasions ⑲ ....
Penetrations ⑲ to ⑳ ....
Historical centres .... ○

ISIDHLOHLO 1
LOUDON............2
KANYENDA............3
MKANDA............4
MANO.................5
KAPHWITI............6
LUNDU.................7

Lake Tanganyika
Lake Mweru
Lake Rukwa
Nkonde
MAPUPO
Songwe R.
KINGA
Luapula R.
Lake Bangweulu
Chambeshi R.
Tumbuka Kamanga
SONGEA
S. Rukuru R.
Lake Malawi
Lujenda R.
Lurio R.
Luangwa R.
Bua R.
Yao
Lomwe
MKOKO
DOMWE
Lomwe
ZUMBO
Zambezi R.
TETE
Shire R.
Sena
QUELIMANE
INDIAN OCEAN

ETHNIC DISTRIBUTIONS

Ankonde....
Atumbuka....
Atonga.....
Angoni.....
Achewa.....
Ayao.....
Alomwe.....
Anyanja....
Asena....

0   50 100 150 200 250 MILES
0 100 200 300 400 KM

BOUNDARY AGREEMENTS and EARLY PROTECTORATE

Lake Tanganyika
Lake Rukwa
Lake Mweru
ANGLO-GERMAN AGREEMENT JULY 1890
AGREEMENT BETWEEN F.O. & B.S.A. Cº. FEB. 1891
Luapula R.
Lake Bangweulu
Chambeshi R.
Luangwa R.
Rovuma R.
Lujenda R.
ANGLO-PORTUGUESE AGREEMENT NOV. 1954 (modifies eastern boundary of 1891)
ANGLO-PORTUGUESE AGREEMENT JUNE 1891
Zambezi R.
1889
Lake Kariba
Umfuli R.
Mazoe R.
Nyangadzi R.
INDIAN OCEAN

0   100   200   300 MILES
0 100 200 300 400 500 KM

BWM

After J.G. Pike

16 ADMINISTRATION: 1891-6 DISTRICTS AND GOVERNMENT STATIONS

British influence in Malawi was represented by a series of Consuls appointed to the eastern part of Central Africa from 1859 onwards. To start with these Consuls were only indirectly concerned with Malawi, being appointed to the East Coast, usually to Moçambique with only vague responsibilities in the interior, and with ill-defined jurisdictions. In 1884, the first Consul to 'the territories of the African Kings and Chiefs in the districts adjacent to Lake Nyasa' was appointed. This appointment was designed to protect the growing number of British settlers, especially missionaries, and commercial interests. Even so, it was not these factors, but the expansion of Portuguese claims into the Shire Highlands, which brought about the declaration of a British Protectorate and the creation of a Civil Administration.

The first Protectorate, over the 'Makololo, Yao and Machinga Countries'—broadly the Shire Highlands area—was declared on 21st September 1889; and the second, over the whole of present-day Malawi, was declared on 14th May 1891. The creation of the Civil Administration was the work of the first Commissioner and Consul-General, Harry Johnston, who set up both a form of district administration and a pattern of central government departments.

In the rural areas Johnston first divided the country into four, and in 1893 into twelve administrative districts, each in the charge of a Collector whose tasks covered a wide executive and judicial field; they were responsible for law and order, for the collection of taxes and the issue of licences, for public works, and for the holding of courts.

At the administrative headquarters, Zomba, the work of the government was co-ordinated in, and directed from, a number of departments. The creation of these departments, each the responsibility of a senior civil servant, took place at an early date: by the end of 1892 there were separate police, medical, postal, scientific, engineering and finance departments. The pattern of central government, despite many changes of detail and emphasis, has persisted to the present day. Important changes, however, have taken place in the field of district administration where that work is concerned with local government.

The location of the early government stations, or 'bomas' were in two major groupings; the one in the Shire Highlands, where at least sixteen bomas were built between 1892 and 1896, and the other along a line of stations, sixteen in number, stretched out along the major waterway of Lake Malawi and the Shire River. A further half dozen were found scattered in the plateau areas to the west of the waterway.

Although Port Herald (now Nsanje) (1) was the only settlement to include the term 'Port' in its name, it was never considered to be a port in any real sense. From a very early date it was the administrative headquarters for the Lower Shire District, but it was not the official port of entry for the country, since Chiromo fulfilled this function.

Chiromo (2) for several years was one of the most important government stations in the country. The first civil servant in British Central Africa was stationed there, as also were the Customs Officers. In 1895-6, nearly half the government revenue derived from customs duties and from road and river dues collected at Chiromo.

A day's river journey upstream north of Chiromo lay Chikwawa (3). The government station was opened in 1892 and it was here that the road from the highlands met the Shire River at the farthest possible point of navigation.

The largest government station in the highlands was Blantyre (4), set up in the early 1890's to be near the Scottish mission and the African Lakes Company at Mandala, both of which pre-dated the Administration by a decade and a half.

Zomba (5) on a site by the Mlunguzi stream descending from Zomba plateau was selected as the administrative capital near a slave caravan route and two days' march from the mission at Blantyre. The slave routes were more closely watched from Fort Lister (6) and Fort Anderson (7) to the north and south of Mulanje Mountain.

Fort Mina (10) and Fort Migoi (11) were small outposts at the southern end of Lake Chilwa, while postal agencies were centred at Pangomani (8) and Thyolo (9). Police posts were established at Fort Roberts (12), Namadzi (13), Thondwe (14), Thuchila (Tuchila) (15), and Lirangwe (16) to guard the main route-ways.

In 1895 in the north of the Shire Highlands, Fort Malemia (17) and Fort Chikala (18) were erected; the first to guard Domasi mission, the second to watch a slave caravan route.

Navigation on the Upper Shire River was resumed at Fort Mpimbe (19), where routes from Blantyre and Zomba converged on the river, and from this point the chain of bomas along the lake-river line was resumed. Above Mpimbe lay Forts Sharpe (20) and Liwonde (21) guarding the line of river transport; up-river was Mvera station (22) set up as a rest-house on the river journey.

The exit from Lake Malawi was protected by Fort Johnston (Mangoche) (23), moved in 1897 to its present site and enlarged to a naval and civil boma with surveyed trading plots. Deep water at Monkey Bay (24) served as a sheltered anchorage and a naval department store-house was set up there for lake vessels.

Ferry routes across the lake, used by dhows and dugout canoes, were surveyed from stations and forts at Leopard Bay (25), Fort Maguire (26), Nkhota Kota (27), Nkata Bay (28), and Deep Bay (29). Karonga boma (30), grew up near the African Lakes Company's trading station, and farther north an administrative station was erected in 1894 on the Songwe River (31) to check the importation of firearms.

Few government stations in this period were erected outside the two major groupings, the Shire Highlands cluster and the Lake-Shire line. However, as the interior was opened routes needed guarding and in 1896 the rise to the Angoni plateau was commanded by Gowa (32), while Dedza (33) was situated where the route emerged onto the plateau. The route coming up the escarpment from Nkhota Kota to Chief Mpezeni's area was controlled from Fort Alston (34) and in the far north Fort Hill, now Chitipa (35), was built in 1896 to guard the road into Tanganyika. On the plateau to the east of the Rift Valley, the strongest fort of all was constructed at Jalasi's town on Mangoche Mountain (36) to bring a halt to the movement of slaves along that route.

Districts, 1894
1. Lower Shire (Port Herald); 2. Ruo (Chiromo); 3. Mulanje (Fort Anderson); 4. Zomba (Zomba); 5. Blantyre (Blantyre); 6. West Shire (Chikwawa); 7. Upper Shire (Liwonde); 8. South Nyasa (Fort Johnston, now Mangoche); 9. Central Angoniland (Tambala); 10. Marimba (Nkhota Kota); 11. West Nyasa (Nkhata Bay); 12. North Nyasa (Deep Bay).
Government Stations, 1891-96
1. Port Herald; 2. Chiromo; 3. Chikwawa; 4. Blantyre; 5. Zomba; 6. Fort Lister; 7. Fort Anderson; 8. Pangomani; 9. Thyolo; 10. Fort Mina; 11. Fort Migoi; 12. Fort Roberts; 13. Namadzi; 14. Thondwe; 15. Thuchila; 16. Lirangwe; 17. Malemia; 18. Fort Chikala; 19. Mpimbe; 20. Fort Sharpe; 21. Fort Liwonde; 22. Mvera; 23. Fort Johnston (Mangoche); 24. Monkey Bay; 25. Leopard Bay; 26. Fort Maguire; 27. Nkhota Kota; 28. Nkhata Bay; 29. Deep Bay; 30. Karonga; 31. Songwe; 32. Gowa; 33. Dedza; 34. Fort Alston; 35. Fort Hill; 36. Fort Mangoche.

C A BAKER

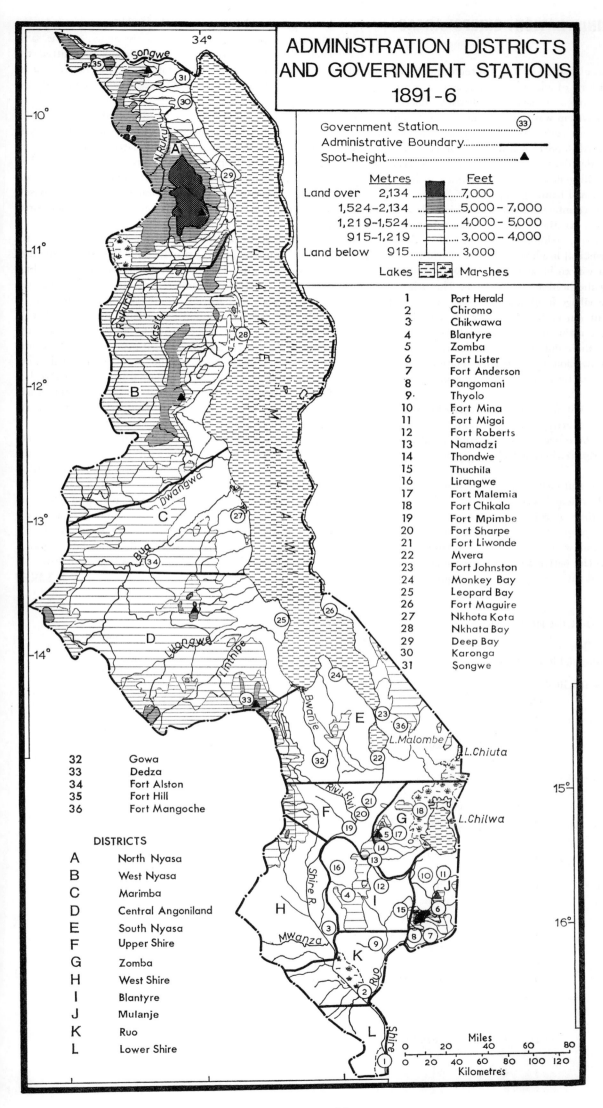

ADMINISTRATION DISTRICTS
AND GOVERNMENT STATIONS
1891-6

Government Station............................⊚33
Administrative Boundary............────
Spot-height.................................▲

Metres		Feet
Land over	2,134	7,000
	1,524–2,134	5,000–7,000
	1,219–1,524	4,000–5,000
	915–1,219	3,000–4,000
Land below	915	3,000

Lakes ⊞ Marshes

1	Port Herald
2	Chiromo
3	Chikwawa
4	Blantyre
5	Zomba
6	Fort Lister
7	Fort Anderson
8	Pangomani
9	Thyolo
10	Fort Mina
11	Fort Migoi
12	Fort Roberts
13	Namadzi
14	Thondwe
15	Thuchila
16	Lirangwe
17	Fort Malemia
18	Fort Chikala
19	Fort Mpimbe
20	Fort Sharpe
21	Fort Liwonde
22	Mvera
23	Fort Johnston
24	Monkey Bay
25	Leopard Bay
26	Fort Maguire
27	Nkhota Kota
28	Nkhata Bay
29	Deep Bay
30	Karonga
31	Songwe

32	Gowa
33	Dedza
34	Fort Alston
35	Fort Hill
36	Fort Mangoche

DISTRICTS

A	North Nyasa
B	West Nyasa
C	Marimba
D	Central Angoniland
E	South Nyasa
F	Upper Shire
G	Zomba
H	West Shire
I	Blantyre
J	Mulanje
K	Ruo
L	Lower Shire

Miles
0 20 40 60 80

0 20 40 60 80 100 120
Kilometres

From the proclamation of the Protectorate in 1891 until 1912 the pattern of administration was one of direct rule through the Collector, later the District Officer, in each district. This system was felt to be necessary because of the weakness of the authority of many of the chiefs. The Colonial Annual Report for Nyasaland for 1911–12 referred to the continuing decay in the power of the chiefs and to the tendency of villagers all over the country to become fragmented into small family groups.

In order to counteract these tendencies a law was introduced, known as the District Administration (Native) Ordinance 1912, which empowered the Governor to appoint a principal headman for each district. Each principal headman was to be assisted by two councillors chosen from among the headmen of his area. The principal headman and the village headmen were responsible to the District Resident (an earlier name for the District Commissioner) for the maintenance of law and order in their areas. In particular their duties included the reporting of crime and the apprehension of criminals, sanitation, control of the movement of cattle and the reporting of the outbreak of epidemic diseases.

In 1933 two important pieces of legislation were passed – the Native Authority Ordinance and the Native Courts Ordinance – the objects of which were to utilize fully the traditional organizations for all purposes of local government.

The Native Authority Ordinance provided for the replacement of principal headmen by native authorities which could be either a chief or a chief-in-council. Native authorities were given powers to make rules for the peace, good order and welfare of Africans within their areas of jurisdiction. The native authorities were appointed by the Governor, and native authority rules required his approval, but in practice the Governor delegated his powers under the Ordinance to the Provincial Commissioners. At the same time the new Native Courts Ordinance permitted the Governor to authorize the establishment of native courts. The effect of the new legislation was to enhance greatly the status of the chiefs.

From 1953 onwards, it became usual for the native authorities together to make rules for the whole district. In most districts the treasuries of the native authorities were 'federated' and from 1951 the practice was adopted of appointing as native authority not the chief as an indidivual but the chief-in-council, thus bringing the chief's advisers and prominent local Africans into the native authority council.

The Local Government (District Councils) Ordinance which was passed in 1953 provided for the establishment of District Councils. The District Councils were to include chiefs as ex-officio members, elected and nominated members with the District Commissioner as chairman.

The first District Council was established in the Thyolo district in May 1954, and by 1962 for all the districts in the country. The native authorities lost many of their functions to the new councils, including the power to make rules, but remained responsible for the maintenance of law and order, for the collection of taxes as agents of the government and for the allocation of African trust land, while the chiefs retained their functions in the African courts.

Amendments to the Local Government (District Councils) Ordinance in 1960 and 1961 further separated the functions of the district councils and the native authorities.

In 1961 the Malawi Congress Party published its election manifesto which advocated, inter alia, the appointment of chiefs as presidents of area and village councils, leaving the day to day business of these councils to elected chairmen.

A list showing the administrative divisions into Regions, Districts, Chiefs' and Sub-Chiefs' areas is given below.

C A BAKER

CHIEFS' AND SUB-CHIEFS' AREAS

C. = Chiefdom
S.C. = Sub-chiefdom

NORTHERN REGION

District	No.	Chief's Area
A. Chitipa	1	C. Kamene
	2	C. Nyondo
	3	C. Mwenisuku
	4	C. Mwenewenya
	5	C. Nthalire
B. Karonga	1	C. Kilupula
	2	C. Kyungu and S.C. Karonga
	3	S.C. Mwirang'ombe
	4	C. Mwafulirwa
C. Rhumphi	1	S.C. Kachulu
	2	S.C. Mwalweni
	3	S.C. Mwalenga
	4	S.C. Mwankunikira
	5	C. Mwamlowe
	6	S.C. Chapinduka
	7	C. Chikulamayembe
	8	C. Katumbi
	9	S.C. Zolokere
D. Mzimba	1	C. Mpherembe
	2	C. Ntwalo
	3	S.C. Munthali
	4	C. Chinde
	5	S.C. Kapingo Sibande
	6	C. Mbelwa
	7	C. Mzukuzuku
	8	C. Mzikubola
	9	C. Mabulabo
E. Nkhata Bay	1	S.C. Mkondowe
	2	C. Bhoghoyo
	3	C. Mbwana
	4	C. Timbiri
	5	S.C. Mkumbira
	6	C. Mankhambira
	7	S.C. Fukamalaza
	8	C. Kabunduli
	9	S.C. Malanda
	10	C. Fukamapiri
	11	S.C. Zilakoma
	12	C. Mpima—Likoma and Chisumula Islands

CENTRAL REGION

District	No.	Chief's Area
F. Kasungu	1	S.C. Chisikwa
	2	C. Kaluluma
	3	S.C. Mnyanja
	4	C. Chulu
	5	S.C. Simlemba
	6	C. Mwase
	7	C. Wimbe
	8	C. Kapelula

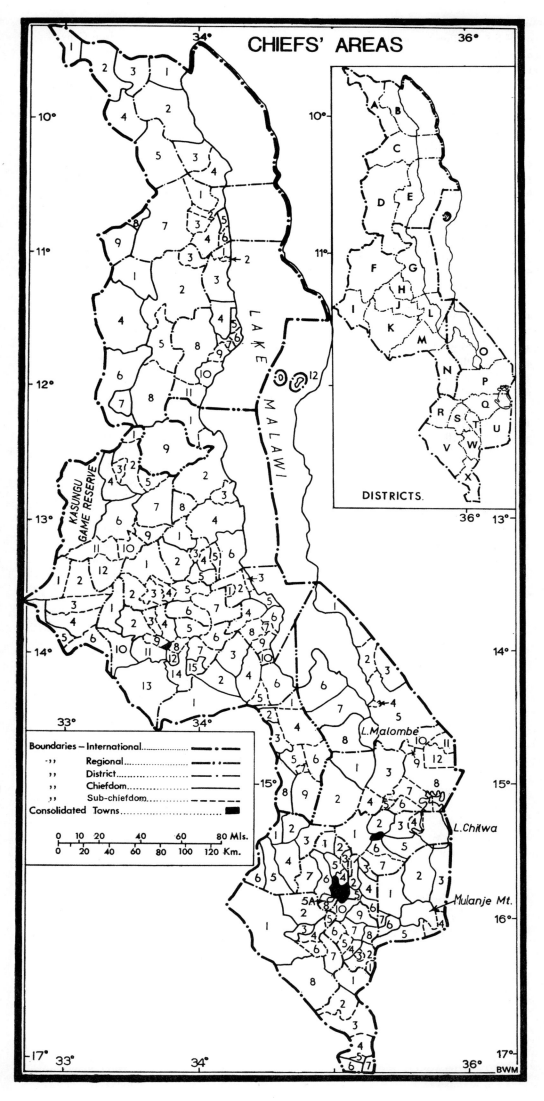

CHIEFS' AREAS

LAKE MALAWI

L. Malombe

L. Chilwa

Mulanje Mt.

KASUNGU GAME RESERVE

DISTRICTS.

Boundaries — International................
,, Regional.....................
,, District........................
,, Chiefdom.....................
,, Sub-chiefdom...............
Consolidated Towns.....................

| 0 | 10 | 20 | | 40 | | 60 | | 80 Mls. |
| 0 | 20 | 40 | 60 | 80 | 100 | 120 Km. |

BWM

District	No.	Chief's Area
	9	S.C. Chilowamatambe
	10	C. Njombwa
	11	C. Kawamba
	12	C. Santhe
G. Nkhota Kota	1	S.C. Kafuzila
	2	C. Kanyenda
	3	S.C. Mphonde
	4	C. Malenga Chanzi
	5	S.C. Mwansambe
	6	C. Mwadzama
H. Ntchisi	1	S.C. Chilooko
	2	C. Kalumo
	3	S.C. Nthondo
	4	C. Kasakula
	5	C. Chikho
I. Mchinji	1	C. Mkanda
	2	S.C. Dambe
	3	S.C. Mduwa
	4	C. Zulu
	5	C. Mlonyeni
	6	S.C. Mavwere
J. Dowa	1	S.C. (G.V.H.) Chakhaza
	2	S.C. (C.R.) Kayembe
	3	C. Dzoole
	4	S.C. (C.R.) Chiponda
	5	C. Msakambewa
	6	S.C. (C.R.) Mkukula
	7	C. Chiwere
K. Lilongwe	1	C. Khongoni
	2	C. Kabudula
	3	S.C. Mtema
	4	C. Chitukula
	5	C. Chimutu
	6	S.C. Chitekwere
	7	C. Mazengera
	8	S.C. Tsabango
	9	S.C. (G.V.H.) Njewa
	10	C. Kalolo
	11	C. Maliri
	12	C. Kalumba
	13	C. Chiseka
	14	C. Chadzamkwenda
	15	C. Kalumbu
L. Salima	1	S.C. Mwanza
	2	C. Khombedza
	3	S.C. Msosa
	4	C. Karonga
	5	C. Kaluunda
	6	C. Maganga
	7	C. Pemba
	8	S.C. Kambwiri
	9	C. Ndindi
	10	S.C. Kambalame
M. Dedza	1	C. Pemba
	2	C. Kaphuka
	3	C. Tambala
	4	C. Kasumbu
	5	S.C. Kamenya Gwaza
	6	C. Kachindamoto
N. Ncheu	1	C. Masasa
	2	C. Mambeya

District	No.	Chief's Area
	3	S.C. Goodson Ganya
	4	C. Njolomole
	5	C. Kwataine
	6	S.C. Makwangwala
	7	S.C. Champiti
	8	C. Mpando
	9	C. Phambala

SOUTHERN REGION

District	No.	Chief's Area
O. Mangoche	1	C. Makanjila
	2	S.C. Namavi
	3	C. Katuli
	4	S.C. Chowe
	5	C. Jalasi
	6	C. Nankhumba
	7	C. Mponda
	8	C. Chimwala
P. Kasupe	1	C. Kalembo
	2	C. Nsamala
	3	C. Liwonde
	4	S.C. Sitola
	5	S.C. Chamba
	6	S.C. Mposa
	7	S.C. Mlomba
	8	C. Kawinga
	9	S.C. Chiwalo
	10	C. Nyambi
	11	S.C. Ngokwe
	12	S.C. Chikweo
Q. Zomba	1	C. Mlumbe
	2	C. Malemia
	3	C. Kumtumanji
	4	S.C. Mkumbira
	5	C. Mwambo
	6	C. Chikowi
	7	S.C. Mbiza
R. Mwanza	1	C. Dambe
	2	S.C. Chekucheku
	3	C. Symon
	4	C. Mlauli
	5	C. Kanduku
	6	C. Ntache
S. Blantyre	1	C. Chigaru
	2	C. Lundu
	3	C. Makata
	4	C. Machinjiri
	5	C. Kapeni (North)
	5A	C. Kapeni (South)
	6	C. Kuntaja
	7	C. Kunthembwe
	8	C. Somba
T. Chiradzulu	1	C. Chitera
	2	C. Mpama
	3	C. Nchema
	4	C. Kadewere
	5	C. Likoswe
	6	C. Nkalo
U. Mulanje	1	C. Nkanda
	2	C. Mkhumba
	3	C. Nazombe
	4	S.C. Laston Njema
	5	C. Mabuka

District	No.	Chief's Area	District	No.	Chief's Area
	6	C. Chikumbu		4	C. Changata
	7	C. Mtiramanja		5	S.C. Kwethemula
				6	S.C. Changata
V. Chikwawa	1	C. Chapananga		7	C. Nchilamwela
	2	C. Kasisi		8	C. Ngamwane
	3	C. Katunga		9	C. Chimaliro
	4	C. Masseah		10	C. Bvumbwe
	5	S.C. Thomas			
	6	C. Lundu	X. Nsanje	1	C. Mlolo
	7	C. Makwira		2	S.C. Mbenje
	8	C. Ngabu		3	C. Tengani
				4	C. Ngabu-Malemia
W. Thyolo	1	S.C. Thukuta		5	C. Chimombo
	2	C. Nsabwe		6	C. Ndamera
	3	S.C. Mbawela		7	C. Nyachikadza

18 ECONOMIC HISTORY

When the Protectorate was founded in 1891 the total annual value of exports was £7000. Ivory was the major export item and grew to reach a peak figure of £18 000 in 1893, when it formed 83% of the value exported. Ivory, however, declined both absolutely and relatively as coffee and rubber became important. Coffee, first introduced in 1878, developed rapidly during the 1890's to reach a maximum of £62 000 in 1900, after which depressed world prices rapidly brought the crop to insignificant proportions. Much the same experience was suffered by rubber which also rose to a peak (£13 000) in 1900 before experiencing a sudden decline. By 1904 ivory, coffee and rubber were no longer of great importance. The first period witnessed the change from indigenous, collected exports, such as ivory, to exotic cultivated items, principally coffee.

The second period, occupying the years 1905 to 1921, was taken up in setting a pattern which to a large extent has prevailed ever since. These were the years during which Malawi's greatest crop, tobacco, rose from forming only 1% of the total exports, with £1000, to 75% with £300 000. Cotton also developed during this period and, although it formed 12% of the total in 1905 and only 16% in 1921, the value increased from £6000 to £66 000. It was during this period too, when the annual value of exports rose from £50 000 to £400 000, that commercial tea exports began, developed steadily but did not yet reach a commanding position.

The third period is a projection over a decade of the position reached at the end of the preceding period. These were the years during which tobacco reigned supreme, rising from an exported value of £300 000 in 1922, when it formed 72% of the total, to over £500 000 in 1932 when it formed 86% of the total value. During this decade African growers entered the market and brought about a great increase of fire-cured tobacco.

Cotton exports declined from £73 000 to £35 000, and this may be attributed partly to the greater interest taken in tea, the export value of which steadily rose from £20 000 to £43 000. This decade also covered the years during which sisal was of importance. First exported in 1908, sisal did not figure as an important export crop until the early 1920's when large areas in the Lower Shire District were opened up. The crop enjoyed popularity and by 1929 £34 000 worth was exported. As had happened previously with coffee and rubber, the decline in sisal exports was rapid, for in 1932 only £3 worth was exported.

Whereas the annual value of exports rose during the third period from £400 000 to £650 000, it rose in the following two decades of the next period to nearly £6 million in 1951. Tobacco continued to be the major export item, rising in value to £2·75 million at the close of the period, but it was beginning to be closely rivalled by tea which continued its steady progress until in 1951 it yielded £2 million. As with tobacco and tea, cotton also increased greatly during these two decades and fetched £330 000 in 1951. A small but significant additional item was added to Malawi's exports during the second half of period four when tung oil was first expressed for export. During this period the annual value of all exports rose from £500 000 to £5·75 million.

During the fifth period, covering the years between 1952 and 1963, the annual export value increased to over £10·5 million. Tea even more closely rivalled tobacco and in 1955, 1957 and 1961, the value of the former exceeded that of the latter; tobacco averaged £3·1 million and tea £3·3 million a year. Cotton, fluctuating annually, generally declined and its place among the 'Big Three' was taken by groundnuts, the rise of which was exceedingly rapid. Groundnuts have been grown since at least 1898 and were exported as early as 1904 but the quantities varied greatly from year to year. In fact the fourth period closed with only £1 worth (97 lb) of nuts being exported in 1951. The following year, however, brought a remarkable change which marks the dividing line between the fourth and fifth periods. The value of groundnuts exported in 1952 exceeded by more than half that of the aggregate value of groundnuts exported during the whole previous history. The £150 000 exported in 1952 formed 2·5% of the total and this was more than doubled in the following year when £350 000 worth left the country, forming 5% of the total value of exports. 1962 was a record year when the £1·9 million exported formed 13% of all exports. During this period the annual exports of groundnuts averaged £762 000 and 8% of the total. Over 60% of the groundnut production is carried out in the Central Province.

During the present, sixth, period, tobacco exports have averaged £4·5 million (17 000 tons) a year, and tobacco is now exported to over 40 different countries, principally the United Kingdom. Tea has averaged £3·8 million (65 000 tons) a year and, again, the United Kingdom is the principal importer. Groundnut exports have averaged £1·3 million (18 000 tons) a year, 86% going to the United Kingdom. Cotton exports have recovered and have averaged £1 million (5000 tons) a year, the United Kingdom taking 75%. Tung oil yields £230 000 (311 000 gallons) annually, and beans and peas £750 000 (23 000 tons) have become important.

The total value of domestic exports in 1969 was £18·3 million.

C A BAKER

EXPORTS

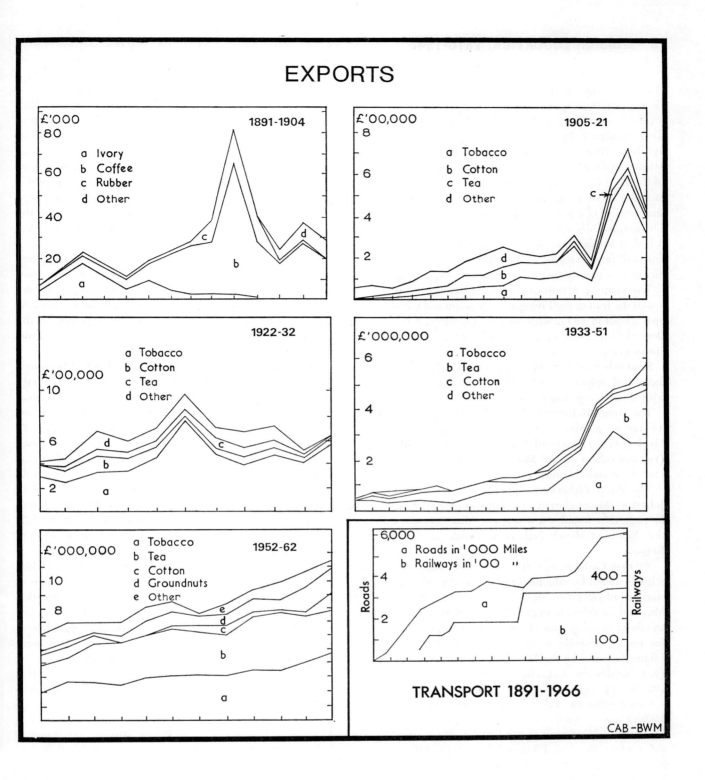

£'000
80
60
40
20

a Ivory
b Coffee
c Rubber
d Other

1891-1904

£'00,000
8
6
4
2

a Tobacco
b Cotton
c Tea
d Other

1905-21

£'00,000
10
6
2

a Tobacco
b Cotton
c Tea
d Other

1922-32

£'000,000
6
4
2

a Tobacco
b Tea
c Cotton
d Other

1933-51

£'000,000
10
8

a Tobacco
b Tea
c Cotton
d Groundnuts
e Other

1952-62

6,000
a Roads in '000 Miles
b Railways in '00 "
Roads
4
2
400
100
Railways

TRANSPORT 1891-1966

CAB-BWM

19 MISSION EDUCATION, 1876-1945

On 21st October 1876, four Africans from the Eastern Province of the Cape Colony landed at Cape Maclear on the south-western shore of Lake Malawi. They were William Koyi, Shadrack Ngunana, Alfred Mapas Ntintili and Isaac Williams Wauchope who had been educated at Lovedale Mission and were members of the second Livingstonia party of the Free Church of Scotland which was led by Dr James Stewart. Their duties at Cape Maclear (1) were to include the running of a school which was started that year by the Livingstonia Mission. This was the first school to be established in Malawi, and other schools followed as the mission founded new stations at Bandawe (2); Khondowe (3); Ekwendeni (4); Kasungu (5); Loudon (6); Karonga (7).

The Blantyre Mission (8) of the Church of Scotland followed the lead of the Livingstonia Mission and founded their own school in 1877, with subsidiary centres at Zomba (9); Domasi (10); Ncheu (11); Mulanje (12); Chiradzulu (13); Lunzu (14).

Soon other missions began operating in Malawi and all of them had important educational programmes connected with their evangelical work.

The Dutch Reformed Church Mission opened schools at its stations at Mvera (15) (1889); Kongwe (16) (1894); Livulezi (17) (1894) and Nkhoma (18) (1896). Malingunde (19) and others on the Malawian border such as Magwero (20) were added before 1906.

The White Fathers attempted to start a mission near Fort Johnston (Mangoche) in 1889 but were forced to withdraw. In 1902 they founded a mission at Mua (21) and called on the Montfort-Marist Fathers to work in the Southern Region.

At first Catholic education relied on networks of bush schools staffed by catechists trained by the priests. A higher standard of education was given at the minor seminaries at Mua and Nankhunda (22) which aimed at the formation of an educated indigenous clergy. In the 1920's normal schools for teacher training were set up by the White Fathers at Likuni (23) and by the Montfort-Marist Fathers at Nguludi (24) besides the Catholic schools at a number of other centres (25-33).

Other missions which started schools in Nyasaland (as Malawi was then called) between 1885 and 1909 were the Universities Mission to Central Africa whose most important centres were at Likoma Island (34), Likwenu (35), Malindi (36), and Nkhota Kota (37); the Zambesi Industrial Mission at Mitsidi (38) near Blantyre and at Dombole (39), Chiole (40) and Dzunge (41) in central Ngoniland; the Baptist Industrial Mission near Ncheu (47) at Gowa (43) and Pantumbi (44); South Africa General Mission at Lulwe (45) and at Port Herald (46), now known as Nsanje; the Nyasa Baptist Mission at Likubula (47) near Blantyre and at

Cholo (now Thyolo) (48); the Seventh Day Adventists near Tholo where the institution adopted the name Malamulo (49); and the Churches of Christ at Namiwawa (50) near Zomba and at Mlanje (now Mulanje) (51).

A few schools were also started by mission-trained Africans. Notable among these was the Providence Industrial Mission school (52), near Chiradzulu, which was opened by John Chilembwe in 1900; a number of schools were opened in the Mzimba (53) district from 1910 onwards by Charles Domingo and financed by the Seventh Day Baptists; the African Methodist Episcopal Church school at Kasungu (54), founded by the Rev. Msokera Phiri in 1925; and the Sazu Home Mission school (55), which was started by the Rev. Charles Chinula in 1934.

A conference of Protestant Missions was held at Livingstonia in 1900 with a view to harmonizing their educational policies. A second conference was held in 1904 which resulted in the publication, in 1905, of an education code. At a third conference held in 1910 positive proposals for the education of women were made and an Education Board was set up to revise the education code of 1905.

Prior to 1908 the entire cost of education had been met by the missions themselves, but in that year the Protectorate Government agreed to make an annual grant towards education of £1000 to be shared among those mission institutions which had subscribed to the 1905 education code. In 1920 the grant was increased to £2000 and in 1924/25 to £3000.

The Phelps-Stokes Commission visited Nyasaland in 1924. One of its recommendations was that village schools should be developed and properly supervised. In order to link village schools with village community life the Jeanes Training Centre was set up at Domasi in 1928. Meanwhile a Director of Education was appointed in 1925 and an Education Department was established the following year.

The Federated Missions which had produced the revised education code in 1910 met to consider ways and means of co-operation between the missions and the Education Department and, in 1927, a Native Education Conference was held, an Education Ordinance was enacted, an Advisory Board was set up and District School Committees were brought into being from the beginning of 1928.

The following statistics show the number of schools that existed in 1927: Universities Mission to Central Africa (Anglican) 163; Dutch Reformed Church Mission 727; Church of Scotland (Blantyre) 343; United Free Church of Scotland (Livingstonia) 399; Nyasa Mission 77; Zambezi Industrial Mission 116; White Fathers 352; Baptist Industrial Mission 42; South African General Mission 60; Montfort Marist Fathers 440; Seventh Day Adventist Mission 64; Providence Industrial Mission 1; African Church of Christ 1; African Episcopal Methodist Church 2; Government Police School 1.

B PACHAI

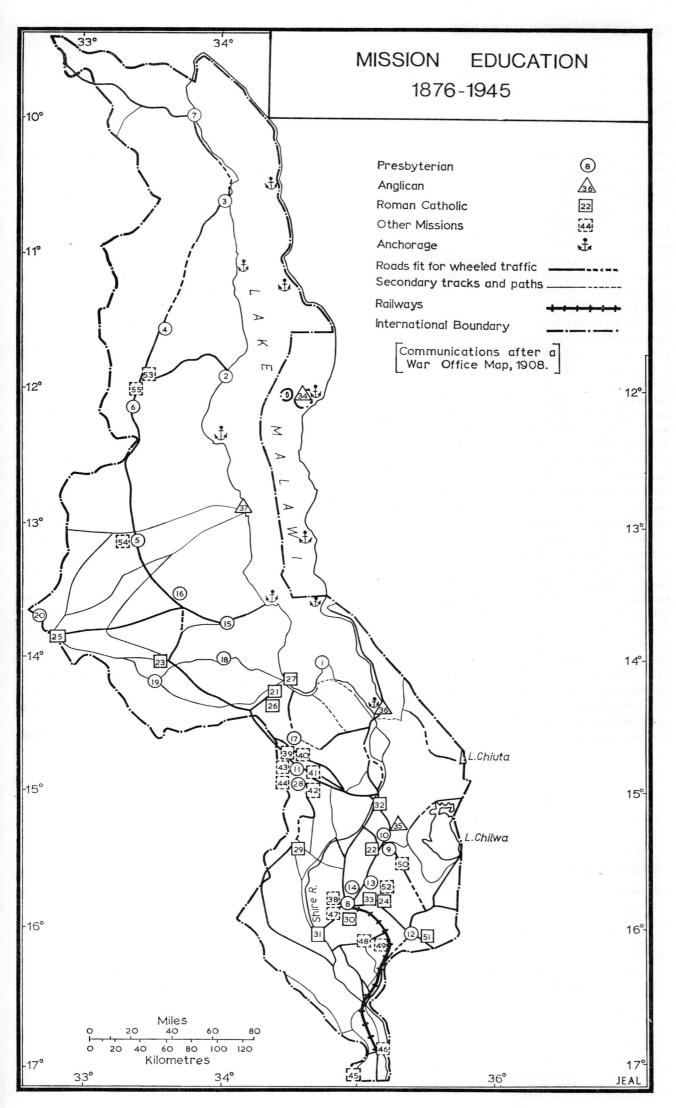

MISSION EDUCATION
1876-1945

Presbyterian ⑧

Anglican △36

Roman Catholic 22

Other Missions 44

Anchorage ⚓

Roads fit for wheeled traffic ━━━━━━

Secondary tracks and paths ━━━━━━

Railways ━┼━┼━┼━

International Boundary ━━·━·━·━

[Communications after a
War Office Map, 1908.]

L A K E   M A L A W I

L.Chiuta

L.Chilwa

Shire R.

Miles
0   20   40   60   80

0 20 40 60 80 100 120
Kilometres

JEAL

53

The Education Ordinance of 1928 brought many initial difficulties to school organization in matters of control, finance, syllabuses and religious instruction developed by the missions. Financial stringency on the part of the government and shortage of money on the part of the missions hindered expansion of the schools and improvements in education at a time when Africans were demanding, particularly through the Native Associations, better schools and also opportunities for higher education.

Two Africans who were appointed to the Advisory Board, Mr Levi Mumba in 1933 and Mr Charles Matinga in 1937, pressed very hard for the introduction of secondary schools and finally obtained the support of government, but the war intervened and it was only in April 1941 that the first secondary school in Malawi, the Blantyre Secondary School, was officially opened. In the next year Zomba Catholic Secondary School was opened, followed by Dedza Government Secondary School in 1951 and Mzuzu Government Secondary School in 1959.

Following the establishment of the Ministry of Education in 1961 and under the stimulus of independence in 1964 education in the post-primary field was greatly expanded and now comprises a four-year secondary school course, teacher training, technical and vocational instruction, sixth form and university courses. A measure of the expansion may be judged by the increase in secondary schools. From the initial two secondary boarding schools in the 1940's, the number of secondary schools has increased to 57, the majority of which were opened since Independence as mixed day-secondary schools.

Nevertheless, limited resources allow no more than 35% of the school age population to attend school. In 1964 of the 30 721 pupils who completed primary school only 2481 pupils or 8·1% passed into secondary school. Increase in the number of secondary schools and a higher teacher/pupil ratio will raise the number of secondary school entrants to 14·1% of the total number of primary school leavers in 1970.

Estimates, calculated by Peter H M Chiwona from pupil/class ratios in secondary schools in 1968, give a projected enrolment of 12 836 pupils in secondary schools in 1975. This is less than half the number (29 837) who are likely to qualify out of the 47 348 candidates for the Primary School Leaving Certificate.

To meet the aspirations of those denied places in secondary schools the Malawi Correspondence College with associated night schools was established in 1966. By 1968, applications for enrolment for correspondence courses had risen to 8500 students which almost equalled the enrolment (8576) into formal secondary education for that year. The lack of secondary school places for the 'unfortunate passers,' as they have been called, is one of the most intractable problems facing the present transitional period in the educational system.

The University of Malawi was opened in September 1965 and, in January 1967, by incorporation with four other institutions of further education, came to consist of five constituent colleges, namely Bunda College of Agriculture, Chancellor College, the Institute of Public Administration which had been started in 1962, the Polytechnic which had been opened in 1964, and Soche Hill College of Education which had been established in 1962. The total student enrolment in the five colleges of the University in 1968–69 was 881.

Entry to the University is at Ordinary Level (C) and the University awards a general degree after four years of study; and diplomas in teaching, engineering, business studies and agriculture are awarded at the completion of three years. Only one school offers sixth form work. Thirty students for the sixth form are selected from the highest passes at School Certificate and on obtaining the British Advanced Level are sent abroad to study for those professions not yet offered by the University. In 1970 over 300 undergraduates were studying abroad.

In Malawi educational costs by type of education are difficult to assess where there are both government assisted and unassisted schools and institutions. In 1968, of the eleven training colleges the government fully supported one only; of the 28 day secondary schools, 26 were government supported and of the boarding schools, many of mission foundation, only five of the 24 claimed full government support.

In 1964, the expenditure on education accounted for 13·2% of the Revenue and Development Account. In 1969 expenditure had risen to 15·3% which can be accounted for by the costs involved in the growth of the University and the continuing expansion in the other sectors of post-primary education. A preliminary estimate for 1970 at 13·5% indicates that expenditure on education is stabilising to a figure more in keeping with the other demands for public money.

SWANZIE AGNEW

ENROLMENT OF PUPILS IN SCHOOLS IN MALAWI* 1959–1970

Number of primary schools	1959	1960	1961	1962	1963	1964	1965	1966	1967	1968	1969	1970
Total primary schools	292 760	285 162	270 382	327 834	367 378	359 841	337 911	286 056	297 456	333 876	333 996	125 222
Total secondary schools	1 306	1 501	1 713	2 587	3 225	5 823	7 996	8 703	7 970	9 283	9 592	10 937
Total schools	294 066	286 663	272 095	330 421	370 603	365 664	345 907	294 959	305 426	343 159	343 588	136 159
Total teacher training course	918	930	972	1 269	1 410	1 368	1 387	1 350	1 180	1 085	719	895
Total technical/vocational training	733	732	671	641	1 369	1 183	1 129	915	551	536	303	339
GRAND TOTAL	295 717	288 325	273 738	332 331	373 382	368 215	348 423	297 224	307 157	344 780	344 610	137 393

* Source: Ministry of Education.

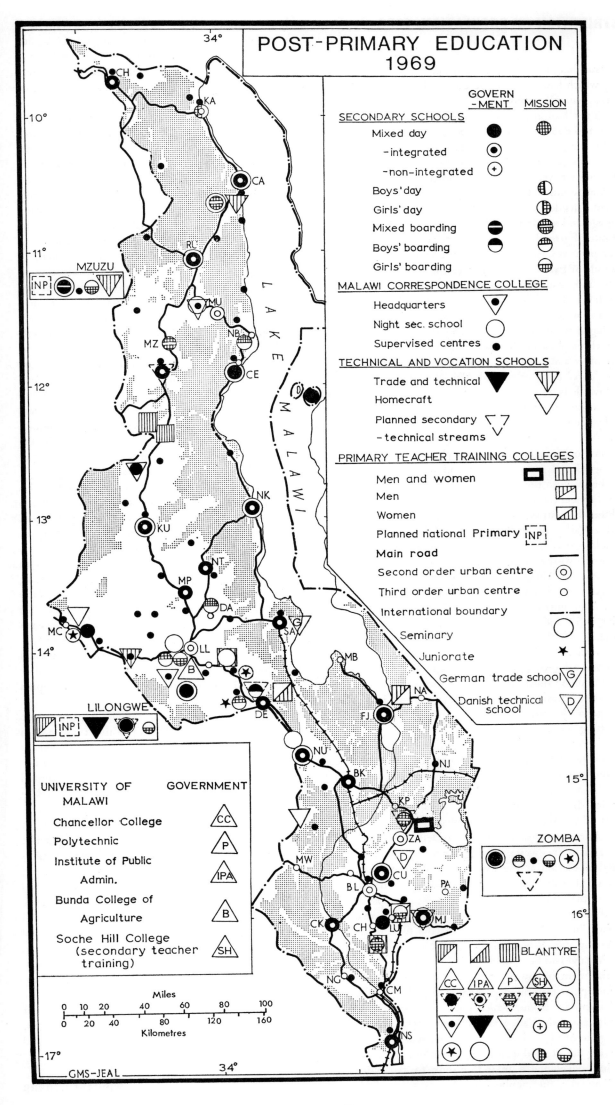

POST-PRIMARY EDUCATION
1969

	GOVERN-MENT	MISSION
SECONDARY SCHOOLS		
Mixed day		
-integrated		
-non-integrated		
Boys' day		
Girls' day		
Mixed boarding		
Boys' boarding		
Girls' boarding		

MALAWI CORRESPONDENCE COLLEGE
Headquarters
Night sec. school
Supervised centres

TECHNICAL AND VOCATION SCHOOLS
Trade and technical
Homecraft
Planned secondary
  -technical streams

PRIMARY TEACHER TRAINING COLLEGES
Men and women
Men
Women
Planned national Primary
Main road
Second order urban centre
Third order urban centre
International boundary
Seminary
Juniorate
German trade school
Danish technical school

MZUZU

LILONGWE

UNIVERSITY OF   GOVERNMENT
MALAWI

Chancellor College
Polytechnic
Institute of Public
  Admin.
Bunda College of
  Agriculture
Soche Hill College
(secondary teacher
training)

ZOMBA

BLANTYRE

Miles
0 10 20   40   60   80   100
0 20 40   80   120   160
Kilometres

GMS-JEAL

21 DISTRIBUTION OF POPULATION, 1966

The first census, held in 1901, indicated a *de jure* population of 737 000, which had risen to 970 000 at the time of the 1911 census, generally considered more reliable. Subsequent growth resulted in the enumeration of a *de jure* population of 1 200 000 in 1921, 1 600 000 in 1931 and 2 183 000 in 1945. In 1966, when the first scientifically conducted census (as opposed to administrative estimates) was conducted two years after Independence, the *de jure* population was found to total 4 305 600, of whom 265 000 were resident outside the country. Upon the basis of data concerning age and sex it was subsequently estimated that the annual rate of growth was about 3·0 per cent. No social or economic process measurable at present or foreseeable in the next decade or two is likely to reduce this rate of growth substantially, and, assuming it remains for the next twenty years at this level, the population of the country will exceed six millions in 1980 and eight millions in 1990.

The existing distribution of population within the country results from three phases in its history. During the first, up to the early nineteenth century, population concentrations grew as the 'core' areas of several African societies, with associated low density extensions, and largely isolated by peripheral unoccupied areas. The first phase was essentially completed by the early nineteenth century. The disruption of most of these cores, and the development of 'refuge' concentrations, constituted the second phase and resulted from the Angoni and Ayao invasions and slave raids. The third phase began with the European occupation.

The largest concentrations of population were, by the end of the eighteenth century, beside Lake Malawi and in the southern Rift Valley on well-watered and fertile alluvial soils: the Ankhonde core in Karonga and the Amaravi core around the south-west arm, and extending southwards into modern Chikwawa. Along the Rhumphi and Nkhata Bay lakeshores settled smaller Citumbuka and Citonga-speaking populations. The northernmost Amaravi settlement was occupied by ivory and slave traders from East Africa at Nkhota Kota. From the Rift Valley cores settlement had spread westwards: in the north along narrow strips of alluvium in the Songwe (Alambya) and the Kasitu-South Rukuru (Atumbuka) valleys: in the centre more extensively over the Lilongwe-Kasungu savannas (Acewa); and in the south and on to the Shire Highlands (Amang'anja). All practised shifting *chitemene* cultivation.

M'mbelwa's Angoni reduced and scattered the populations of the Lilongwe plateau, settled among the Atumbuka to the north, and commenced a movement southwards away from the alluvial strips into Mzimba. The Maseko Angoni, having disturbed the Lilongwe areas and, having travelled east of the lake, passed through and reduced the Amaravi lakeshore core area, settling in the Dedza and Dowa areas above and to the west. Raiding for slaves and food increased its population at the expense of adjacent areas, which became virtually depopulated. Over the southern lakeshore and the Shire Highlands successive groups of Ayao moved from their westward-extending core area north of Lake Chilwa and east of Lake Malawi to raid the remaining Amang'anja. When Europeans first arrived much of southern Malawi had been depopulated.

The establishment of towns and agricultural estates and the use of porters, within the depopulated Shire Highlands, created a demand for labour which could not be satisfied from the adjacent Rift Valley floor. Very early mission efforts among the Atonga and Angoni-Atumbuka had created there a growing literate and educated population, which by the 1890s had developed a migration link to the Shire Highlands. However, the numbers involved were insuffici-ent. Early attempts to use the Dedza-Dowa concentration for labour met with resistance from the Angoni chiefs, but after punitive expeditions a regular movement developed from the southernmost parts. These seasonal labour movements did little either to reduce growth in source areas, or to increase growth in the Shire Highlands. The large-scale permanent immigration of the Alomwe into the Shire Highlands and the Asena into the southern parts of the Lower Shire eventually provided a solution. The Ayao of the south-central region contributed both temporary and permanent migrants to the Shire Highlands. These immigrants, and their subsequent natural increase, were almost entirely responsible for the development of the large concentration of population here, and only a small proportion may be attributed to permanent migration from the Northern and Central administrative Regions, except that from Ncheu.

During the 1920s development of tobacco production on the Lilongwe plateau stimulated a movement from the Dowa-Dedza area of less fertile soils, from the southernmost areas of the Northern Region and from Moçambique. Post-1945 developments in the Mzuzu area stimulated only minor concentrations of population. From Salima to Karonga the lakeshore populations grew after movements from the plateau surfaces above, while from the growing densities of the Shire Highlands there has been a movement down into the rift valley floor. Local moves towards main roads and areas with wells and boreholes have been common.

By 1966 these accumulated effects had resulted in the concentration of exactly one-third of the then *de facto* population (1 340 000 out of 4 040 000) in the Shire Highlands. The adjacent Ntaja and Namwera hinterlands contained a further 198 000. The second largest concentration, 987 000 (one-quarter of the *de facto* total), occupied a larger area at lower densities, in the Lilongwe area. A further 204 000 were enumerated in the still lower density Mchinji and Kasungu hinterlands. Nearly sixty per cent of the Malawian population was concentrated in these modern 'core' areas. The remainder were resident either on the plateaux to the north in extensive low density areas, or within the Rift Valley in restricted areas of medium to high density, each separated by largely unoccupied areas. Of the former type the Mzimba, Rumphi and Mzuzu hinterlands contained 292 000 persons, and was separated from the much smaller Chitipa concentration of 65 000 persons by the unoccupied Nyika plateau.

Thirty per cent of the *de facto* population, 1 204 000 persons, were resident within the Rift Valley: 573 000 in the lakeshore plains, 208 000 persons in the hinterlands of Ncheu, Balaka and Liwonde on the main Lilongwe-Shire Highlands routes, while in the Lower Shire, separated from the foregoing by the infertile and forested middle Shire area, a further 274 000.

The population potential surface reflects the degree of concentration around Lilongwe and the Shire Highlands, which have peaks of 642 000 and 418 000 persons-miles respectively, in contrast to the uniformly low potential elsewhere. Of particular interest is the area of low potential between the two peaks, and the extension of the Lilongwe positive anomaly into Moçambique. Assuming the mutual attraction of the two peaks, the area between Lilongwe and Blantyre is the most likely to yield the greatest benefits from investment in regional population immigration and transportation and service provision. In fact during the inter-censal period 1945–66 it was this area which showed the highest net increase, 117 per cent, compared to 104 per cent in the Lower Shire, 100 per cent in the Shire Highlands, 97 per cent in the central and central lakeshore areas, and only 71 per cent in the Northern Region.

MICHAEL STUBBS

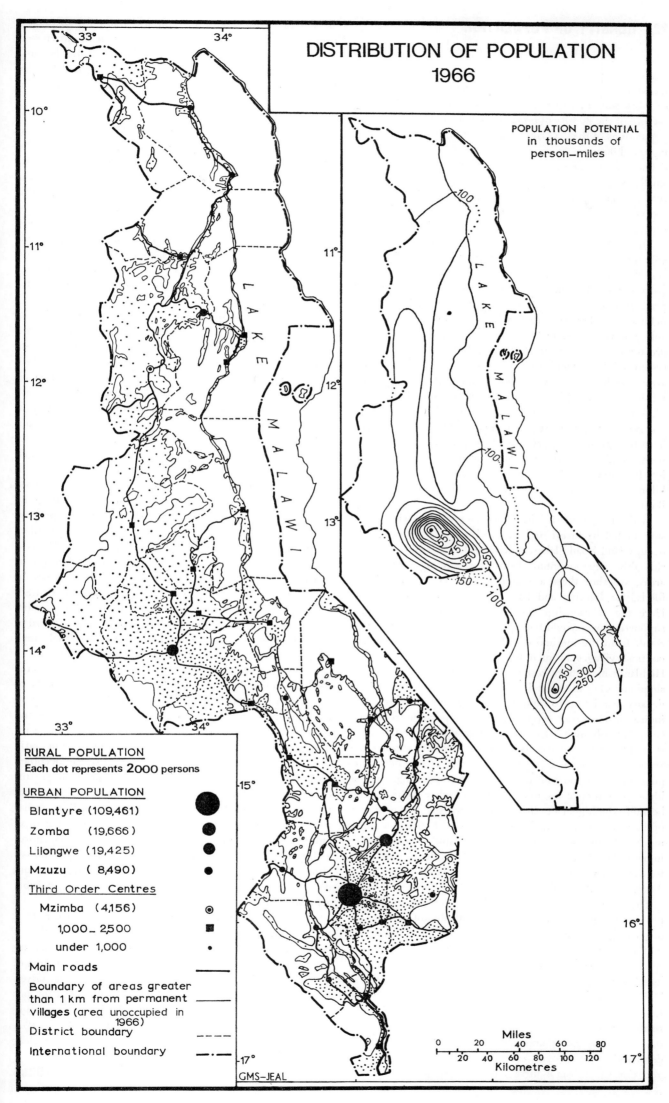

DISTRIBUTION OF POPULATION
1966

POPULATION POTENTIAL
in thousands of
person–miles

LAKE MALAWI

RURAL POPULATION
Each dot represents 2000 persons

URBAN POPULATION
Blantyre (109,461)
Zomba (19,666)
Lilongwe (19,425)
Mzuzu (8,490)
Third Order Centres
Mzimba (4,156)
1,000 _ 2,500
under 1,000
Main roads
Boundary of areas greater
than 1 km from permanent
villages (area unoccupied in
1966)
District boundary
International boundary

Miles
0   20   40   60   80
20 40 60 80 100 120
Kilometres

GMS–JEAL

57

22 DENSITY OF POPULATION

For the purposes of the 1966 census maps were prepared showing the locations of all hamlets and villages at the scale of 1/50 000. In order to obtain a uniform and detailed picture of the density of population in 1966 the enumerated populations of these villages were related to an area extending one kilometre from each. Within the occupied area so defined actual densities were calculated for all but the smaller strips of land by aggregating the population within two overlapping sets of coterminous 10 kilometre squares, the centres of one set forming the corners of the second series.

The choice of a distance of one kilometre from an enumerated hamlet as the definition of the occupied area rested upon data relating to distance lapse of intensity of use collated by Chisholm (1962). It was asumed that a very high proportion of food requirements were produced within the defined area. It is true that, where cultivable land is available and villages sufficiently distant, cultivation occurs at greater distances, particularly in relation to the *chitemene* system of shifting cultivation still practised in low density areas, particularly those of the Northern Region. Such extensions are rarely coterminous and comprise scattered plots temporarily occupied and producing crops which do not require, or are not given, high inputs of labour. Even here the greater proportion of food produced comes from permanently cultivated plots adjacent to the village or hamlet. It is assumed that the cultivated area farther than one kilometre is balanced by uncultivated areas within that limit.

In the lower density areas, where groups of villages are surrounded by forest or bush, and where lines of villages occupy land beside lakes, cultivated food supplies are considerably supplemented from surrounding unoccupied areas, whether these are used for the collection of wild foods, for hunting and fishing, or for livestock grazing. Here the relationship between population and the total supporting area would be expressed by lower densities than result from the method of calculation described above. In contrast villages in such high density areas as the Shire Highlands have more restricted opportunities for similarly supplementing their food supplies, and for this reason the density in relation to supporting area is approximately that indicated. However, supplementation is possible from wage and salary labour in adjacent urban areas and in estates, and is used to import foodstuffs from lower density areas. These areas are also more accessible to sources of production inputs and to opportunities for urban marketing, and so higher intensity of use has resulted in higher yields making bearable the higher densities. However, low cost provision of domestic water-supply materials and fuel is becoming more difficult and requires considerable investment in improved facilities and commercialized production. Domestic water supply, more than soil fertility, has been the major determinant of population concentration.

The density ratio is also very relevant to the most efficient provision of inputs and services and diffusion of information originating in the urban centres. Higher densities, combined with location near to an urban centre, permit a much greater return in productivity and social satisfaction than an equivalent investment in lower density areas. The largest areas of high densities are clearly associated with urban growth, at Lilongwe and particularly around Zomba, Blantyre and the smaller third order urban centres of the Shire Highlands. In the dormitory commuter zones for Blantyre and Zomba densities rise to 232 and 270 persons per sq. km. (600 and 700 per sq. mile). A further factor here, and in the Mulanje area, is the source of domestic water for so great a concentration of population which exists in the numerous streams emerging from the residual massifs. These become buried in alluvial deposits, particularly during the dry season, within a short distance of their emergence on to the plateau.

A different approach to the calculation of population density is that of relating population to the area described as 'of clear field pattern'. This method, developed by the Ministry of Agriculture, is based upon the analysis of aerial photographs and the delimitation of all areas having clear evidence of cultivation. The method relates population both to recently abandoned cultivated land and to land currently in use, and thereby lowers the density ratio. Available good land is defined as land which can give medium to high yields with minimum expenditure of labour or capital. Moderate quality land is that which will give medium yields but requires greater investment, being of lower fertility, more broken and less accessible.

The resultant density surface, expressed in acres of clear field pattern per person, is similar to that obtained from the alternative method of calculation. Important contrasts emerge with respect to the amount of good and moderate land remaining available. In the Shire Highlands area all available good and moderate land is utilized in Thyolo and Chiradzulu Districts, and over three-quarters utilized in Zomba, Mulanje and probably in the Shire Highlands section of Blantyre District. The Central Region moderate density area has in most of its constituent districts just under half of the total good and moderate land still available, while in the peripheries of these two concentrations of higher densities, the Lower Shire, and south-central region, the central lakeshore, and in Mchinji and Kasungu, the proportion of suitable land still available is considerably higher. The greater acreage available in the north-central and Northern Regions is probably a reflection of the inclusion of fallow. Probably the actual cultivated land used is not so greatly different from that available to the peasant in Chiradzulu, and the productivity per acre of the latter is possibly greater. Apart from Karonga District, where only a third of available good and moderate land remains, similarly high proportions exist in the Northern Region districts.

Although this possibility exists, however, the factor likely to determine future densities will be accessibility to urban markets and to transportation networks leading to external markets. Increasing use of unoccupied areas and increased densities in occupied areas which meet these requirements costs will yield a greater cost-benefit ratio than would a uniformly spread extension of the occupied area. This factor, together with the future probable greater concentration of population in urban areas, indicates that the future surface of rural population density will be similar to the existing one, although with still higher densities in an enlarged area around Lilongwe, in the central lakeshore, and particularly in the south central region and the Lower Shire. Within the Shire Highlands the existing medium density area of the Chilwa-Palombe plain will probably achieve higher densities.

The total land area is 94 079 sq. km. (36 324 sq. miles), and the clear field pattern 21·3 per cent of this, that is 20 239 sq. km. (7737 sq. miles), giving an average density per total land area of 111 and per clear field pattern area of 522 in 1966—very high average densities for Africa. Given the present rate of population growth, 3·0 per cent per annum and an even distribution of density it would be 1991 before all available good and moderate land (44·1%, 41 489 sq. km. or 16 019 sq. miles) supported this clear field pattern density.

MICHAEL STUBBS

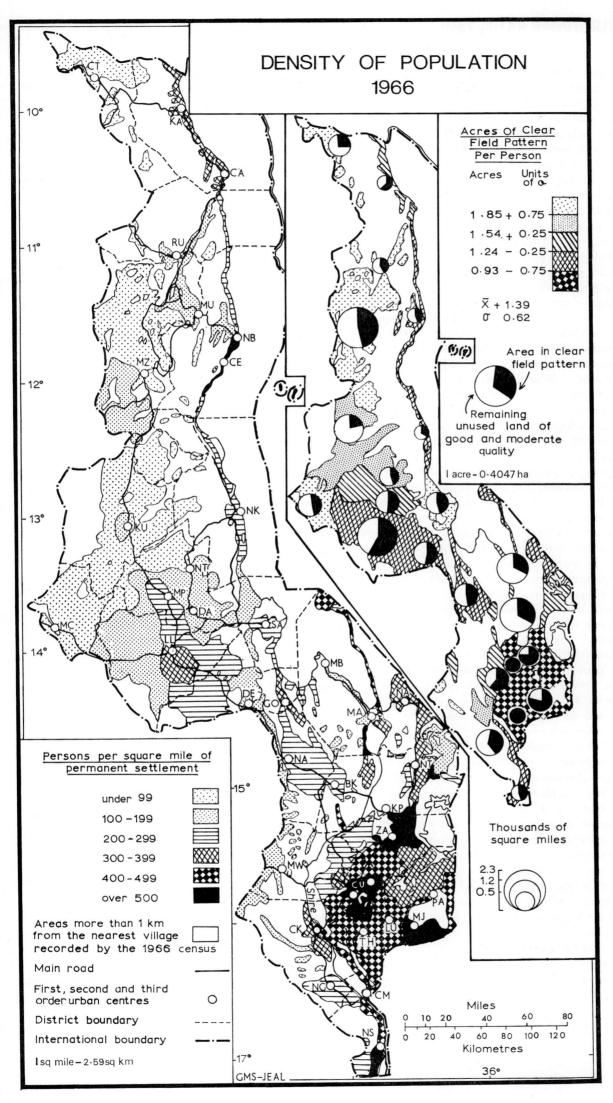

DENSITY OF POPULATION
1966

Acres Of Clear Field Pattern Per Person

Acres	Units of α
1·85 + 0·75	
1·54 + 0·25	
1·24 − 0·25	
0·93 − 0·75	

$\bar{X}$ + 1·39
σ   0·62

Area in clear field pattern

Remaining unused land of good and moderate quality

1 acre - 0·4047 ha

Thousands of square miles

2·3
1·2
0·5

Persons per square mile of permanent settlement

under 99	
100 - 199	
200 - 299	
300 - 399	
400 - 499	
over 500	

Areas more than 1 km from the nearest village recorded by the 1966 census

Main road

First, second and third order urban centres   ○

District boundary

International boundary

1 sq mile - 2·59 sq km

Miles
0 10 20   40   60   80

0   20   40   60   80   100   120
Kilometres

36°

GMS-JEAL

23 CHILD–WOMAN RATIO, 1966

No questions concerning fertility and mortality were included in the 1966 census enquiries. The only information relevant to these two processes was that derived from the response to questions on age and sex. The child–woman ratio was the only indicator which could be obtained from the source. It measured the numerical relationship between women stating their age to be between, and including, 15 and 49 years in August 1966, and the survivors, whose age was stated to be less than 5 years, of those assumed therefore, to have been conceived during the period November 1961 to November 1965. Both levels of fertility and of foetal, infant, and child mortality might have changed during this period of 5½ years prior to the census enumeration. The child–woman ratio might measure, therefore, either a rapidly changing situation or a static one. It is probable that the incidence of age misreporting for children with real ages 4 to 6 was low, as the risk of memory lapse would be small. Age misreporting for females, particularly at the older boundary of the class at risk of child-bearing, was probably greater although the distorting effect would be reduced because of the smaller numbers of older females. It is plausible to consider that both female and child age misreporting, particularly that of females, would be greater in areas of lower educational attainment. Spatial variations in this level are analysed in another section, and if the assumed relationship is real, suggest those areas where distortion might be greatest. However, the direction of over-enumeration remains unknown. The child–woman ratio is, therefore, a crude indicator which can be used, with care, as a measure of survival to the age 5, but not for separate measurement of either fertility or mortality. There was some reason to believe that in Malawi the ratio was primarily determined by mortality, and that variations in the ratio between information areas indicates variations in the level of mortality between conception and age 5.

Most non-quantified information points to the tentative conclusion that levels of fertility were uniform throughout Malawi, as well as being, more obviously, high. For almost all of the ninety-five per cent of the national population resident in rural areas high levels of fertility were the most appropriate. Frequent pregnancies were essential to compensate for the high incidence of miscarriages, stillbirths, and infant and child mortality. Human labour, whether used on peasant subsistence or commercial holdings or exported to areas of employment within or outside Malawi, brought benefits usually greater than costs of support. Very high prestige value was attached by parents to large families and by village headmen and chiefs to large populations within the area of their authority. The losses of the slave raids and attendant epidemics and famines had continued up to the beginning of the century, and had reinforced the level of preference for high fertility rates.

The incidence of disease and of malnutrition in females was relevant to levels of fertility, and varied considerably within the country in relation to a whole complex of factors.

Male labour migration had a varied but possibly small effect, possible frequency of visits to the home being a determining factor. Labour contracted by the W.N.L.A. organization for work in South Africa was usually absent for two years, a period slightly longer than the average spacing between conceptions but less than the period of absence sufficient to warrant the wife's remarriage. Thus the size of completed family where the husband was contracted for several periods during early marriage, was likely to be slightly less. The less formal migrations of males to Rhodesia, Zambia and to urban centres and other places of employment in Malawi appeared to have little effect, as either the husband or wife was able to make sufficiently frequent visits to each other.

Commercial agriculture was still very much labour intensive. Higher incomes in this sector and in urban employment were used to support larger families at a slightly higher standard of living, rather than concentrated upon an even higher standard for a smaller family. It would seem that a very much greater use of machinery on commercial peasant holdings would be necessary before the benefits of the labour of a large family were no longer valuable. In urban areas this labour factor was less important and costs were higher, particularly for primary education. With reduction of mortality through proximity to medical facilities, some of the more permanently established urban workers considered limitation of family size to 3 or 4 children. This proportion of the total population was very small, and even with a more rapid shift to urban areas is likely to remain less than 25 per cent at least until the end of the century. Levels of fertility are likely to remain at their present high level, therefore, or even to become higher with improved health and nutrition for the female population at risk.

Mortality and disease appeared to be highest in areas of high heat strain and optimal temperature conditions for germ reproduction and transmission, that is, in the lakeshore and Shire valleys of the Rift Valley floor. Levels of sanitation and hygiene were generally low, being related to ignorance of basic hygiene processes, and shortage of domestic water, particularly during the dry season. Where densities were high the risks involved in poor sanitation and inadequate water were greatest.

The frequency of marshes and lagoons considerably increased the incidence of malaria and bilharzia, while the use of polluted lake waters for domestic purposes greatly increased the incidence of dysentery. A high proportion of infant deaths resulted from these diseases. In contrast the plateau surfaces above the Rift Valley had rather better conditions with lower densities, lower temperatures and hence lower incidence of malaria and other hot-humid tropical diseases. Close to urban centres, particularly in the suburbs of Blantyre, very high densities and inadequate sanitation and water supplies again occur.

The provision of health facilities, and of general education, had an important effect upon mortality. Regular visits to maternity and health clinics and births in hospitals greatly reduce mortality.

The surface which results from the grouping of the child–woman ratio for information areas into seven classes defined in terms of units of the standard deviation around a mean, reveals the contrast between low density plateau areas with high child–woman ratios and the Rift Valley and Palombe-Chilwa Plains areas, and areas of high density close to Blantyre, where ratios are much lower, presumably indicating high mortality.

MICHAEL STUBBS

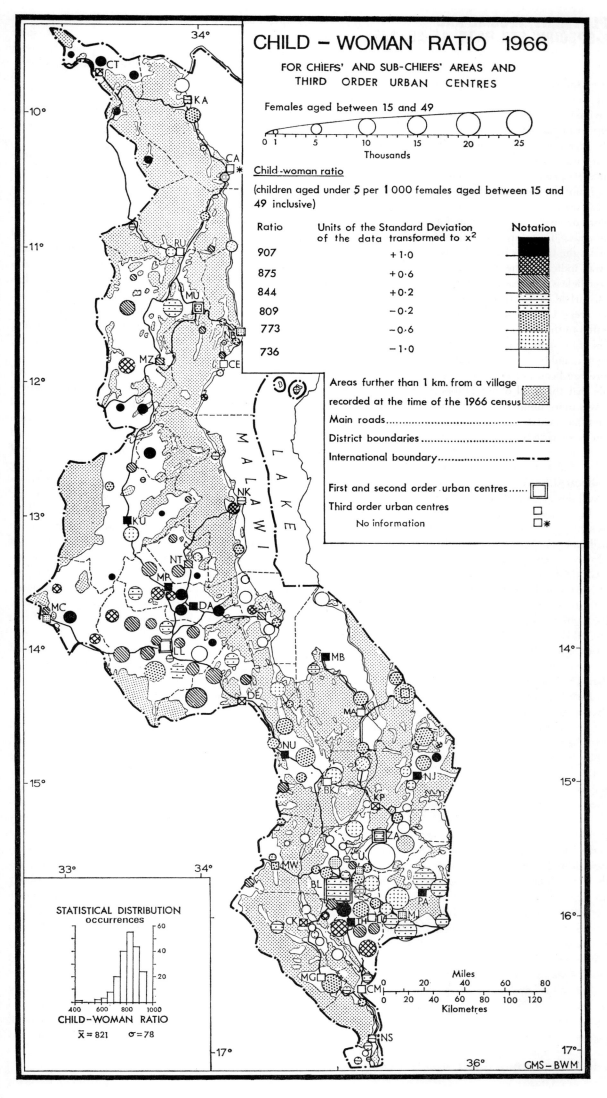

CHILD – WOMAN RATIO 1966

FOR CHIEFS' AND SUB-CHIEFS' AREAS AND THIRD ORDER URBAN CENTRES

Females aged between 15 and 49

0 1   5   10   15   20   25

Thousands

Child-woman ratio

(children aged under 5 per 1 000 females aged between 15 and 49 inclusive)

Ratio	Units of the Standard Deviation of the data transformed to x^2	Notation
907	+ 1·0	
875	+ 0·6	
844	+ 0·2	
809	− 0·2	
773	− 0·6	
736	− 1·0	

Areas further than 1 km. from a village recorded at the time of the 1966 census

Main roads ....

District boundaries ....

International boundary ....

First and second order urban centres ......

Third order urban centres

No information

STATISTICAL DISTRIBUTION
occurrences

CHILD–WOMAN RATIO

$\bar{x} = 821$ $\sigma = 78$

Miles

0   20   40   60   80

0 20 40 60 80 100 120

Kilometres

GMS – BWM

LAKE MALAWI

24 EMPLOYMENT, INCOME AND AGE-SPECIFIC SEX RATE, 15–29, 1966

An analysis of spatial variations in the sex ratio specific to the age group 15–29 by chiefs' areas and third order urban centres provided a sensitive indicator of certain of the factors relevant to migration.

Use of the measure assumed that the female population of the age group was static, and that parity existed between the sexes at age 15 and would have continued to exist up to age 29 were it not for the effect of migration. It was known, however, that small numbers of young females migrated in search of work or further education, and many more accompanied husbands. Therefore where analysis indicated a deficit of males the true loss was probably larger, and where a surplus was indicated the true gain was also probably larger. Nevertheless the spatial pattern was assumed to be much less disturbed by this than the actual value of the ratio in any one area. Upon marriage in matrilocal societies males migrated to the wife's village, but it was assumed that the numbers of out-going and incoming males balanced. All values were net, and it was known that, in some areas of net deficit, there had been in fact considerable in-migration. It was possible that the level of actual loss from the resident population was more uniform than appears from analysis of this ratio and that variations in the amount of compensating in-migration were largely responsible for the spatial variations.

The values of this ratio for the 198 information areas used were allocated to five classes defined in terms of units of the standard deviation and arranged symmetrically about the mean. These classes were then mapped. The resultant surface was strongly characterized by a core-periphery pattern at third and particularly at second order levels, with evidence also of a similar pattern at first order, national, level. The two highest classes occupied core areas, and the two lowest classes peripheral areas.

At the third order level almost all urban centres had values in the highest class with a net surplus, while Kasungu, Mzimba and Nkhata Bay had values in the second highest class. This was so even in peripheral areas where all adjacent chiefs' areas had values in the lowest class – for example in Mchinji, Nsanje, Ncheu and Mangoche. Rumphi, Kasupe and Nkhota Kota had values in the lowest class, suggesting a complete lack of attraction to young male migrants. Rumphi and Kasupe are both recently established administrative centres which have attracted little supplementary economic activity, while the Nkhota Kota rice mill had been closed just before the census date.

At the second order level the combination of reduced loss and increased numbers of immigrant young males finding employment was reflected in higher values in chiefs' areas adjacent to Blantyre, Zomba, Lilongwe, and Mzuzu, those adjacent to the latter being in the second highest and not the highest class, an indication of a national first order gradient northwards. In the Southern Region the special attraction of the Nchalo Sugar Estate (C.A. Lundu), the Thyolo and Mulanje tea estates, and the Lake Chilwa fisheries (C.A. Mkumbira) was reflected in an extension of the higher values of the ratio to these areas. In the Central Region the areas of considerable in-migration and high farm incomes in western Lilongwe and Dowa and in southern Kasungu were reflected again by higher values, operating against the regional trend away from Lilongwe. In the Northern Region the analogous area connects Mzuzu to Nkhata Bay.

Extensions of the higher value core areas around Lilongwe and Blantyre occur along the main road between the two centres in the Dedza and Balaka areas, slightly reducing the generally very low values which characterize the whole area of Kasupe, Mangoche, Ncheu, Dedza and Salima, which constituted the periphery between the two second order cores. The analogous second order periphery between Lilongwe and Mzuzu had generally higher values, and provided much smaller net surpluses. This naturally reflected the fact that the population of the area was smaller, but may reasonably be taken as a reflection of a weaker influence exerted over the area by core areas with less power of attraction than Blantyre.

Within the Southern Region secondary core area, the intermediate third order peripheries between Blantyre and Zomba, between Thyolo-Luchenza and Mulanje, between Thyolo and Chiromo, and between Zomba and Mulanje were clearly revealed. The second order periphery was also visible in Nsanje south of Chiromo, in C.A. Chapananga and western Blantyre District, and to a less extent in the Palombe plains. Nkhota Kota and rural Salima, eastern parts of Ntchisi, Dowa and Lilongwe, and Mchinji appeared as the eastern and western peripheries of the Central Region. Western Mzimba and western Chitipa appeared as peripheries to Mzuzu and Karonga respectively, while much of Rumphi appeared as a periphery between these two centres. Loudon and Chilumba appeared as smaller core areas.

Thus the surface suggested that at the first order national level there was a gradient of attraction which sloped downwards from Blantyre, and that at the second order level there were similar but steeper gradients sloping from Blantyre, Lilongwe and Mzuzu, but with reduced initial power. The third order centres exerted very weak fields of influence. The effect in each field was to detach young males from the rural populations, the higher proportions leaving from nearer and not farther locations. However, the employment opportunities generated by, and almost all in, the various centres also extended outwards over a much smaller area, within which there was both a reduced rate of exodus, and a balancing in-migration from the outer areas. In these adjacent areas opportunities for the marketing of primary produce, stimulation of local business and possibilities for commuting to urban areas combined to increase their attractiveness to both immigrants and potential emigrants.

The Southern Region and Chikwawa were characterized by a relatively high proportion of both males and females with wages and salaries as their main source of cash income. Outside this area only Lilongwe, Mzimba and Karonga Districts had relatively high proportions of males with wages and salaries, while female proportions were very small everywhere outside the Southern Region. The Central Region had high proportions of both sexes with sales of their own farm produce as their principal source of income. This contrasted particularly with the Northern Region, although proportions in the Southern Region were also lower. Possibly at a considerable distance from Blantyre there were only limited sales from the farms, while within a short distance of this first order centre the much higher densities and consequent reduction in the availability of land, alternative employment opportunities and related withdrawal of labour from agriculture reduced the relative and actual importance of sales of own farm produce, except immediately adjacent to the city. Only in the medium distance Central Region were most of the relevant factors favourable. In Zomba District a particularly high proportion of females had 'other' sources of cash income, and this might have represented income from fish-processing and beer-brewing around Lake Chilwa. The proportions of both sexes with no source of cash income at all was considerable in all parts of the country except the Central Region and Zomba, and was particularly high in the Northern Region.

MICHAEL STUBBS

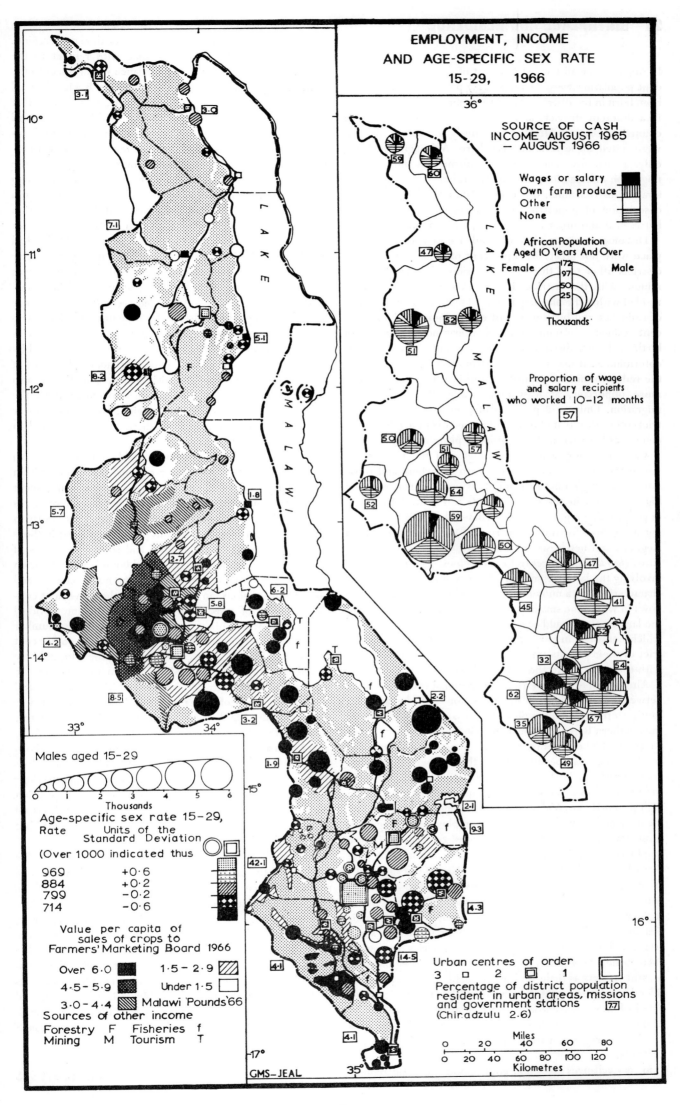

EMPLOYMENT, INCOME
AND AGE-SPECIFIC SEX RATE
15-29, 1966

SOURCE OF CASH
INCOME AUGUST 1965
– AUGUST 1966

Wages or salary
Own farm produce
Other
None

African Population
Aged 10 Years And Over
Female   Male
172
97
50
25
Thousands

Proportion of wage
and salary recipients
who worked 10–12 months
57

Males aged 15-29

0   1   2   3   4   5   6
Thousands

Age-specific sex rate 15–29,
Rate   Units of the
            Standard Deviation
(Over 1000 indicated thus

969	+0·6
884	+0·2
799	−0·2
714	−0·6

Value per capita of
sales of crops to
Farmers' Marketing Board 1966

Over 6·0   1·5 – 2·9
4·5 – 5·9   Under 1·5
3·0 – 4·4   Malawi Pounds'66

Sources of other income
Forestry F   Fisheries f
Mining   M   Tourism   T

Urban centres of order
3   2   1
Percentage of district population
resident in urban areas, missions
and government stations
(Chiradzulu 2·6)   7·7

Miles
0   20   40   60   80
0 20 40 60 80 100 120
Kilometres

GMS–JEAL

L A K E   M A L A W I

25 BIRTHPLACE AND RESIDENCE

In August 1966 all but 0·5 per cent of the enumerated resident population were Africans, 81·7 per cent of whom had been born in the district of their enumeration, 11·3 per cent in a different district, and 7·1 per cent in other African countries. 265 000 Africans, previously resident in Malawi, were stated to be resident elsewhere. Although consisting only of birthplace and residence information and not true migration information, for only the relatively large administrative district units, this census data provided a summary description of population movements within Malawi and between it and other countries in southern Africa.

Distances between place of residence in 1966 and birthplace were not great: 67·0 per cent of persons resident in districts other than that of birth resided in districts coterminous with the district of birth. A further 3·9 per cent resided within the planning region of birth although districts of residence and birth were not coterminous, and 17·3 per cent resided in planning regions coterminous with that of birth, although districts of residence and birth were not coterminous. It may be deduced from this information that the redistribution of population within rural areas was still more important, at least numerically, than rural-urban migration. Only 11·8 per cent of persons resident in districts other than that of birth had moved over long distances, defined as between non-coterminous planning regions.

Calculation for each planning region of the balance between the numbers of residents born elsewhere and those born in the region but resident elsewhere (= 100) revealed highest values in the central (158) and central lakeshore (149) planning regions; smaller values—but still representing net gains—for the Northern (118) and Southern (113) Regions, and net losses for the south central (88), Lower Shire (67) and north central (31) regions. Except for those involving the latter region each inter-regional exchange was characterized by a numerical relationship between the two flows in which the smaller was never less than two-thirds of the larger. This would suggest a circular migration pattern, which consisted in part of those children born in the district of their parents' migrant residence who had returned with their parents to the latters' district of origin.

Almost half of the 233 194 inter-regional exchanges were between the southern planning region and the adjacent south central and Lower Shire regions. 44 625 residents of the Southern Region had been born in the south central, and 14 591 in the Lower Shire region. The reverse exchange had resulted in 43 040 persons born in the Southern Region becoming resident in the south central region, and 13 997 in the Lower Shire. The southern planning region contained a high proportion of Malawi's secondary and tertiary employment, together with considerable employment in agricultural estates, and resident migrants consisted largely of those employed or seeking employment in these sectors. The relatively high density areas of Ncheu and Nsanje had supplied a greater proportion of this inward movement than had lower density districts of the south central and Lower Shire regions, in two of which there were alternative opportunities in expanding peasant cotton production and a sugar estate (Chikwawa) and tourism and fisheries expansion (Mangoche). Few immigrants to the Southern Region were peasant farmers as little land was available there, and a considerable proportion of those who had left this region consisted of those leaving land shortage areas, particularly in Chiradzulu and Cholo Districts, for the lower density areas of adjacent regions, particularly in Kasupe and Chikwawa Districts.

In its exchanges with non-coterminous planning regions the Southern Region enjoyed a considerable positive balance only with respect to the Northern and north central region. It had only a slight positive balance with respect to the central lakeshore, and a negative balance with respect to the Central Region. The net gain to the Central Region from all other planning regions, 19 100 persons, was double that achieved by the Southern Region. Within the Central Region the low density areas of the western parts of Lilongwe, Dowa and Ntchisi Districts and much of Kasungu District were most attractive to farmers moving from the higher density areas of Mzimba in the north central planning region, from the eastern parts of Ntchisi, Dowa and Dedza Districts themselves, and from areas of high population density and land shortage in the south central and southern planning regions. Eastern Ntchisi, Dowa and Dedza had relatively high densities of population during the early colonial period, firstly because they had served as refuges for the populations of the adjacent plateau and plains devastated by the Angoni and Ayao, and secondly because they had been occupied by the Maseko Angoni themselves, who had then brought back slaves captured as far away as in Blantyre and Zomba Districts. The movement measured by the census represented a compensating modern flow out of these less fertile areas. Ntchisi, Dowa and Dedza also furnished a high proportion of the movement from the central to the central lakeshore region, which was greater than the return movement, which was largely directed to the western 'frontier' areas.

The number of residents born outside Malawi (283 854) was greater than the total inter-regional movement within the country (233 190), and for all planning regions except the central and central lakeshore the number of residents born outside the country was greater than those born in other regions. The difference was particularly great in those regions peripheral to the central and southern centres of attraction but with long international boundaries in relation to their area – that is the Northern, north central and Lower Shire regions, an indication that the movement consisted largely of peasant farmers across the international boundaries. Moçambique had supplied the greatest number of residents born outside Malawi: 206 260, and 90 per cent of these resided in districts adjacent to the Moçambique boundary. Of the 11 170 residents born in Tanzania, 90 per cent were resident in coterminous Chitipa, Karonga and Nkhata Bay, while of the 21 944 born in Zambia the greater proportion lived in districts coterminous with that country. Some of the Zambia-born, and a high proportion of the 33 584 persons born in Rhodesia and the 9083 persons born in South Africa were presumed to be the wives and children of Malawians who had returned home subsequently to their marriage. The total sex ratio for the resident population born outside Malawi was 999 and 913 males per thousand females for those born in Moçambique and Tanzania, but only 789 for all other countries.

As a result of these movements there was a considerable variation in the proportion of the population both born and resident in each district. In some over 90 per cent of the resident population had been born in the district, the highest proportion, 93 per cent, being in Mzimba. In contrast, over a third of the population in Blantyre District were born elsewhere in Malawi. There was also a considerable contrast between districts in the extent to which the population born there had subsequently dispersed to other parts of the country. Lilongwe and Mchinji, Chikwawa, and Karonga and Chitipa were areas of least dispersal; Chiradzulu, Blantyre, Zomba and Ncheu and Rumphi the areas of greatest dispersal.

MICHAEL STUBBS

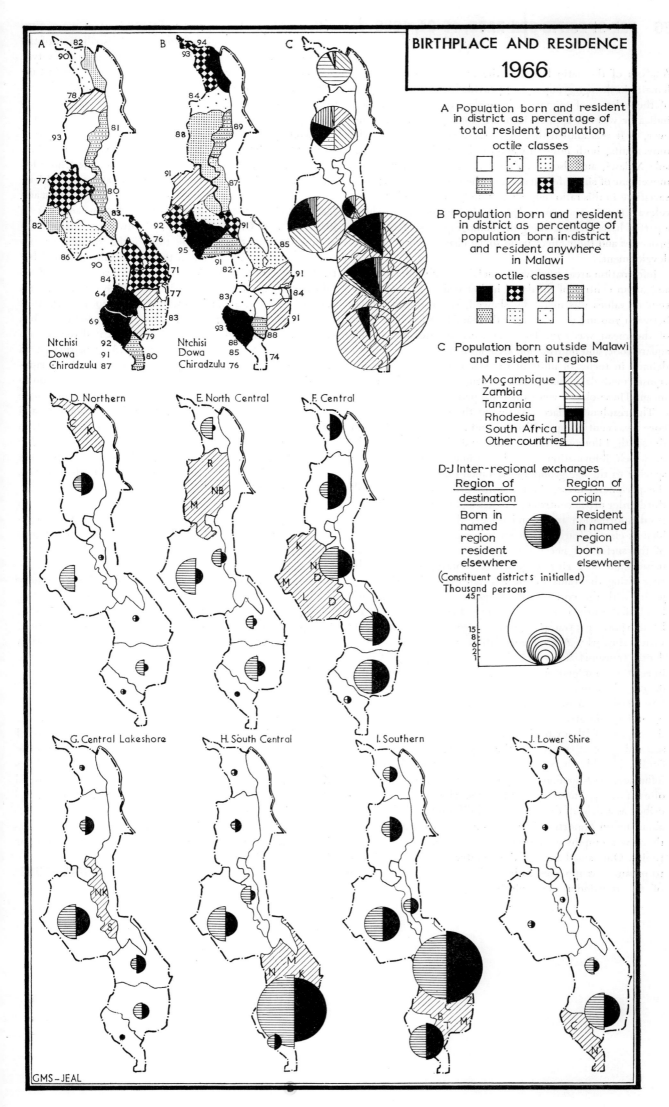

BIRTHPLACE AND RESIDENCE
1966

A Population born and resident
in district as percentage of
total resident population
octile classes

B Population born and resident
in district as percentage of
population born in district
and resident anywhere
in Malawi
octile classes

C Population born outside Malawi
and resident in regions

Moçambique
Zambia
Tanzania
Rhodesia
South Africa
Other countries

D-J Inter-regional exchanges

Region of   Region of
destination   origin

Born in   Resident
named   in named
region   region
resident   born
elsewhere   elsewhere

(Constituent districts initialled)
Thousand persons

A   82
    90
    78
    93
    81
    77
    80
    83
    82
    86
    90
    84
    64
    69
    79
Ntchisi   92
Dowa   91
Chiradzulu 87   80

B   94
    93
    84
    88   89
    91
    87
    92
    76
    95
    91
    82   91
    71   85
    77   84
    83   91
    93   88
Ntchisi   88   88
Dowa   85
Chiradzulu 76   74

D. Northern

E. North Central

F. Central

G. Central Lakeshore

H. South Central

I. Southern

J. Lower Shire

GMS–JEAL

Analysis of the ratio between the numbers of males and females in the age group 15–64 provided a general indicator of the balance of migration by males moving alone. The indicator was not applicable to the total population, however, as it was known that there were considerable family movements, both internally and to places of attraction outside Malawi, and also that there was a small but growing movement of single females. Nevertheless analysis of spatial variations in this ratio suggested a number of possible factors relevant to migration, notably urban influence, and provided a partial basis for describing the demographic structure and processes and their effect upon social change and economic development.

Information areas used were chiefs' and sub-chiefs' areas, and urban centres of third and higher order. The distribution of values was markedly skewed, the majority falling between 700 and 900 males per thousand females. The value of the mean was 877. The data were transformed to the square root, and information areas allocated to seven classes defined in terms of units of the standard deviation of the transformed data, and arranged symmetrically about the mean. These classes were then mapped.

The resultant surface revealed at the second order level core areas centred upon Blantyre and the Shire Highlands in the south, Lilongwe in the centre, and Mzuzu in the north, in which information areas had values of the sex ratio specific to the age group 15–64 much higher than those in the peripheral areas. At the third order level almost all third order urban centres had values higher than the adjacent rural information areas, and usually the value was in the highest class. Clearly a primary factor controlling the value of the surface of net male migration was accessibility to urban influence. This suggested relationship was tested by correlating the value of the sex ratio specific to this age group with the cost of public passenger transport at each level of the urban system. Although the measure used related to passenger transport, costs for goods transport largely varied similarly. A high correlation was discovered. Evidently transportation cost in itself was not a primary factor, in relation to migration, but only a measure of the probable degree of economic development in each area. As transportation costs increased from urban centres so did the costs of operating commercial enterprises, thus making necessary the export of labour to those areas in which its application secured greater returns to the migrant, or his extended family. Possibly there were two surfaces related to urban influence, with gradients sloping away from urban centres of each order, but at different levels. The first may be described as a field of disturbance and diffusion of information about urban opportunities; the second, that within which there was employment or commercial agriculture opportunity. Only small areas of the country within and adjacent to urban areas appeared to be within the latter field. Much of the remainder was within the field of disturbance and causation, but outside the area of opportunity.

Examination of spatial variation in the distribution of the seven classes showed that the average value of the Blantyre core area was higher than that of Lilongwe, which in turn was higher than that of Mzuzu. In the Shire Highlands area the values for all urban centres except Chiradzulu were in the highest class. In addition, four chiefs' areas had values in the two highest classes, both with excess males. These were C.A.s Machinjili and Likoswe, adjacent to Blantyre, C.A. Nchilamwera in which were the majority of the Cholo tea estates, and C.A. Mkhumbira. There were also seven chiefs' areas with values in the third class: C.A.s Laston Njema and Mabuka; C.A.s Somba, Bvumbwe and Kapeni adjacent to Blantyre; and C.A.s Malemia and Mwambo adjacent to Zomba. Within this area the third order peripheries between Blantyre and Zomba in the Chiradzulu area, and between Thyolo and Mulanje east of Luchenza were visible as information areas with values in the fourth class. Adjacent parts of Chikwawa and northern Nsanje appear with most information areas in the fourth class, except for the urban centres and C.A. Lundu, in which was located the Nchalo Sugar Estate. Southern Nsanje and C.A. Chapananga in western Chikwawa appear as parts of a second order periphery which extends from C.A. Nsabwe in southern Thyolo to western Blantyre District, in which Mwanza urban centre had a value in the third class, to Ncheu, Mangoche and Kasupe in which was the largest concentration of information areas with values in the lowest classes, with a considerable deficit of males. Within this area, however, the Balaka and Kasupe areas had slightly higher values and all urban centres had values in the highest class.

In the Lilongwe area a core of information areas with higher values extended through central and western Lilongwe, western Dowa and north-western Ntchisi into eastern Kasungu District. Almost all information areas in this core had values in the fourth class, and only two in the third class. This core was bounded by a marked periphery with area values in the fifth and sixth class, extending through Mchinji and Kasungu into eastern Ntchisi, Dowa, Lilongwe and Dedza to connect with the south-central peripheral area already noted. Kasungu and Dowa urban centres had values in the second class, and Mchinji in the third.

In the Mzuzu area only two adjacent chiefs' areas had values in the fourth class, and the urban impact of Mzuzu was clearly much more restricted than that of Lilongwe. Values for Mzimba and Rumphi urban centres were only of third and fourth class respectively, while that for Chinteche was in the fifth class. In Karonga, and Chitipa C.A.s Kilupula, Mwirang'ombe, and Nthalire had values around the national mean, and only one chief's area, Kameme, had a value higher than the fifth class. Although peripheral to both primary and secondary core areas, values were not as low as were expected in relation to accessibility to urban influence.

MICHAEL STUBBS

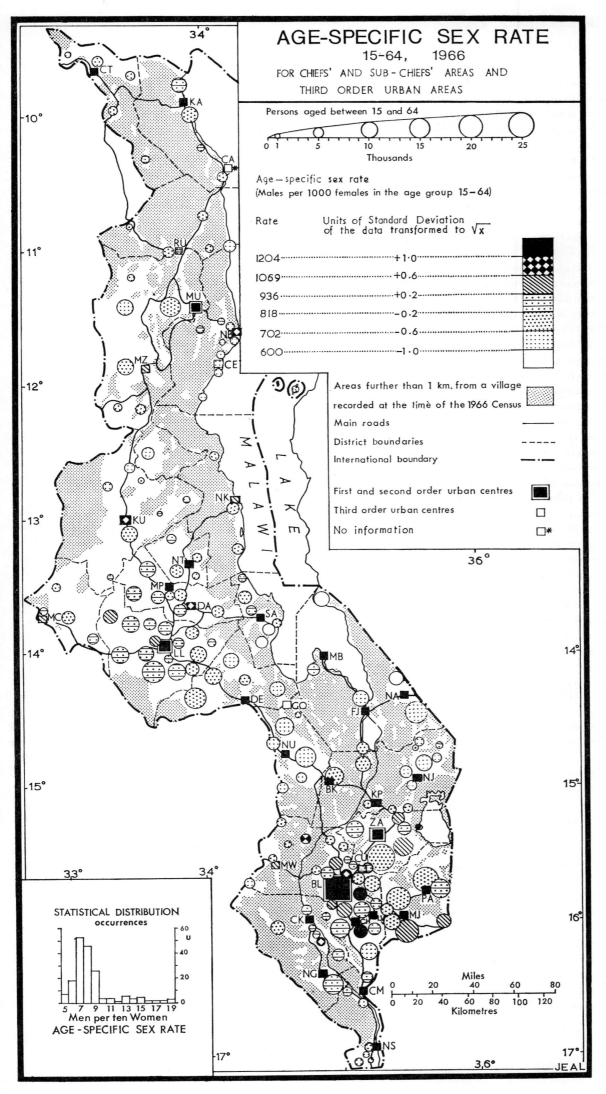

AGE-SPECIFIC SEX RATE
15-64, 1966
FOR CHIEFS' AND SUB-CHIEFS' AREAS AND
THIRD ORDER URBAN AREAS

Persons aged between 15 and 64

0 1   5   10   15   20   25
Thousands

Age—specific sex rate
(Males per 1000 females in the age group 15—64)

Rate	Units of Standard Deviation of the data transformed to $\sqrt{x}$
1204	+1·0
1069	+0·6
936	+0·2
818	−0·2
702	−0·6
600	−1·0

Areas further than 1 km. from a village recorded at the time of the 1966 Census

Main roads
District boundaries
International boundary

First and second order urban centres
Third order urban centres
No information

LAKE MALAWI

STATISTICAL DISTRIBUTION
occurrences

5 7 9 11 13 15 17 19
Men per ten Women
AGE-SPECIFIC SEX RATE

Miles
0   20   40   60   80
0   20   40   60   80 100 120
Kilometres

JEAL

67

27 DEPENDENCY RATE, 1966

For the purpose of this analysis the economically active population was defined as that aged 15–64 inclusive, this being assumed to be the group supporting a dependent population aged under 15 and over 64. The dependency rate expressed the ratio between the dependent and the supporting populations, and was expressed as dependent persons per thousand of the supporting population. In this predominantly rural population, which still has a strong subsistence economic base, both the lower and the upper age boundaries of the economically active population are somewhat arbitrary, for even very young children have important roles within the production process, and older persons continue to contribute at least some work until incapable for reasons of health or old age. Nevertheless, as a means of showing significant differences within the country with respect to the general relationship between supporting and supported population these definitions are acceptable. The ratio was calculated for 204 information areas, including all chiefs' and sub-chiefs' areas, and all but one of the defined third order urban centres. The statistical distribution was slightly skewed, but no transformation of the data was applied, and the rates were allocated to seven classes defined in terms of units of the standard deviation, which was 151, arranged symmetrically about the mean of 908.

The dependency rate is a secondary demographic index. The proportion of persons aged over 64 was small, and the numbers of the dependent population were largely controlled by the balance of fertility and foetal, infant, and child mortality. This balance is discussed in the section on the 'Child–Woman Ratio'. The size of the supporting, economically active population, was largely affected by the loss of adult males by migration, discussed under both the sections 'Age-Specific sex rate, 15–64,' and 'Employment, Income and Age-Specific sex rate, 15–29'. The spatial variations which resulted from the analysis reflected, therefore, a wide range of processes, each affected by a multiplicity of factors, and there is little benefit in using the spatial variations as an aid in explanation. Nevertheless the considerable variation between different parts of the country did reflect the real level of pressures of economic and social importance upon the resident active population.

Areas with high dependency rates were those in which large numbers of surviving children (a reflection more usually of low infant and child mortality) were combined with a moderate to considerable loss by migration of adult males. Such areas (with rates in the two highest statistical classes) included: the whole of Chitipa, and two adjacent chiefs' areas to the south along the Zambian border – Katumbi in Rumphi, and Mpherembe in Mzimba Districts; in southern Mzimba and in C.A. Kaluluma in northern Kasungu; some parts of the Rumphi and Nkhata Bay lakeshore, including Likoma Islands; the whole of Mchinji District, and the adjacent C.A. Santhe in southern Kasungu; an extensive belt stretching from eastern Ntchisi District through the eastern chiefs' areas of Dowa and Lilongwe into Dedza, Ncheu and western Blantyre; parts of north-east Kasupe District, and C.A. Nsabwe in southern Thyolo. All of these areas were within second order peripheries; none were within core areas. High dependency rates may be taken, therefore, to be characteristic of peripheral parts of the country in 1966.

Dependency rates became lower either as the numbers of children decreased (because of lower fertility, or more usually because of increased mortality), or as the numbers of male emigrants decreased, or as a result of a combination of both. The presumed higher mortality noted in the lower lying lakeshore and Rift Valley areas was therefore largely responsible for the medium to low rates evident in C.A. Kilupula in northern Karonga District, in the Nkhota Kota, Salima and Mangoche lakeshore, in the Middle Shire areas of Kasupe and Blantyre Districts, and in the Lower Shire. The Nkhata Bay and southern Karonga lakeshore had contrasting higher dependency rates, largely the result of higher child–woman ratios, possibly attributable to lower mortality.

Within the Central Region a core area of lower rates was apparent in much of Lilongwe District, and in the western part of Dowa District, with intermediate values between this and the peripheral areas of higher dependency previously noted. Although an area of relatively high child–woman ratios, this is compensated by low to moderate net loss of adult males.

As opposed to the lower dependency rates of those chiefs' areas of Zomba District on the Shire Highlands plateau, which had low dependency values, because of net immigration and relatively low child–woman ratios, much of Chiradzulu, Thyolo and Mulanje had moderate to moderately high values. This reflected the lower child and infant mortality in most of these areas together with considerable net loss of adult males, particularly in the Chiradzulu third order periphery between Blantyre and Zomba.

Partly because of the low values of the child–woman ratio, but largely owing to the effect of the concentration of adult males, urban areas had usually lower dependency rates than rural areas. Two-thirds of the third order urban centres and Blantyre, Zomba, Lilongwe and Mzuzu had rates in the lowest of the seven defined classes.

Chiefs' areas with rates in the lowest class were few, and included those adjacent to Zomba, Blantyre and Thyolo urban areas, the fishing communities of C.A. Mkhumbira on Lake Chilwa and C.A. Kaluunda in Salima District, and two areas of agricultural expansion and immigration in the Lower Shire valley, C.A.s Ngabu and Chapananga.

The economic and social consequences of high dependency rates in Malawi have not been fully investigated. In general terms greater dependency in a predominantly subsistence society implies that available resources have to be spread among a greater number of people, and per head consumption is reduced, with consequent unfortunate effects upon levels of health and nutrition. The economic effect might to a certain extent be mitigated by remittances from the migrant males where high dependency is largely the result of a high rate of male migration. It is at least possible, however, that the value of the remittance received, which is certainly less than the small amount earned at the place of migration destination, whether within Malawi or outside, is also less than the value of the productive contribution made by the male if he had remained within the home community. The social effect is even more in need of investigation. Larger numbers of dependents makes it conceivable that parental or other adult control and influence is reduced, and this might be particularly significant with respect to education.

If in most parts of Malawi the greatest cause of high dependency is high fertility together with low mortality, then the consequences of high dependency may be attributed very largely to high fertility rates. As mortality is reduced among infants and children, therefore, the burden of dependency will increase in rural areas, unless the productivity of the economically active population increases at least at the same rate.

MICHAEL STUBBS

68

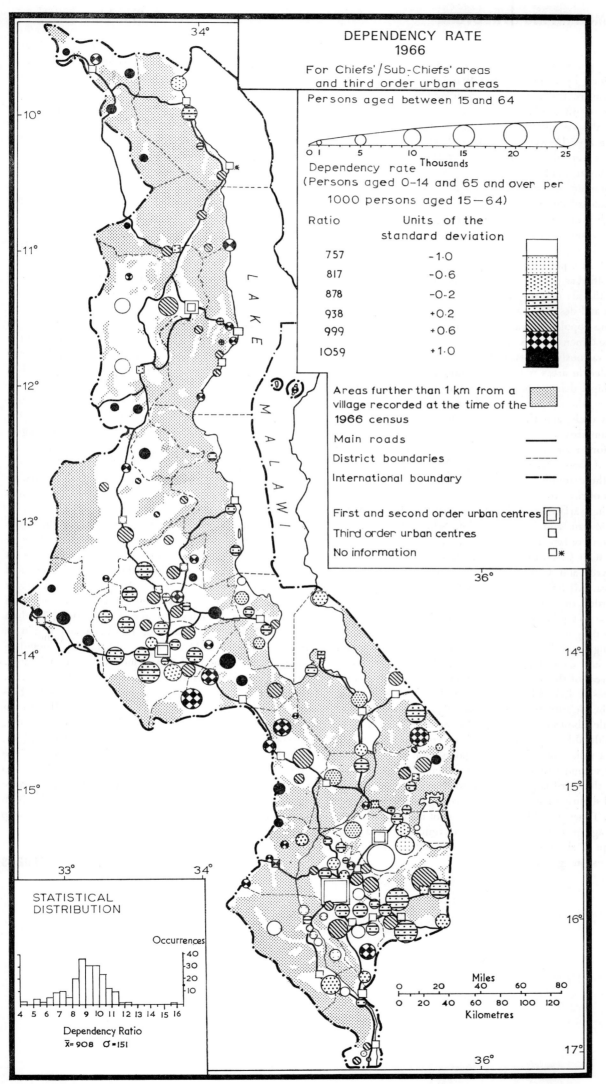

DEPENDENCY RATE
1966

For Chiefs'/Sub-Chiefs' areas
and third order urban areas

Persons aged between 15 and 64

O 1   5   10   15   20   25
Thousands

Dependency rate
(Persons aged 0–14 and 65 and over per
1000 persons aged 15—64)

Ratio	Units of the standard deviation
757	-1·0
817	-0·6
878	-0·2
938	+0·2
999	+0·6
1059	+1·0

Areas further than 1 km from a
village recorded at the time of the
1966 census

Main roads

District boundaries

International boundary

First and second order urban centres

Third order urban centres

No information

LAKE MALAWI

STATISTICAL
DISTRIBUTION

Occurrences

Dependency Ratio
x̄ = 908   σ = 151

Miles
0   20   40   60   80
0   20   40   60   80   100   120
Kilometres

A simple typology of demographic structural characteristics was obtained by combining the two indices which most nearly measure the three basic demographic processes—fertility, mortality, and migration—that is the child–woman ratio and the sex rate specific to the economically active population aged between 15 and 64. High, moderate, and low classes were defined for each in terms of units of the standard deviation of the transformed values, and nine types of demographic structure were isolated. The choice of the ± 0·6 standard deviation values as class boundaries meant that a high proportion of information areas were classified, at least in one dimension, as 'moderate'. (see table on p. 140.)

In 1966 44·6 per cent of the population resided in those areas classified as of type E, in which both the child–woman ratio and the sex rate specific to age 15–64 were both about the mean and described as 'moderate'. A further 49·5 per cent of the population was resident in information areas in which one dimension was of moderate value, and these were classified variously as of type B, D, F, and H. Only 5·9 per cent resided in areas with neither dimensions 'moderate'. The principal demographic indices for each of these structural types, the proportion of the national population included in each, and the numbers and locational types of information areas, are shown in the table below.

All information areas classified as of type A, and the majority of those classified as of types B and C, were urban centres, the common factor being an excess of adult males as a result of rural to urban migration, and the differentiating factor being variations in the child–woman ratio. Blantyre, Zomba, Mzuzu, and Nsanje, Ngabu, Salima, Karonga and Ntchisi were of type B, with moderate child–woman ratios, together with C.A.s Likoswe and Machinjili both adjacent to Blantyre, and C.A. Nchilamwera in the Thyolo tea estate area. All but one of the urban areas were either of second order, or were within the Rift Valley floor. The six urban areas of type C with low child–woman ratios included Chiromo-Bangula, Mulanje, Luchenza, Nkhata Bay, Balaka and Lilongwe. All had some industrial or transportation functions and associated labour forces. The two rural information areas of this type, C.A. Mkhumbira, a fishing community beside Lake Chilwa, and C.A. Lundu in which was located the Nchalo Sugar Estate, had high concentrations of single male labourers. In the 14 urban areas of Type A there was considerable disparity in the three younger age groups, possibly a reflection of the small population size. Type B, with the second largest sex rate specific to the age 15–29, but only the third largest specific to the age group 15–64, appeared slightly more attractive to young males than Types A and C. Types A and B showed excess of males in all quinquennial age groups over 15, with a maximum at age 25–29, while type C showed a similar pattern, with an additional large excess in age 35–39.

Information areas in Types D, E, and F were almost entirely rural. All were characterized by moderate or low sex rates specific to the age group 15–64, indicating loss of adult males by migration. Type D information areas, all rural, were concentrated in Chitipa, south Mzimba, Mchinji and adjacent C.A.s Santhe and Khongoni, central Dowa and eastern parts of Kasungu, Ntchisi, Dowa and Lilongwe, with adjacent C.A.s Malenga Chanzi in Nkhota Kota and Karonga in Salima Districts, C.A.s Dambe and Mlauli in western Blantyre, Ngokwe in north-eastern Kasupe, and areas in western Thyolo including the adjacent C.A. Thomas in Chikwawa.

Type E, which may be considered the 'normal' demographic structural type, was concentrated predominantly in the Lilongwe-Dowa-Ntchisi and southern Kasungu areas, in northern Mzimba and parts of southern Rumphi, in parts of the Karonga, Nkhota Kota, Salima and Mangoche lakeshore, in the chiefs' areas to the north of Blantyre, in Thyolo and Mulanje, largely away from the tea estate areas, in Chapananga and Kanduku, and in the Ngabu-Chiromo area.

Type F was concentrated in the Karonga and northern Salima lakeshore, in the Kasupe and Blantyre sections of the Rift floor, in chiefs' areas around the Chilwa-Palombe plains in Kasupe, Zomba, Chiradzulu and Mulanje, and in parts of the Lower River.

All information areas of types D, E, and F had the greatest deficit of males in the age group 25–29, that for type F being very considerable, equivalent to 2·7 per cent of the aggregate population for the type. There was a progressive shortening of the period for which deficits occurred, however, between type D, in which all above 15 showed deficits, to type E in which only those 15–54 and to type F in which only those aged 15–49 showed deficits.

Types G, H, and I had the lowest sex ratio specific to the age 15–64, and all but one, Chinteche, were rural. Type G occurred only in four information areas: C.A.s Kameme in Chitipa, Mabulabo in Mzimba, Chikweo in Kasupe and Zilakoma in Nkhata Bay. Type H occurred in a larger number of information areas, with a notable concentration in the Mangoche, Ncheu and eastern Kasupe areas, Tambala in Dedza, Nthache in Blantyre, Kaluluma and Chulu in Kasungu, Chinde in Mzimba, in Nkhata Bay, including Likoma Islands, and in Tengani and Ndamera in Nsanje. Type I occurred in Chinteche Urban and adjacent C.A. Fukamapiri in Nkhata Bay, in the southern Salima-Kachindamoto and Makanjila area, Liwonde and Mlomba in Kasupe, Chigaru in Blantyre, and Chomombo in Nsanje. For type G, the male deficit extending between 15 and 64, reached a maximum between age 20 and 24, while for Type H there was an anomolous slight male excess in the group 30–34, which might reflect a return migration of more temporary migrants from the Shire Highlands. In both Types H and I the greatest male loss was in the age group 25–29.

MICHAEL STUBBS

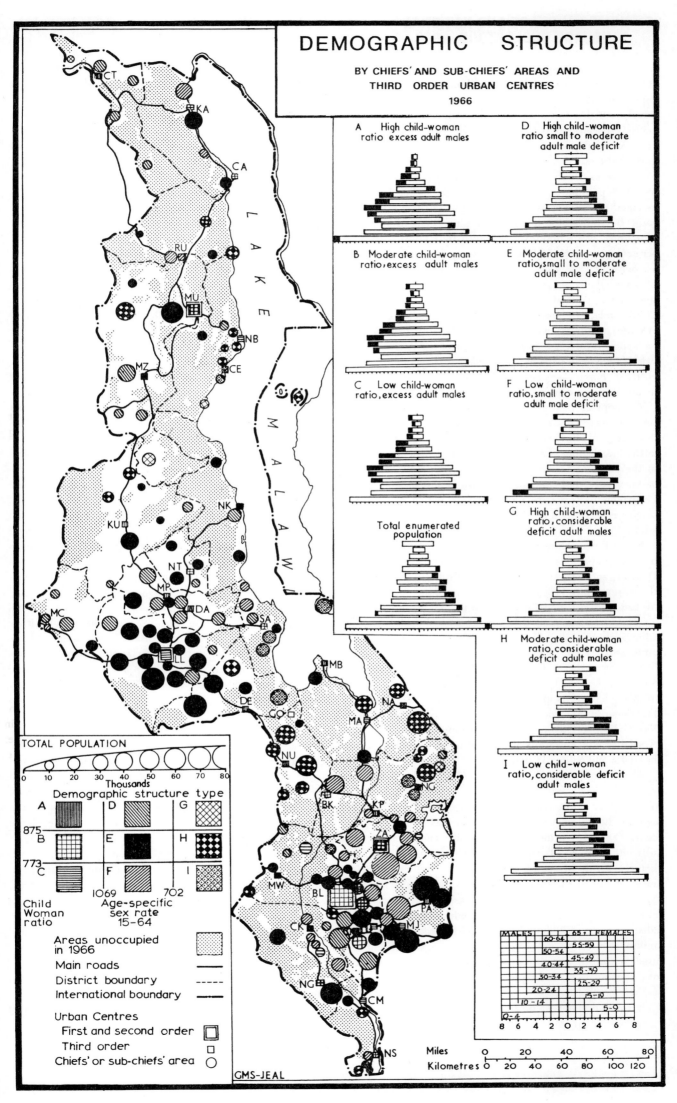

DEMOGRAPHIC STRUCTURE

BY CHIEFS' AND SUB-CHIEFS' AREAS AND THIRD ORDER URBAN CENTRES
1966

A High child-woman ratio excess adult males

D High child-woman ratio small to moderate adult male deficit

B Moderate child-woman ratio, excess adult males

E Moderate child-woman ratio, small to moderate adult male deficit

C Low child-woman ratio, excess adult males

F Low child-woman ratio, small to moderate adult male deficit

Total enumerated population

G High child-woman ratio, considerable deficit adult males

H Moderate child-woman ratio, considerable deficit adult males

I Low child-woman ratio, considerable deficit adult males

TOTAL POPULATION

Thousands
0 10 20 30 40 50 60 70 80

Demographic structure type

A	D	G
B	E	H
C	F	I

875
773

1069   702

Child Woman ratio

Age-specific sex rate 15-64

Areas unoccupied in 1966

Main roads

District boundary

International boundary

Urban Centres
First and second order
Third order
Chiefs' or sub-chiefs' area

GMS-JEAL

MALES   60-64   65+ FEMALES
              55-59
        50-54
              45-49
        40-44
              35-39
        30-34
              25-29
        20-24
              15-19
        10-14
              5-9
        0-4
8 6 4 2 0 2 4 6 8

Miles   0   20   40   60   80
Kilometres 0 20 40 60 80 100 120

LAKE MALAWI

CT KA CA RU MU NB MZ CE NK KU NT MP DA SA MC LL MB NA MA DE GO NU NC BK KP ZA MW BL PA CK MJ NG CM NS

71

29 HOME LANGUAGE AND NATIONAL LANGUAGE UNDERSTOOD, 1966

The language usually spoken in the home is the single most important indicator of the cultural attachment of the individual, and the only one available uniformly over Malawi for the African population over the age of 5. The census of 1966 revealed that by far the largest home language group spoke what was then termed Chinyanja, and what was later designated as Chichewa, the national language of the country, in September 1968. Of the thirteen other languages specified in the census the one spoken as their home language by the largest number, 14·5 per cent of the total (476 300), was Chilomwe, followed by Chiyao with 13·8 per cent (452 300). Chitumbuka was spoken in the home by 9·1 per cent (298 900), Chisena by 3·5 per cent (115 100), Chikhokhola by 2·3 per cent (74 500), Chitonga by 1·9 per cent (62 213), and Chingoni by 1·1 per cent (37 480). Chinkhonde, (31 000), Chilambya (18 600), Chisukwa (18 000), Chinyakyusa (3000), and Kiswahili (2900) were each spoken by less than one per cent of the African population. Only 209 persons indicated that they spoke English as their home language. Other African languages, not specified in the census, were spoken by 39 500 persons.

The population which employed Chichewa as their home language were concentrated in the central and central lakeshore regions, in the Shire Highlands, and to a lesser extent in the intervening Ncheu, Kasupe, and Mangoche areas and in the adjacent Lower Shire. These areas represented the national core, and contained the two largest urban centres. Peripheral to this core were areas in which other home languages were used by significant proportions of the population.

In the Lower Shire region Chisena was used in the home by 103 500 persons, 73 per cent of the population in Nsanje District, and 34 per cent of that in Chikwawa District. In the eastern Shire Highlands 67 per cent of the population in Mulanje District used Chilomwe in the home, and a total of 455 500 persons used this language in Mulanje, Thyolo, Chiradzulu, Zomba, Blantyre and Kasupe Districts. In the same area 72 600 persons reported Chikhokhola as their home language. The fourth home language used within the Southern Region, Chiyao, was spoken by 384 500 persons in Mangoche, Kasupe, Zomba, Chiradzulu and Blantyre Districts. In Mangoche District 79·7 per cent, and in Kasupe District 50·7 per cent of the population used Chiyao. A smaller concentration of persons using Chiyao occurred in Dedza and Salima Districts.

The second area in which languages other than Chichewa were used in the home was the Northern Region, in which only 2·5 per cent of the population aged 5 and over used it as their home language. Chitumbuka was used by 64 per cent, (258 500) principally in Mzimba and Rumphi, and adjacent areas of Nkhata Bay and southern Karonga, the latter a result of recent migration. In Kasungu District, adjacent but in the Central Region, Chitumbuka was used by 29 000 persons. Chitonga was used by 13 per cent, almost entirely within Nkhata Bay, with small numbers in adjacent areas of Nkhota Kota District. Chinkhonde, Chilambya, Chisukwa and Chinyakyusa were almost entirely used in Chitipa and Karonga Districts, where 62 per cent of the population over 5 years of age used one of these four as their home language.

A small number of persons, predominantly around the lakeshore, used Kiswahili as home language. Most of the very small number of Africans who used English as a home language were enumerated in Blantyre and Zomba. The other home languages, not specified in the census, were spoken largely in Chitipa and Karonga, in Mchinji, and in Chikwawa.

As no comparable information about ethnic origin was obtained at the time of the census, and as it would be in any case extremely difficult to make meaningful distinctions in view of the ease and rapidity of inter-marriage, particularly in the Southern Region, no analysis of the extent of cultural assimilation can be attempted. Some indication can be obtained, however, from a comparison of home language and language understood for the four largest language groups – Chichewa, Chilomwe, Chiyao and Chitumbuka. Although only 50·2 per cent of the population aged over 5 used Chichewa as home language, 76·6 per cent understood it: 750 000 persons used languages other than Chichewa as their home language, but were able to understand it. These numbers and proportion have increased very considerably since the census date, so that Chichewa has become the undisputed national language for most persons who previously used other languages in their homes.

While 71·7 per cent understood Chichewa alone, 4·9 per cent in addition understood English, 22·5 per cent understood only an African language other than Chichewa, and a further 0·9 per cent understood English and another language but not Chichewa. Thus in 1966 slightly over one in five of the population aged 5 and over were unable to understand either of the languages in which information was diffused and administration and business conducted. The greater proportion of such persons were resident in the Northern Region and in adjacent areas of Kasungu and Nkhota Kota, with a second and smaller concentration in Mangoche and Kasupe Districts, and much smaller groups in Nsanje and in the Shire Highlands. In the Shire Highlands there are considerable inter-mixing of groups and opportunities to hear and use the language. The relatively small proportion of non-Chichewa speakers in the area in 1966 suggests that very soon inability to understand either Chichewa or English will disappear in that area, and has probably already disappeared as far as the younger generations are concerned. The problem in the Mangoche and Kasupe areas and in the Northern Region is much greater. In the Northern Region 83·4 per cent of the population (337 395) could not understand either Chichewa or English. In Chitipa and Karonga Districts this percentage reached 89 and 87 respectively. In Mangoche and Kasupe Districts in 1966, 209 000 persons, 56 per cent of the population aged 5 and over, did not understand either Chichewa or English. In Mangoche District the proportion reached 69 per cent. For full economic and social integration with the remainder of the country an understanding of one of the two national languages is essential. Considerable efforts have been made since Independence, and particularly since 1968, to bring an understanding of Chichewa and English to these populations, by means of the formal education system, and particularly through the media of the Malawi Broadcasting Corporation.

In all instances the proportion of females understanding languages other than the home language was considerably less than that of males. This might have been a result of the much more restricted opportunities for travel, education and employment.

MICHAEL STUBBS

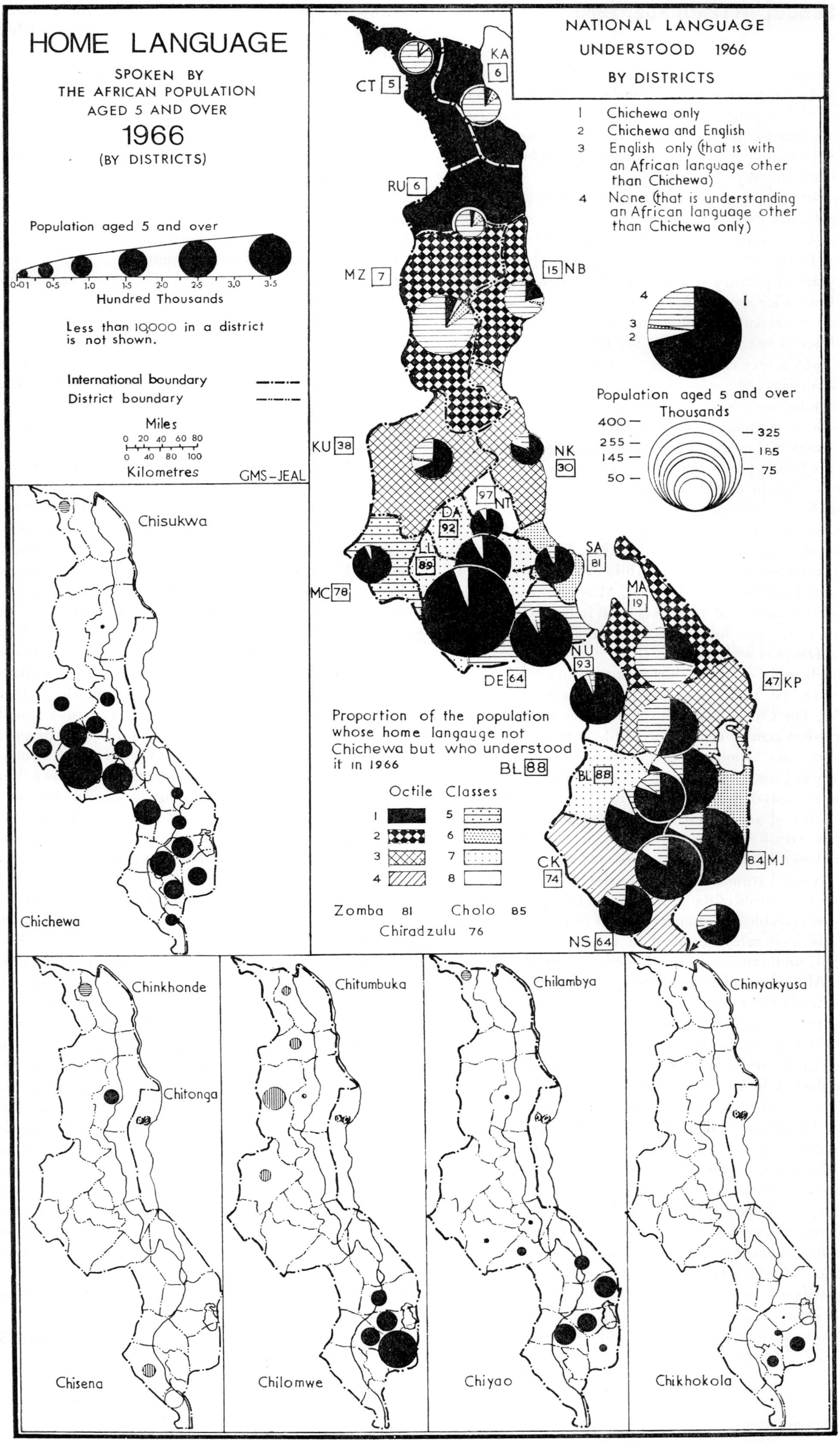
HOME LANGUAGE
SPOKEN BY
THE AFRICAN POPULATION
AGED 5 AND OVER
1966
(BY DISTRICTS)
Population aged 5 and over
0·01 0·5 1·0 1·5 2·0 2·5 3·0 3·5
Hundred Thousands
Less than 10,000 in a district is not shown.
International boundary
District boundary
Miles
0 20 40 60 80
0 40 80 100
Kilometres
GMS-JEAL
Chisukwa
Chichewa
NATIONAL LANGUAGE
UNDERSTOOD 1966
BY DISTRICTS
1 Chichewa only
2 Chichewa and English
3 English only (that is with an African language other than Chichewa)
4 None (that is understanding an African language other than Chichewa only)
Population aged 5 and over
Thousands
400 — 255 — 145 — 50 —
— 325 — 165 — 75
KA 6
CT 5
RU 6
MZ 7
15 NB
KU 38
NK 30
97 NT
DA 92
LL 89
SA 81
MC 78
MA 19
NU 93
DE 64
47 KP
BL 88
84 MJ
CK 74
NS 64
Proportion of the population whose home langauge not Chichewa but who understood it in 1966
Octile Classes
1 2 3 4 5 6 7 8
Zomba 81 Cholo 85
Chiradzulu 76
Chinkhonde
Chitonga
Chisena
Chitumbuka
Chilomwe
Chilambya
Chiyao
Chinyakyusa
Chikhokola

30 SCHOOL ATTENDANCE, 1966

The 1966 census enquiry revealed that 23·1 per cent of the male and 12·5 per cent of the female populations aged between 5 and 24 years were attending school. Comparison of the proportions for males and females for single years showed that although female attendance lagged behind male attendance only slightly at the youngest age, the gap became larger with age, until age 11, after which female proportions declined while male attendance continued to rise to a peak proportion at age 15. This reflected the then still very limited female attendance at secondary school and in the later years of primary school. The still considerable male attendance after age 18 resulted both from very late completion of secondary and even primary education, and attendance at vocational and higher education institutions. Since 1966 a very considerable expansion of both primary and secondary education has occurred, and particular attention has been given to education for girls.

Levels of attendance of both males and females varied very considerably within the country, although in almost all cases the female proportion in any one area was lower than the male. For the country as a whole, and for the age group 10–14, female attendance was 75 per cent of that of the males. In 11 of the 23 districts, this ratio was between 70 and 80 per cent. In Rumphi, and Ntchisi, Dowa, and Dedza the ratio was over 80 per cent, while in Lilongwe it was 99 per cent. In Mchinji and Kasungu, Mangoche and Kasupe, it was between 60 and 70 per cent and in Nkhota Kota only 52 per cent. The lowest ratios were in Chikwawa and Nsanje Districts with only 36 and 38 per cent respectively. For single years of age the highest attendance level was between 11 and 17 for males and between 11 and 14 for females. For Chiefs' and Sub-Chiefs' areas and most third order urban centres data was available only as an aggregate attendance for quinquennial age groups. The age group 10–14 was chosen for mapping. Analysis for 198 areas revealed a skewed distribution, with a mean of 43 and a modal class of 30–39 per cent. For mapping purposes the data was transformed to the square root and allocated to seven classes defined in terms of units of the standard deviation arranged symmetrically about the mean.

Over two-thirds of the urban centres for which information was available had attendance rates in the highest class. Similarly high rates occurred in rural areas of Chitipa, Rumphi, southern Karonga and north-eastern Mzimba Districts. All but one of the remaining urban areas had attendance rates in the second class, as had chiefs' areas adjacent to the rural areas mentioned above. The concentration of the highest attendance rates in these parts of the Northern Region has its origin in the primary education system introduced during the last decades of the nineteenth century by the Free Church of Scotland missions centred at Livingstonia, Ekwendeni and Loudon. It would seem that high levels of attendance had diffused by 1966 to almost all parts of the Northern Region. It is interesting to note, however, that the Chinteche lakeshore area of southern Nkhata Bay District, which was the first area to have a missionary primary school system, had only moderate levels of attendance. A possible contributory factor, the precise method of operation of which has been insufficiently investigated, is the patrilineal and patrilocal social organization of the populations of this region, which contrasts with the matrilineal and matrilocal social organization of most societies in the Central and Southern regions. It is conceivable that a more direct male parental responsibility and control has resulted in a greater pressure to attend school. Areas of considerable but rather later mission education influence in other parts of the country have not had the same degree of impact. Further factors include a lower level of employment opportunities and a slow development of commercial agriculture in 1966 and the early establishment of a tradition of long distance migration to fill skilled and clerical occupations all over central and southern Africa which required at least a primary education.

High values in urban areas reflected both the greater provision of primary schools, early commencement of secondary school attendance, and the generally greater opportunities for the children of urban households who usually have higher incomes than rural households. For these reasons many children resident in the more distant villages, which may be defined as any place over 5 to 8 km. (3–5 miles) distant because of limited public transportation facilities, resided in hostels or with relatives in the third order centres. Although the census was held during school holidays it is possible that some of these children were still resident in the urban areas, thereby increasing proportions there and reducing them in the rural areas.

The lowest proportions of males attending school were found in parts of Dedza and Salima Districts, in Mangoche and in all parts of Kasupe except the Balaka area. These areas have high proportions of Ayao, together with Alomwe in Kasupe and Achewa in Dedza and Salima Districts. The Ayao are largely Moslem, as are many members of other groups in the same area. Because of the early association of education with Christian missions and the early opposition by the Ayao chiefs to colonial occupation, the Ayao have been reluctant to make use of educational facilities, either mission or government. Consequently even in 1966 school attendance was very limited, in one chief's area the proportion falling to less than one per cent. It is interesting to note that notwithstanding these low levels the urban areas had attendance levels within the two highest classes. The only urban area with a value in the third class was Salima.

Areas with rates in the next to the lowest class were concentrated in Salima and Dedza Districts adjacent to those in the lowest, and in the Palombe-Chilwa area, in parts of Chikwawa District, and in western Lilongwe District, Mchinji and in southern Kasungu where C.A. Santhe had an attendance level in the lowest class. Attendance rates close to the mean occur in chiefs' areas around Blantyre and Zomba, in the Ngabu-Chiromo areas and southern Nsanje, in Ncheu, and in Dowa, Ntchisi and southern Kasungu.

With the increasing momentum of the self-help programme of primary school construction, and increased interest in attending school, the levels of school attendance have increased considerably even during the four years since the census. The objectives of the Ministry of Education's primary education programme is to maintain the level of attendance in districts with rates above the national average of 35 per cent, and to raise the level in other districts as rapidly as possible towards this level. The greatest efforts have been necessary in Mangoche and Kasupe Districts which in 1966 had only 11 and 18 per cent male attendance, and in Salime 24, Mchinji 26, Mulanje 27, Dedza 27, and Lilongwe 29.

A table of the enrolment of pupils in schools is given on p. 141.

MICHAEL STUBBS

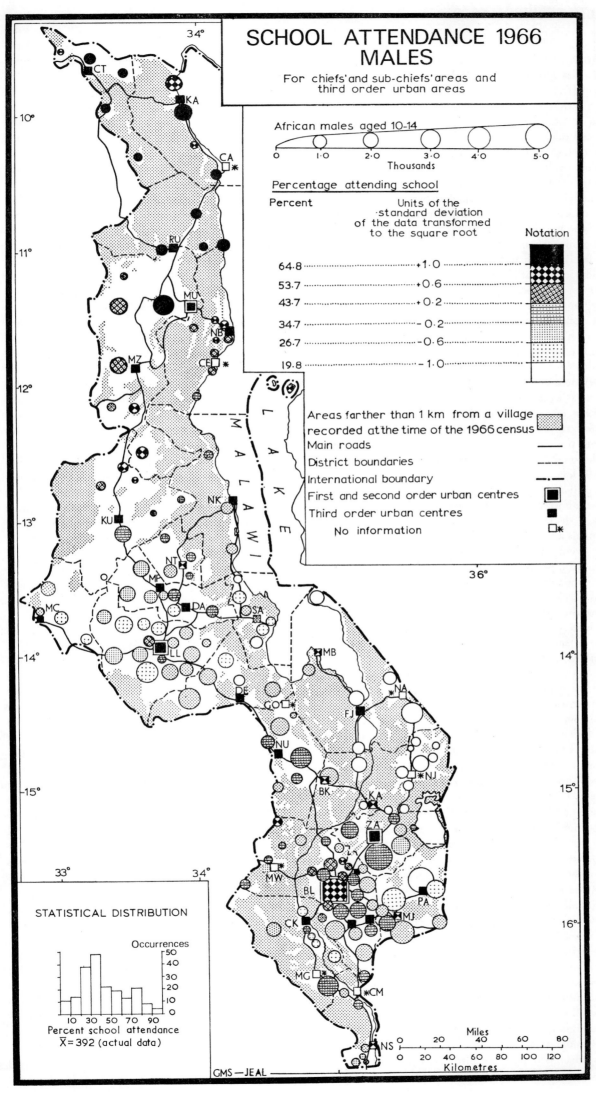

SCHOOL ATTENDANCE 1966 MALES

For chiefs' and sub-chiefs' areas and third order urban areas

African males aged 10-14

Thousands

Percentage attending school

Percent	Units of the standard deviation of the data transformed to the square root	Notation
64.8	+1.0	
53.7	+0.6	
43.7	+0.2	
34.7	−0.2	
26.7	−0.6	
19.8	−1.0	

Areas farther than 1 km from a village recorded at the time of the 1966 census

Main roads

District boundaries

International boundary

First and second order urban centres

Third order urban centres

No information

LAKE MALAWI

STATISTICAL DISTRIBUTION

Occurrences

Percent school attendance
X̄ = 392 (actual data)

Miles

Kilometres

GMS—JEAL

75

31 HEALTH SERVICES, 1969

The population of Malawi suffers from the characteristic range of diseases found in a tropical developing country. Dysentery, malaria and hookworm are common throughout the country, although levels are considerably increased in the hot, humid and marshy lakeshore and Rift Valley floor regions. In addition such diseases as leprosy, sleeping sickness, elephantiasis and trachoma achieve serious levels here. The healthiest ecological regions are the plateau surfaces above the Rift Valley, particularly those of low and medium density, although the Shire Highlands experiences, in the cool season, cool and wet weather which increases the levels of rheumatism and influenza. Tuberculosis is endemic. Those areas of higher population density and restricted area of land per family suffer most from diseases related to malnutrition and poor sanitation and hygiene caused by shortage of and pollution of domestic water.

At the beginning of 1969 there were 6593 hospital beds of which 84 per cent were in government, mission and private hospitals, a little under six per cent in a psychiatric hospital and five leprosaria, and the remaining ten per cent in rural health centres, clinics, dispensaries and maternity units. Government units accounted for 53 per cent of beds. In Malawi in 1963 there was one bed for 644 persons, one doctor for 51 000 persons, and one health centre or dispensary for 26 570 persons. Between Independence in 1964 and 1968 there had been an increase of one-third in the number of hospital beds, of which missions contributed 62 per cent. Missions accounted for 46 per cent of beds, and private companies 1 per cent.

Government hospitals and health units were organized by administrative districts. A central hospital at Blantyre, general hospitals at Zomba and Lilongwe, and district hospitals in the twenty remaining administrative centres supervised 13 rural hospitals and 95 rural health centres. The Northern Region capital, Mzuzu, had no government hospital, and was served by mission hospitals there and at Ekwendeni, nearby, and all but the district hospitals at Liwonde, which served Kasupe District, were located in the third order urban centre which functioned as district headquarters. Both of these anomalies resulted from recent administrative relocations. Of the 13 third order centres which were not district administrative centres, and therefore did not have district hospitals, six had rural hospitals (Chilumba, Chinteche, Mponela, Mwanza, Balaka and Ngabu) and four were served by adjacent mission hospitals (Monkey Bay, Chiromo, Palombe and Mtakataka). Luchenza, without a district hospital or nearby mission, was served by facilities at Thyolo and Mulanje. Ntaja and Namwera, newly developed urban centres on the eastern periphery of the Southern Region, were farthest from district level hospitals and most in need of additional facilities. A military and a psychiatric hospital were located in the capital, Zomba, and a government leprosarium, with 28 beds and accommodation for 640 ambulatory patients, at Kochirira near Mchinji. The central and general hospitals were equipped with all but the most specialized equipment (normally provided in Salisbury, Rhodesia), and only eight of the 20 district hospitals were without X-ray facilities. Central government facilities were supported by 42 district council maternity units.

Mission organizations controlled 43 ordinary hospitals and one maternity hospital (at Nkhota Kota), 26 maternity units, almost all with general dispensaries, 31 ordinary dispensaries and clinics, 4 leprosaria and 2 leprosy dispensaries. The older missions ante-dated the development of the administrative urban system, while many later missions have chosen locations at some distance from established centres. Consequently government and mission facilities are not spatially coincident, and mission hospitals tend to fill the spatial gaps between government centres, thereby bringing most areas within at most 24 km. (15 miles) of a hospital facility. However, an estimated total of 482 000 persons in 1969, 12 per cent of the national population, resided farther away than this. These were mostly on the peripheries of the several regions, adjacent to the national frontiers, and along the lakeshore in areas distant from existing administrative centres. The Namwera, Ntaja and Lake Chilwa-Palombe areas with relatively dense populations contained the greater proportion of this population. A distance of 24 km. was still considerable given the problems of passenger transportation.

Just over 27 per cent of Malawi's hospital beds were located in the southern 'core', the Shire Highlands, and a further 21 per cent in the central 'core', in the Lilongwe, Dedza, Dowa, Mponela and Ntchisi areas. A core-periphery pattern was observable with respect to the ratio of persons to hospital beds. In the Northern and North Central Regions lower than average ratios were characteristic of the Karonga and the Mzuzu-Rumphi-Mzimba-Nkhata Bay cores, and similar lower ratios were observable in the Lilongwe and the Blantyre-Zomba cores.

Hospital facilities are supplemented by a variety of smaller health facilities. In order to facilitate spatial comparisons, government health centres and mission dispensaries have been defined as single units, mission, private and district council maternity units as equivalent to only two-thirds, and the stopping places of mobile mission clinics only one-third of a unit. In most areas the relationship between population and the resultant clinic equivalents is similar to that between population and hospital beds, but in some areas low bed/population ratios are partially compensated for by higher than average clinic equivalent/population ratios.

Until recently little preventive resources had been available, but pilot projects at Ngabu in the Lower Shire and at Namitambo on the edge of the Palombe-Chilwa plains will be used as prototypes for regional preventive health programmes.

Three types of agricultural development are crucial to the future development of the country: comprehensive rural reorganization in the long dry season and non-irrigable plateau areas; development of urban-market-oriented mixed agriculture around the larger towns; and, perhaps most important, development of the irrigable areas of highest potential in the Rift Valley, lakeshore and Palombe-Chilwa plains. Of these the third is likely to be most dependent upon a very considerable improvement in human productivity and health status, because of these regions' high levels of disease and present greater than average shortage of health facilities. Possibly in these areas the greatest benefit would result from concentration upon environmental and preventive health programmes supported by expanded hospital facilities in the relevant third order urban centres. Because Blantyre is one of the key functional units in the country's industrial development, similar programmes are likely to be most beneficial there also.

As national and regional transportation systems improve, and urban centres develop, the advantages of close spatial co-ordination of health services with them becomes greater. External economies are achieved by locating health facilities at appropriate urban centres, in which adequate supporting services and utilities exist. Economies of scale grow as population migrates into urban and adjacent areas. Transportation improvements constantly improve the accessibility of urban centres both absolutely and in relation to non-urban locations.

MICHAEL STUBBS

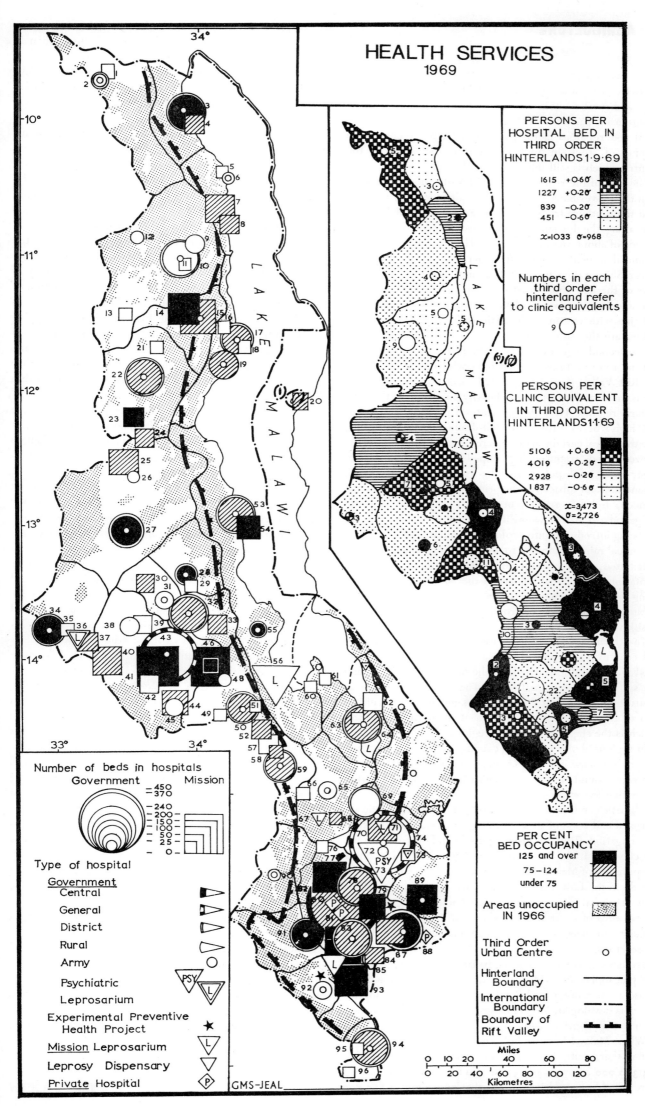

HEALTH SERVICES
1969

PERSONS PER HOSPITAL BED IN THIRD ORDER HINTERLANDS 1·9·69

1615	+0·6σ
1227	+0·2σ
839	−0·2σ
451	−0·6σ

$x=1033 \quad σ=968$

Numbers in each third order hinterland refer to clinic equivalents

9 ◯

PERSONS PER CLINIC EQUIVALENT IN THIRD ORDER HINTERLANDS 11·69

5106	+0·6σ
4019	+0·2σ
2928	−0·2σ
1837	−0·6σ

$x=3,473 \quad σ=2,726$

PER CENT BED OCCUPANCY

125 and over	■
75–124	▨
under 75	□

Areas unoccupied IN 1966

Third Order Urban Centre ◯

Hinterland Boundary ——

International Boundary —·—·—

Boundary of Rift Valley ▰▰ ▰▰

Number of beds in hospitals

Government — Mission

450
370
240
200
150
100
50
25
0

Type of hospital

Government
Central
General
District
Rural
Army
Psychiatric PSY
Leprosarium L

Experimental Preventive Health Project ★

Mission Leprosarium L

Leprosy Dispensary L

Private Hospital P

LAKE MALAWI

GMS–JEAL

Miles
0 10 20 40 60 80
0 20 40 60 80 100 120
Kilometres

34° 33° 34°

10° 11° 12° 13° 14°

32 AGRICULTURE

Three major agricultural regions can be distinguished in Malawi, each showing differences in climate, soil series, crops and rural economy. The presence or absence of cattle or pigs in any part of any of the regions depends mainly upon social and religious factors, although tsetse precludes the keeping of stock in approximately 12 per cent of the country which is still infested with the fly.

The first of the regions is the Rift Valley floor extending from the Lower Shire valley, with an altitude of 37 m. (120 ft) at the southern frontier, northwards to Lake Malawi and then along the lowlands of the western lake shore to an altitude of about 762 m. (2500 ft). There is a wide variation in annual rainfall, ranging from 635 mm. (25 in.) in the Lower Shire valley to over 2540 mm. (100 in.) in those parts of the lake shore lowlands facing rain-bearing winds. Characteristic cultivated plants are bulrush-millet, cassava and rice with cotton as the main cash crop. Rice, cotton and tea are the cash crops.

The second region consists of the plateau, lying between 762 and 1372 m. (2500 and 4500 ft), which is separated from the Rift Valley floor by dissected escarpments and which forms the most important and heavily populated of the agricultural regions. Here the agricultural potential is particularly high wherever there are well-drained ferruginous soils, but there are certain areas where leached sands, lateritic horizons and waterlogging impede cultivation. Maize, finger-millet and pulses are the traditional staples with groundnuts and tobacco as the principal cash crops. Oriental tobacco, upland varieties of cotton, and *ninde*, a shrub indigenous to Africa whose flowers contain essential oils, are being introduced into ecologically suitable areas. Where the annual rainfall amounts to 1270 mm. (50 in.) and is well distributed, tea, tung oil and saligna gum are grown as plantation crops. Smallholders in the Northern Region are being encouraged to grow coffee and it is proposed to investigate the prospects of growing mulberry trees as a base to silk-worm culture.

The third region comprises the hill zones between 1372 and 1539 m. (4500 and 5500 ft) above sea level which have good agricultural soils wherever the slopes are moderate and the soils are deeply weathered. The relatively low mean annual temperatures at these altitudes encourage the cultivation of legumes, potatoes and wheat in addition to maize, which is the staple crop in this region.

In regions above 1539 m. (5500 ft) cultivation is sparse, but the montane grasslands, indigenous forests and planted softwoods found in these highlands play an important part in protecting the water-divides.

Climatic conditions for cocoa, oil palm and sugar-cane are marginal and none of these can be grown successfully without irrigation. Trials in growing cocoa and oil palm are being conducted by the Ministry of Agriculture. The Sugar Corporation of Malawi has been operating a sugar scheme at Nchalo in the Lower Shire valley since 1965. In 1969 there were 2509 ha. (6200 acres) of cane under irrigation and 29 836 tons of sugar were produced which was more than sufficient to meet Malawi's present annual consumption of 20 000 tons.

Fruits such as avocado pears, bananas, mangoes, pawpaws and pineapples are widely grown and production will increase as marketing facilities improve and the canning industry is developed. Vegetable-growing on a small scale is a feature of peri-urban areas.

When Malawi became independent in 1964 it was estimated that, out of a total land area of 10 268 310 ha. (23 300 000 acres), some 5 261 100 ha. (13 000 000 acres) were suitable for cultivation but that only about 2 860 800 ha. (6 400 000 acres) of the land suitable for cultivation could be utilized under the methods of agriculture then in use and without large scale capital investment.

With 2 860 800 ha. (6 400 000 acres) immediately available for cultivation and a population of about 4 million people, the average amount of productive land per head was 0·65 ha. (1·6 acres).

With the traditional methods of farming, the actual amount of land cultivated by a peasant family depends upon the availability of unoccupied woodland for new fields, local population pressure, and the amount of labour available. When oxen are used for ploughing, an innovation that is being actively encouraged by the government, more land can be brought under cultivation than is possible by hoe.

In Malawi it is common to find a catena, or connected series, of soils from interfluve to valley floor, each series differing in texture, moisture retention and availability of nutrients. The peasant farmers have a keen appreciation of the different qualities of the soils, and dispose their gardens accordingly, cultivation ranging from continuous cropping on the strongest soils to cropping rotating with fallow of varying length on the weaker soils. This has led to extreme fragmentation of family land and, within each plot, further subdivision has taken place in accordance with kinship obligations and the laws of inheritance.

Since independence substantial development funds have been devoted to land reorganization and agricultural settlement schemes which are bringing about fundamental changes and innovations in land usage, agricultural practices, settlement patterns and communication networks.

The largest of these schemes is the Lilongwe Land Development Project which initially covered an area of over 202 450 ha. (500 000 acres) and involved 190 000 people occupying 38 000 farms. The project is designed to increase production of crops and livestock. The plan will cover a thirteen-year period during which roads, drains, waterways and bridges will be built; three hundred new boreholes will be provided; twenty-one new markets with storage facilities will be erected; twenty-five properly planned small townships will be built; extension services will be increased; and credit facilities will be made available.

Other important schemes are the Salima Lakeshore Development Project, affecting some 3000 cotton growers, and the Chikwawa Cotton Development Project, involving 15 000 farmers in the lower Shire Valley. The aims of both these projects are to increase cotton production in the areas concerned through the provision of training facilities for growers, extra boreholes and crop-extraction roads.

In addition to these large scale projects, the agricultural programme is concerned with the development of particular crops, including maize, groundnuts, tobacco, rice and coffee.

Since independence it has also been the policy of government to repurchase freehold land, which exists primarily as a result of land grants made in the early days of the British protectorate, and to use it for such purposes as farm training bases for the Malawi Young Pioneers, experimental farms, beef and dairy farms, and resettlement schemes.

Agricultural progress is therefore taking place along a broad front, supported by rapidly increasing extension and technical services, improved marketing facilities and greater availability of credit.

Agriculture, including livestock, fishing and forestry, is the most important sector of the economy which engages more than 95 per cent of the population. In 1969 agriculture contributed 40 per cent of the gross domestic product, and almost 94 per cent of the total value of Malawi's exports was derived from agricultural products.

SWANZIE AGNEW

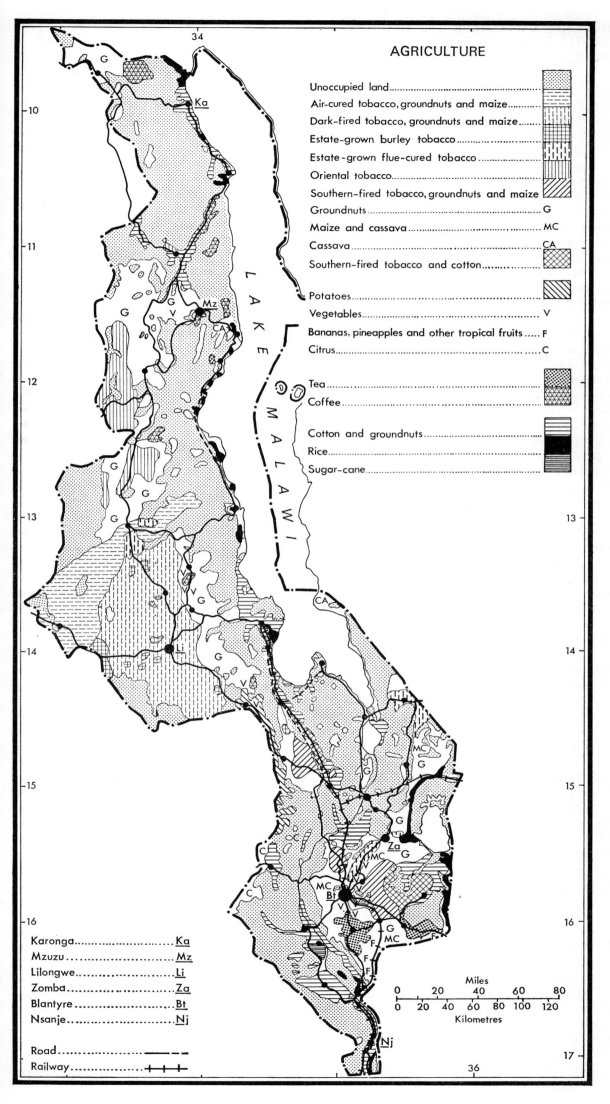

AGRICULTURE

Unoccupied land..
Air-cured tobacco, groundnuts and maize............
Dark-fired tobacco, groundnuts and maize........
Estate-grown burley tobacco..............................
Estate-grown flue-cured tobacco.....................
Oriental tobacco...
Southern-fired tobacco, groundnuts and maize
Groundnuts... G
Maize and cassava... MC
Cassava... CA
Southern-fired tobacco and cotton.................

Potatoes...
Vegetables.. V
Bananas, pineapples and other tropical fruits..... F
Citrus.. C

Tea..
Coffee...

Cotton and groundnuts.....................................
Rice..
Sugar-cane...

LAKE MALAWI

Karonga.........................Ka
Mzuzu............................Mz
Lilongwe.........................Li
Zomba............................Za
Blantyre..........................Bt
Nsanje............................Nj

Road...................... ___ __ __
Railway.................. ┼┼┼

Miles
0   20   40   60   80
0 20 40 60 80 100 120
Kilometres

33 AGRICULTURAL RESEARCH AND TRAINING FACILITIES AND MALAWI YOUNG PIONEERS, 1969

The programme of agricultural modernization within Malawi consisted of basic research conducted by the Agricultural Research Council of Malawi, the Tea Research Foundation and the University of Malawi, applied research in the Ministry of Agriculture, training of agricultural, scientific, technical and administrative staffs in the University of Malawi and Ministry of Agriculture, practical training of peasant commercial farmers and members of the Malawi Young Pioneers organization, and general agricultural training for children within Malawi's educational programmes.

The Agricultural Research Council of Malawi was established in 1967 as a statutory body to take over the work of the former Agricultural Research Council of Central Africa. Its headquarters and Cotton Pest Research Unit were at Makoka south of Zomba. A Grain Legume Breeding and Research Unit was located at the Ministry of Agriculture's research station at Chitedze, west of Lilongwe. The Council was also responsible for a soil physicist engaged upon the irrigability of tea soils with the Tea Research Foundation, and a biometrics unit shared with the Ministry of Agriculture's research services. The Tea Research Foundation of Central Africa had its headquarters near Malosa in the Mulanje tea-growing area, with additional research sub-stations in each of the Thyolo and Mulanje tea-producing areas. In Blantyre the University of Malawi's Chancellor College and the Farmers' Marketing Board also conducted agricultural and ecological research.

The Ministry of Agriculture concentrated its research efforts upon the development of economic farming systems adapted to the varied ecological conditions within Malawi, and research and experimental stations and sub-stations were located in each ecological region. The principal research stations in the Southern Region were at Bvumbwe south of Blantyre, and at Makanga near Chiromo in the lower Shire valley. Research sub-stations were located at Ngabu in the Chikwawa cotton development area, and in the Kirk Range. In the Central Region Chitedze west of Lilongwe and Lisasadzi south of Kasungu were the principal stations. Chitala constituted the station for the central lakeshore region. In the Northern and north central regions a research station at Mzuzu, and sub-stations at Mbawa south of Mzimba, at Thulwe near Rumphi, at Nchenachena, in the Limphasa dambo and at Karonga and Misuku formed a research network for the varied ecological conditions of the north. In addition to work upon the staple, maize, and upon the principal export crops—tobacco, groundnuts, coffee and rice—attention was given to horticultural production, grain storage, legumes, hill farming, animal husbandry and soil surveys.

The demand for trained Malawian scientific, professional and technical staff grew with the expansion of modern agriculture, particularly as there were few such staff at the time of Independence. The University of Malawi's College of Agriculture south of Lilongwe was responsible for the training of agriculturalists to diploma and degree levels, while its Chancellor College was responsible for the initial general training of scientists, many of whom were subsequently employed in agricultural research and experimentation. Technical and extension staff were trained in the Ministry of Agriculture's Colby School of Agriculture, also near Lilongwe.

Education of peasant farmers expanded considerably with independence. In 1966 there were only 686 student days of attendance at rural area training centres and 12 276 student days at divisional residential training centres. By 1968 these figures had increased respectively to 26 541 and 40 168. A Farmer's Institute within each of the administrative regions (Hora in the north, Chitala in the centre, Thuchila in the south), 15 divisional and 53 area training centres existed. In addition to education in improved agricultural methods courses relating to the whole range of rural development, including health and community development and adult literacy, were offered. Some of the divisional centres but few of the area centres were located in third order urban places. These centres therefore became additional nuclei for the diffusion of modernization within the rural areas.

Increased emphasis was placed in 1969 upon the encouragement of selected 'progressive' farmers, the *achikumbe*, by concentrating upon them extension and technical services both in order to maximize the impact of government scarce manpower, and to develop nuclear farms from which modernization might spread to neighbours more likely to accept innovations from farmers within their own community. Another important element in the government's rural development strategy was the contribution by the Malawi Young Pioneers organization, established in 1963 and trained by Israeli teams. In this both boys and girls were given basic education and trained in improved methods of agriculture, home economics, youth leadership, hygiene and health. Some continued to vocational training programmes as carpenters, builders, blacksmiths, drivers and motor mechanics and pilots. The basic programme was provided in 21 training bases, one in each administrative district except Mulanje and Chiradzulu, while vocational training was provided at two technical bases, one at Nasawa supported by Danish technical assistance, the other at Chitala supported by West German technical assistance. Although some trained Pioneers returned to their villages and acted as disseminators of modern methods of agriculture there, many others joined government-supported settlement schemes, associated with existing agricultural development projects or with areas of great potential previously neglected. Eleven settlement schemes were established by 1969. Three were concerned with irrigated rice production: Hara and Limpasa in the northern lakeshore and Likangala on alluvial soils near Lake Chilwa. Each was supported by Taiwanese rice demonstration teams, and constituted prototypes for the development of many other potential sites along the lakeshore. Schemes at Thulwe near Rumphi and three near Namitete west of Lilongwe were concerned with tobacco production. Remaining projects were concerned with cotton production at Chitala in the Salima lakeshore, at Rivi Rivi in the upper Shire section of the Rift Valley, and at Mangulenje and Chikonje in the lower Shire section. Whereas peasant farmers' average yields were 165 kg. per hectare (147 lb. of rice per acre), average yields in settlement projects were 773 kg. (690 lb. per acre). During the two-year period 1967–9 3440 men and 140 girls completed their training. 1000 pioneers were engaged in existing settlement schemes in 1969, and it was planned to allocate between 700 and 800 annually during succeeding years. Pioneer trainees were also being educated in modern fisheries methods at the Mpepwe Fisheries Training School near Mangoche. Pioneers who had specialized in youth and physical education were attached to primary and secondary schools, with the further objective of helping to remove the existing prejudice against rural employment. In this way the Malawi Government hoped to solve the problems of rural and urban unemployment and underemployment, and to develop the country's still largely unused potential.

A key to the map is given on p. 141.

MICHAEL STUBBS

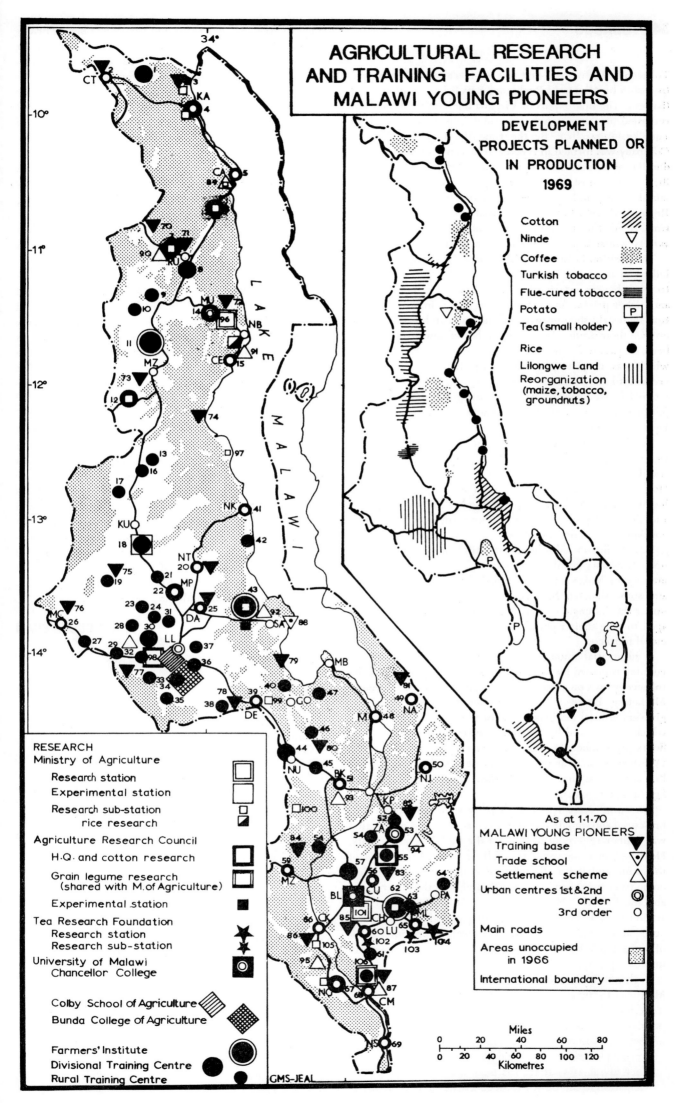

AGRICULTURAL RESEARCH AND TRAINING FACILITIES AND MALAWI YOUNG PIONEERS

DEVELOPMENT PROJECTS PLANNED OR IN PRODUCTION 1969

Cotton	
Ninde	▽
Coffee	
Turkish tobacco	
Flue-cured tobacco	
Potato	P
Tea (small holder)	▼
Rice	●
Lilongwe Land Reorganization (maize, tobacco, groundnuts)	

RESEARCH

Ministry of Agriculture

Research station ☐
Experimental station ☐
Research sub-station rice research ◨

Agriculture Research Council

H·Q· and cotton research ☐
Grain legume research (shared with M. of Agriculture) ☐
Experimental station ■

Tea Research Foundation
Research station ✦
Research sub-station ✦

University of Malawi Chancellor College ◉

Colby School of Agriculture
Bunda College of Agriculture

Farmers' Institute
Divisional Training Centre
Rural Training Centre

As at 1·1·70
MALAWI YOUNG PIONEERS

Training base ▼
Trade school ▽
Settlement scheme △
Urban centres 1st & 2nd order ◎
3rd order ○
Main roads ——
Areas unoccupied in 1966 ▨
International boundary —·—

Miles
0 20 40 60 80
0 20 40 60 80 100 120
Kilometres

GMS-JEAL

LAKE MALAWI

34 TOBACCO

Tobacco in Malawi was first planted in 1889 in the Blantyre township by Mr David Buchanan, a well known pioneer of that era. The first export of Virginia flue-cured tobacco was recorded in 1899 when the total export amounted to 1009 kg. (2240 lb.). By the time the Imperial Tobacco Company was formed in Nyasaland in 1907, the annual production of tobacco had risen to some 272 160 kg. (600 000 lb.). At first most of the tobacco produced was of the flue-cured variety and was produced entirely in the Southern Region, whereas today a substantial percentage of production is of the fire-cured and sun/air-cured (Western) variety which is produced mainly in the Central Region.

The position in Rhodesia following UDI and sanctions has led to an increased interest in Malawi flue-cured tobacco, to more buyers entering the market, stronger competition and higher prices. As a consequence of this improved situation the established growers of flue-cured tobacco have increased their production and a number of new growers have been registered. The production of flue-cured tobacco which was 1 231 614 kg. (2 715 640 lb.) in 1965 had increased to 2 771 482 kg. (6 109 959 lb.) in 1969 which fetched an average price of 104 pence per kg. (47·33 pence per lb.) and in 1970 production reached a figure of 4 675 781 kg. (10 308 160 lb.).

For the last few years Malawi tobacco has been considered to be a very usable tobacco but, as production was low, it was difficult to persuade buyers to enter the Malawi market. However, it is now believed that, if annual production can be maintained at least at 4 536 000 kg. (10 000 000 lb.), and the quality of the crop is improved, buyers will then continue to support the Malawi market.

In 1969 flue-cured tobacco was still being grown entirely on estates and mainly by European growers. However, a number of Malawian growers had already been registered and some selected Malawian growers were being trained under the Kasungu Tobacco Growers' Scheme and encouraged to take their rightful place in the production of flue-cured tobacco.

A substantial amount of all the tobacco produced in the country is grown by Malawians on customary land. All the tobacco grown on customary land is bought by the Farmers' Marketing Board which purchases the crop from the growers in local markets, transports and grades the tobacco which is then sold by the Board over the licensed auction floors in Limbe. In 1970 the production of fire-cured (Western) tobacco ammounted to 9 985 260 kg. (22 013 405 lb.) and of sun/air-cured (Western) tobacco to 1 841 241 kg. (4 059 170 lb.).

For some years recently there was over-production of fire-cured and sun/air-cured tobacco and in 1968 production was deliberately reduced to meet the trade's requirements. However, in 1969 production fell far short of the needs of the trade and it was therefore decided that the time had come to increase production again and both the government and the Farmers' Marketing Board took measures to help attain this end. There is undoubtedly a good future for fire-cured and sun/air-cured tobacco in Malawi provided levels of production can be controlled and steps are taken to improve quality.

Burley tobacco is now produced on estates, mainly by Malawian tenant farmers by agreement with and under the direction of the estate owner who purchases the leaf and prepares it for sale over the auction floors. The production of Burley tobacco in 1970 amounted to 5 674 644 kg. (12 510 238 lb.), the highest figure ever recorded.

Since about 1967 there has been increased interest and participation in the Burley tobacco market in Malawi which has led to greater competition and very much higher prices being realized for Burley tobacco. This interest has led to higher production by the established Burley growers and to the registration of a number of new growers. For the future there appears to be no reason why Malawi should not firmly establish itself in the Burley markets of the world provided steps are taken to maintain and improve the quality of Burley tobacco with particular emphasis on coloured Burley for which there is today a world demand.

By law all tobacco grown in Malawi has to be sold over the auction floors, except Turkish (oriental) tobacco which is bought by the Farmers' Marketing Board and is, at present, sold by private treaty. The Turkish crop is almost entirely grown in the Northern Region. Production in 1969 was 89 294 kg. (196 875 lb.) and seems likely to increase in future years.

The auction floors in Malawi were started in 1938. The floors in Limbe usually open in about the last week of April and sales are conducted daily until about the middle of September, depending on the size of the various crops. Many local and overseas visitors come to see the auction floors during the selling season and are always fascinated by the familiar 'sing-song' chant of the auctioneer and the speed at which the bales are sold. An average of 3200 bales, of some 272 160 kg. (600 000 lb.) in weight, are sold daily.

The marketing of tobacco in Malawi is controlled by the Tobacco Control Commission which is a statutory body appointed by the Ministry of Agriculture in terms of the Tobacco Control Commission Ordinance. The Commission consists of four representatives of grower interests and four representatives of buyer interests. The Commission's powers under the Ordinance include the organization and supervision of auction sales of all types of tobacco other than Turkish; the licensing of auction floors, buyers and commercial graders; the formulation of rules governing the packing, presentation and sale of all types of tobacco except Turkish; and the collection of relevant statistics.

An analysis of tobacco sales is given on p. 84.

R W D BUCKINGHAM

FARMERS' MARKETING BOARD CENTRES 1970
(Agricultural Areas)

REGIONS

NORTH

1 Misuku Hills	8 Mzimba North-East
2 Karonga North	9 Nkhata Bay
3 Chitipa Lowlands	10 Kasitu Perekezi
4 Karongi South	11 Mzimba North
5 Rumphi Lowlands	12 Mzimba Central
6 Rumphi Highlands	13 Mzimba South-West
7 Mzimba North-West	14 Mzimba South-East

CENTRAL

15 Kasungu North	31 Dowa Hills
16 Kasungu Central	32 Chimutu
17 Nkhota Kota	33 Salima Central
18 Salima North	34 Nathenje
19 Ntchisi	35 Malangalanga
20 Madisi	36 Mpingo
21 Kasungu South	37 Chileka
22 Mchinji West	38 Sinyala
23 Mchinji East	39 Mkwinda
24 Chisepo	40 Kampini
25 Kasiya	41 Tiwi/Maonde
26 Nsaru	42 Dedza Hills
27 Nambuma	43 Salima South
28 Lumbadzi	44 Kirk Range
29 Ngwangwa	45 Nsipe Rivulezi
30 Mponela	46 Bwanje Valley

SOUTH

47 Mangoche West	50 Kasupe West
48 Mangoche East	51 Blantyre West
49 Kasupe East	52 Blantyre East

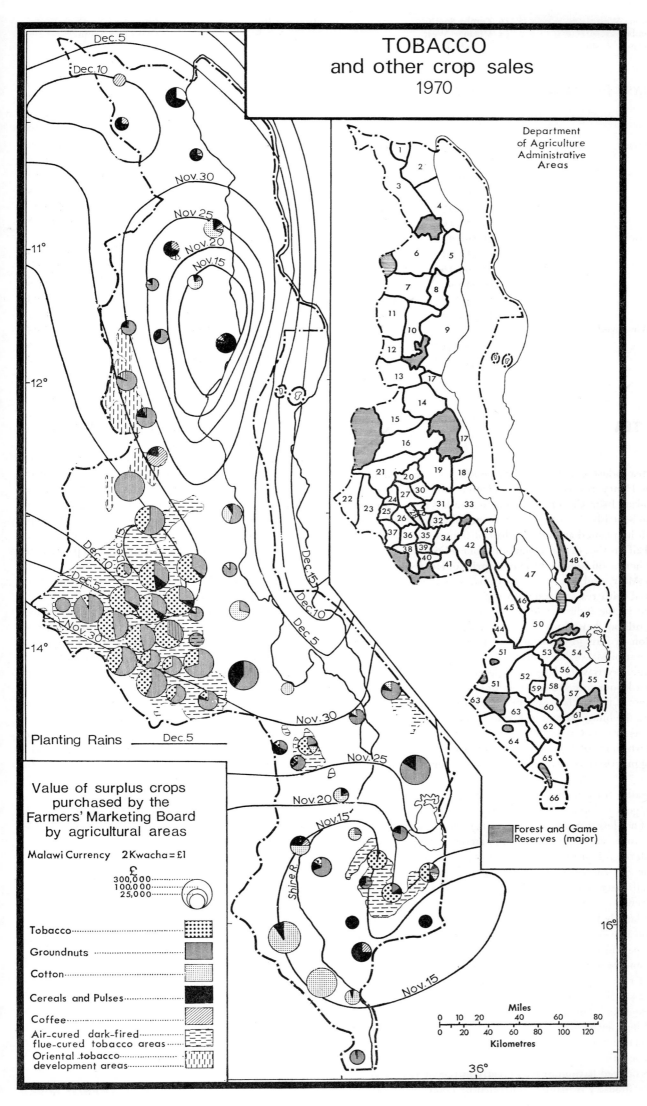

TOBACCO
and other crop sales
1970

Department
of Agriculture
Administrative
Areas

Planting Rains ———— Dec.5

Value of surplus crops
purchased by the
Farmers' Marketing Board
by agricultural areas

Malawi Currency   2 Kwacha = £1

£
300,000
100,000
25,000

Tobacco

Groundnuts

Cotton

Cereals and Pulses

Coffee

Air-cured dark-fired
flue-cured tobacco areas

Oriental tobacco
development areas

Forest and Game
Reserves (major)

Miles
0   10   20   40   60   80
0   20   40   60   80   100   120
Kilometres

ANALYSIS OF MALAWI TOBACCO SALES

	Year	Weight lb.	Value £
Flue-cured	1965	2 715 640	368 663
	1966	2 704 365	426 470
	1967	4 040 383	873 277
	1968	6 060 679	1 088 759
	1969	6 109 959	1 204 914
	1970	10 308 160	1 956 275
Fire-cured	1965	31 496 334	2 565 367
	1966	26 718 721	2 156 271
	1967	23 165 263	1 358 225
	1968	16 839 902	1 456 498
	1969	10 544 752	1 352 017
	1970	22 013 405	2 919 159
Sun/Air-cured	1965	10 118 299	705 940
	1966	6 087 568	300 781
	1967	2 517 212	144 377

	1968	2 329 861	238 671
	1969	2 134 794	295 357
	1970	4 059 170	546 301
Burley	1965	5 765 890	562 891
	1966	5 335 159	543 619
	1967	5 874 333	458 461
	1968	6 672 956	837 749
	1969	7 631 898	1 409 953
	1970	12 510 238	1 775 583

			Av. price in pence per lb.
Turkish (oriental)	1965	213 053	24·98
	1966	207 438	19·31
	1967	127 575	19·74
	1968	99 787	29·59
	1969	153 690	31·90
	1970	N.A.	N.A.

35 TEA

The tea industry in Malawi may be said to date from 1891 when Henry Brown, a coffee planter who had come to Nyasaland from Ceylon, saw some tea bushes in the grounds of the Scottish Mission at Blantyre and obtained a few seeds which he planted at Mulanje, half of them on his own land and half on that of his neighbour, John Muir.

Others soon followed the enterprise of Henry Brown and John Muir, and by 1970 15 214 ha. (37 593 acres) were planted with tea and more than £15 million had been invested in the industry. In 1970 more than 17 million kg. (38 million lb.) of tea was exported, earning above £4·5 million in foreign exchange which accounted for over 30 per cent of Malawi's export earnings. At the same time the tea industry was the largest single employer in the country with a labour force of some 34 000.

Most of the tea is grown in the Thyolo and Mulanje areas where the humidity and soil conditions are suitable, but tea gardens are now being developed near Nkata Bay on the western shore of Lake Malawi where overhead irrigation is being practised to make up for the deficiency of winter rainfall.

Ideally, tea requires deep, permeable, well-drained acid soils, gently sloping land, and fairly evenly distributed rainfall of not less than 1 270 mm. (50 in.) a year. There does not seem to be an upper limit to the amount of rainfall under which tea will grow vigorously. In Malawi a most important factor for successful tea growing is a minimum winter rainfall (between April and October) of 168 mm. (7 in.).

Conditions for the production of tea in Malawi are not ideal largely because most of the rainfall occurs during the period November to April which makes for a similar short peak period for plucking. During these months it is usual for some 80 per cent of the whole year's crop to be plucked. In the remaining months crop activity is at a minimum and only a small amount is plucked and processed. During years of less than normal or badly distributed rainfall the peak plucking period may be contracted into an even shorter period than the normal. Despite the lack of ideal conditions, however, the efficiency of production and the quality of the tea produced have improved greatly in recent years.

The industry is mainly controlled by companies who to-day own all of the 51 tea estates throughout Malawi, 30 of which have their own factories.

However, the government is now encouraging the establishment of African smallholder schemes. In 1967 government approval was given for the appointment of a Tea Authority to co-ordinate work among the smallholder tea growers and to assist them with marketing their crops. Prospective smallholder teagrowers are carefully selected before they are allowed to begin planting and all preparatory work on each small holding is inspected by officials of the Ministry of Agriculture. A tea nursery has already been established for the benefit of smallholders.

The two main tea areas of Thyolo and Mulanje are well served by communications. The railway line to the port of Beira in Moçambique runs between them with Luchenza as the main loading point. Tea from the Nkhata Bay area is transported by lake steamer to Chipoka and thence by rail to Luchenza and Beira.

The largest proportion of Malawi tea is still sold in London though exports are increasing to a number of other countries, notably the United States, South Africa, Canada and the Continent of Europe. There is also some demand in other African countries and a certain amount is sold at the Nairobi auctions.

At present the local market for Malawi tea is only 2 per cent of the total production, an average of 226 800 kg. (500 000 lb.) of tea being sold locally each year under numerous brand names.

TEA PRODUCTION IN MALAWI 1940–70

Year	Acres under tea	Production lb.	Export lb.	Value of exports £ Sterling
1940	18 257	12 879 000	12 794 312	481 688
1945	19 807	13 639 000	13 717 261	685 493
1950	23 510	15 407 000	15 157 065	1 690 712
1955	26 500	17 500 000	17 190 378	3 128 166
1960	28 680	26 079 000	24 253 209	3 805 978
1965	33 801	28 657 697	28 448 973	3 788 422
1970	37 593	41 295 823	38 500 000	N.A.

SWANZIE AGNEW

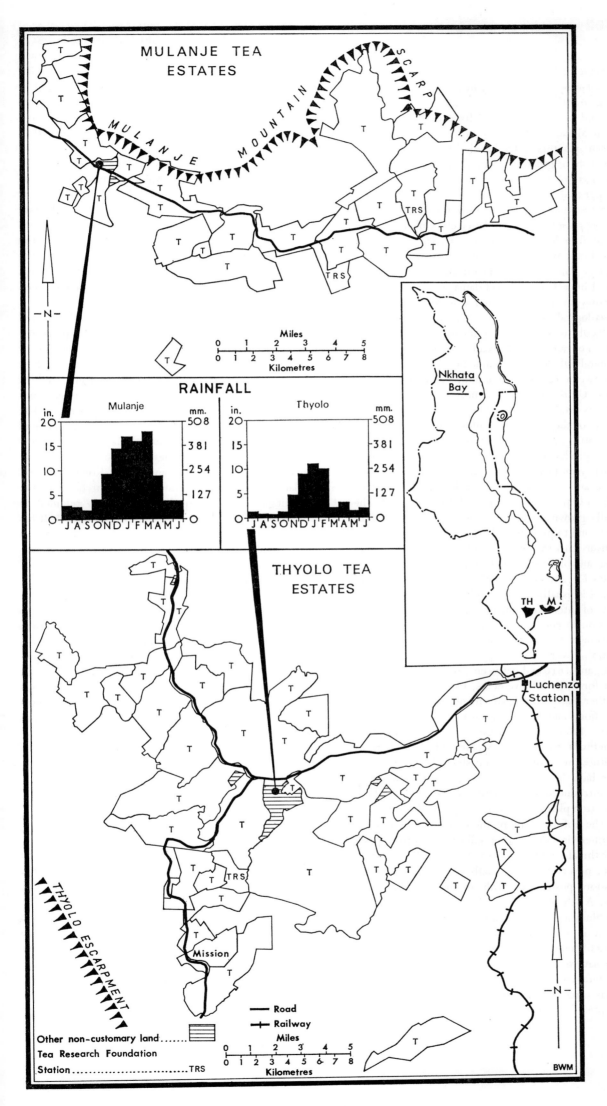

MULANJE TEA ESTATES

MULANJE MOUNTAIN SCARP

Miles
0 1 2 3 4 5
0 1 2 3 4 5 6 7 8
Kilometres

-N-

RAINFALL

Mulanje

in.   mm.
20   508
15   381
10   254
5   127
0   J A S O N D J F M A M J   0

Thyolo

in.   mm.
20   508
15   381
10   254
5   127
0   J A S O N D J F M A M J   0

Nkhata Bay

TH M

THYOLO TEA ESTATES

Luchenza Station

THYOLO ESCARPMENT

Mission

-N-

Other non-customary land........

Tea Research Foundation

Station.................................TRS

Road
Railway

Miles
0 1 2 3 4 5
0 1 2 3 4 5 6 7 8
Kilometres

BWM

36 COTTON

Cotton has been cultivated in Malawi for several decades. One variety, *tonje kaja* was probably introduced to Africa by Arab traders. Another variety, *tonje manga* is native to Brazil and found its way to Malawi from early Portuguese settlements in Moçambique. Later in the nineteenth century European planters introduced 'American Upland' varieties which have greater commercial usefulness. Since 1902 Malawi has grown these new varieties and now *tonje kaja* has disappeared and *tonje manga* is very rarely found. The principal commercial variety now grown almost exclusively is *Gossypium hirsutum*, an American Upland variety. The variety bred in Malawi is 'Alba 637', which has been well received in the world market. Its lint is slightly longer than the average American Upland varieties and is bred to resist bacterial infection and jassid damage.

Cotton grows satisfactorily under a wide range of climatic and ecological conditions in Malawi and the exact limits are difficult to define. Among the inter-related factors are distribution of rainfall, soil texture, drainage, depth and fertility. Generally the crop is confined to areas receiving an average of between 508 and 1016 mm. (20 and 40 in.) of rainfall a year. Until about 1965 almost 80% of the country's cotton was produced in the lower Shire valley area in the south, part of the great Rift Valley which in Malawi is only 60 to 90 m. (200 to 300 ft) above sea level. In 1968 only 60% was produced from this area, more cotton being produced each year in the upland areas between 457 and 762 m. (1500 and 2500 ft) above sea level. This is attributed largely to improved techniques of insect control. The crop is usually grown on raised ridges, primarily to conserve moisture and to prevent soil erosion. Every endeavour is made to ensure that the crop is planted as early as possible after the first suitable rains which usually fall in mid-November or early December. Harvesting of the crop begins in early April and is usually completed by the middle of July.

The results of intensive campaigns for increased agricultural production in general are illustrated by the achievement of an average annual rate of increase of cotton production of about 7% over a 15-year period in spite of declines between 1953 and 1956 and between 1966 and 1968. Much of the credit for these achievements, based largely on area expansion rather than yield improvement, can be ascribed to nation-wide efforts and the extension work of the Ministry of Agriculture. Efforts are now being made to introduce improved methods to increase yields and destroy pests which constitute the most important single limiting factor. Good results have been obtained by the enforcement of regulations, introduced in the late 1950's, under which remnants of cotton plants must be destroyed by burning by a given date. The enforcement of these regulations has reduced the otherwise devastating effects of cotton pests which earlier threatened the very existence of the industry. This measure, nevertheless, still falls short of what is required and more positive controls are necessary to raise cotton yields. A scheme for supplying subsidized knapsack spraying machines and insecticides to smallholder farmers has now been in operation since 1954. Because of the different types of pests, both the timing of the spray application and the nature of the insecticide used is critical. To ensure complete coverage over all parts of the plant, a knapsack spray machine with a specially designed tail boom has been adopted for general use in Malawi.

The average yield of slightly more than 392 kg. of seed cotton per ha. (350 lb. per acre), although not the lowest in Africa, leaves considerable room for improvement. Since 1964, following trials on research stations and an increasing number of smallholders using improved techniques, it is now accepted that progressive farmers who regularly spray their cotton crop can achieve yields of 1009 kg. per ha. (900 lb. per acre), rising with experience to more than 1121 kg. per ha. (1000 lb. per acre).

The most serious cotton pests in Malawi are the boll-worms, leaf-eaters and jassids. Aphids, mites and stainers also cause a great deal of damage. Several leaf-eating insects cause early and often serious harm. Heavy attacks of jassid (*Empoasca fascialis*) often occur early in the season. Cotton-stainers (*Dysdercus spp.*) cause widespread damage to the cotton crop, transmitting a fungus disease which stains the lint yellow and weakens the fibre. Damage by cotton-stainers is the most common cause of the downgrading of seed cotton.

The price paid to the farmer for cotton is greatly affected by a proportion of lower grade cottons. Insect pests and plant diseases account for as much as 20% of the lower grades. As a result of an increase in insect pests, the average price to the grower for the period 1964 to 1966 declined from about 12·8 to 12·1 pence per kg. (5·8 to 5·5 pence per lb.). Cotton is sold both on local and export markets. The traditional market for cotton was Rhodesia, but increased production in that country has caused Malawi to seek new markets. In 1966 small quantities of grade A cotton were sold in France, Germany, Holland, Hong Kong, Italy and Switzerland, but the bulk of the crop was purchased by the United Kingdom. Lower quality cotton was retained to meet the demands of the new textile mill in Malawi. It has been estimated that internal consumption will reach a maximum of about 10 000 bales of lint or 6000 short tons of seed cotton per annum. The demand from the United Kingdom is also expected to increase, provided high classification standards are maintained.

The market value of seed cotton over the period 1957 to 1965 ranged from K122·6 to K145·4 per ton, but in 1970 considerable additional gains were made not only in production but also in value of the crop following the implementation of the Chikwawa Cotton Development Project. In 1966 production fell to 14 270 short tons, giving a market value of seed cotton of K1·2 million; in 1970 production stood at the record level of 23 500 short tons valued at K2·3 million.

The annual production of seed cotton since 1955 has been as follows:

Year	Production short tons	Year	Production short tons
1955	9580	1963	11 000
1956	3430	1964	14 730
1957	4630	1965	22 680
1958	6120	1966	14 270
1959	10 760	1967	13 070
1960	13 570	1968	12 770
1961	12 960	1969	19 911
1962	19 030	1970	23 500

J HALL

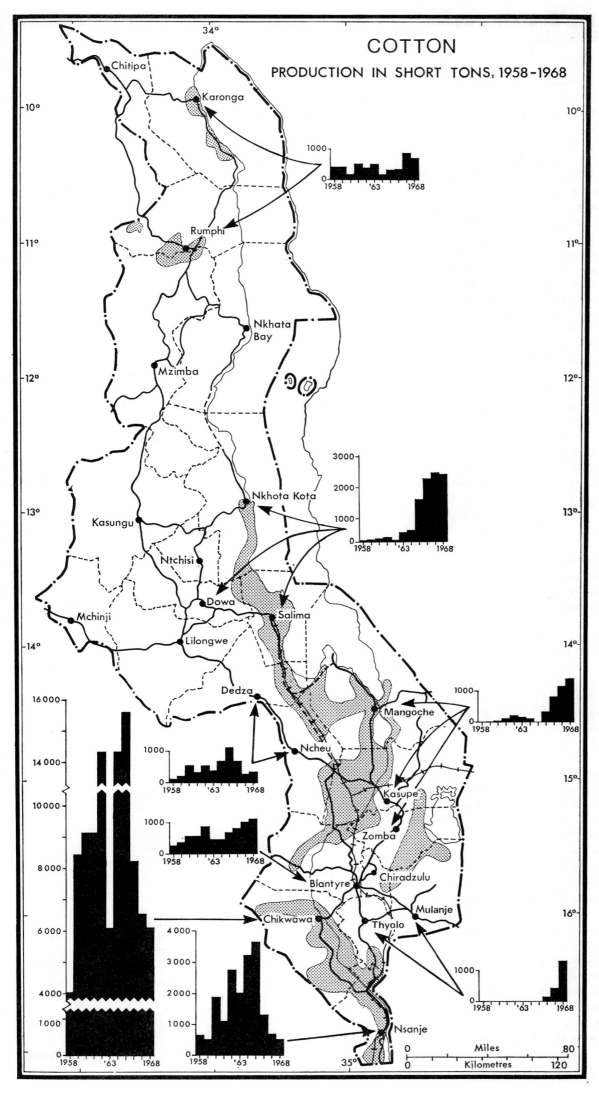

COTTON

PRODUCTION IN SHORT TONS, 1958-1968

37 FARMERS' MARKETING BOARD CENTRES, 1970

In 1968 the Farmers' Marketing Board was operating 52 permanent markets and over 700 temporary buying stations for the purchase of farm products. The products were stored in depots maintained throughout the country with space for more than 120 000 tons of agricultural produce. The Board was also operating a ginnery at Chikwawa, a groundnut grading factory at Limbe, a Turkish tobacco-handling depot at Mbawa as well as three large tobacco-grading factories at Lilongwe, Limbe and Sedi. In addition the Board owns a farm at Toleza near Balaka which produces improved seeds of the most suitable varieties for distribution to farmers in different parts of the country.

The present Board is the successor of the three former Tobacco, Cotton and Produce Marketing Boards which amalgamated in March 1956 to form the Agricultural Production and Marketing Board that has since been renamed the Farmers' Marketing Board.

The Farmers' Marketing Board is a statutory body charged with the following responsibilities:

1 The marketing, processing or manufacturing and disposal of agricultural produce grown on land other than that which is privately owned.
2 The provision and maintenance of reserves of foodstuffs on behalf of government.
3 The maintaining of adequate price stabilization funds with the twofold purpose of first protecting the farmer from violent price fluctuations of world commodity markets and, second, by means of continued price stability increasing the agricultural output of the country.
4 The provision at cost, or below cost prices, of such aids as are necessary for the increased production of economic crops.
5 The provision of bursaries for the study of agriculture or other matters connected with the Board's responsibilities.

Tobacco was the first cash crop to be widely grown by Africans on Trust Land. By law tobacco had to be sold over a registered auction floor. With the object of supervising and assisting African growers, the Native Tobacco Board was set up in 1926. This Board did not, at first, market the tobacco but supervised the purchase of it by licensed buyers and provided advice on growing, curing and setting up marketing stations. Later the Board was empowered by Government to buy all tobacco produced on Trust Land and the crop from African growers was then sold by the Board over the licensed auction floors in Limbe. The Board employed both African and European staff who assisted the Department of Agriculture in advisory work among tobacco growers for about 9 months of the year, the other 3 months being taken up with marketing duties.

From the beginning the Tobacco Board, and the Cotton and the Produce Marketing Boards which were set up later, had two objects in view: first to encourage the production of better crops and to introduce marketing schemes with strict grading of products purchased to ensure uniform standards of goods offered for sale and, secondly, to organize an export market for graded primary products which would bring in revenue for the country.

In order to stimulate the production of better crops the Boards undertook the further role of selling to farmers at cost or, for some items at very much below cost, such aids as fertilizer, pesticides, spraying equipment, farm carts and tools.

The establishment by the Boards of rural markets led to the extension of the district road system and to the opening of access roads in remoter areas.

Up to and including 1956 it was the policy of the Board or Boards to pay the producer prices which were considered to give him a reasonable return and no more.

Among the reasons for this policy were that the assistance given by the Boards to African growers was expensive and also that the Boards carried the risk of loss from a fall in prices or failure to sell on the export market.

Moreover, until 1956 the Boards paid £48 000 per annum into government revenue in return for services rendered by the Department of Agriculture and, between 1948 and 1958, they contributed £2 104 000 to the African Development and Welfare Fund. The contribution to this fund was mainly used for agricultural development, road-building and maintenance, and the improvement of water supplies.

The policy followed until 1956 was undoubtedly to the advantage of the national agricultural economy as a whole. However, the low prices paid for produce and the fact that the prices paid were the same in all parts of the country discriminated against the better situated and progressive farmers. It probably did much to hinder the settlement of master farmers on freehold land because it was seen that most of the profits from good farming were taken by the Boards. Moreover, the monopoly exercised by the Boards in buying produce prevented the emergence of an entrepreneur class.

In 1957 the Board changed its price policy and thereafter, except in the case of tobacco, it published guaranteed minimum prices before each planting season. In the case of tobacco, prices for each of the grades were announced at the beginning of the picking season. The prices offered were related as closely as possible to world market trends. This guarantee of prices was made possible by virtue of the substantial reserves accumulated over a number of years.

The Farmers' Marketing Board has always had a monopoly of trade in the principal agricultural products. Despite any disadvantages which may have arisen from this, the Board has always been a valuable means of introducing improved agricultural techniques to the remotest areas and an organization that has done much to promote production of more and better crops; this in addition to organizing a valuable export trade in agricultural products.

The value to growers of produce purchased by the Farmers' Marketing Board in the years 1964 to 1970 is as follows:

PURCHASES BY THE FARMERS' MARKETING BOARD

	VALUE £'000					
COMMODITY	1964	1965	1966	1967	1968	1969	1970
Tobacco	768	1925	1337	1601	573	470	1463
Cotton	763	1115	620	536	560	899	1029
Maize	277	226	866	1048	1268	790	1208
Wheat	13	14	17	21	18	18	N.A.
Groundnuts	768	1050	2323	2361	1057	1783	1408
Paddy rice	64	104	84	97	43	262	3024
Coffee	20	19	30	34	23	23	30
Pulses	417	691	530	478	120	523	N.A.
	3090	5144	5807	6176	3662	4768	8162

Note The key to the numbers by the bar chart on the right of the map opposite is to be found on pp. 82 and 84.

SWANZIE AGNEW

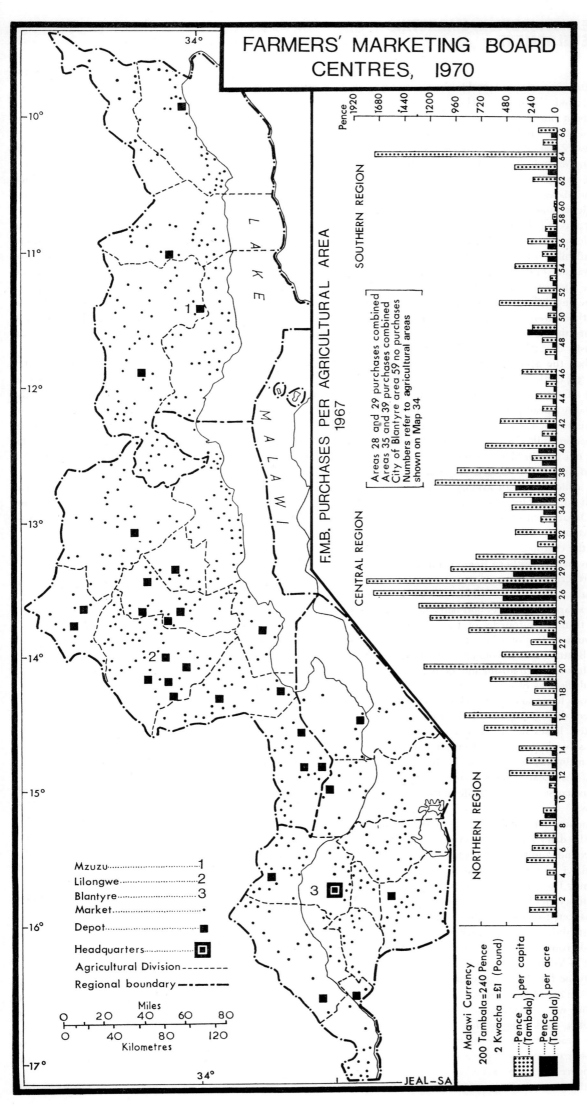

FARMERS' MARKETING BOARD
CENTRES, 1970

F.M.B. PURCHASES PER AGRICULTURAL AREA
1967

SOUTHERN REGION

CENTRAL REGION

NORTHERN REGION

Areas 28 and 29 purchases combined
Areas 35 and 39 purchases combined
City of Blantyre area 59 no purchases
Numbers refer to agricultural areas
shown on Map 34

Mzuzu.................1
Lilongwe.............2
Blantyre.............3
Market...............·
Depot................■
Headquarters........▣
Agricultural Division-------
Regional boundary—··—··—

Miles
0   20
40   60
0   40   80
Kilometres   120

Malawi Currency
200 Tambala=240 Pence
2 Kwacha =£1 (Pound)

Pence
(Tambala) } per capita
Pence
(Tambala) } per acre

JEAL-SA

L A K E   M A L A W I

34°

34°

89

38 CATTLE DISTRIBUTION, MARKETING AND DEVELOPMENT

Almost half Malawi's cattle are found in the Central Region, particularly around Lilongwe. The Northern Region accounts for about one-third of the cattle raised, and the more densely settled Southern Region for less than one-fifth. The Malawi Zebu (*Bos indicus*) is the dominant type of cattle found in Malawi. The Zebu type cattle are well adapted to the conditions existing in Malawi. The main attributes of the Malawi Zebu are its tolerance of humidity, drought and ticks, and its ability to utilize poor quality roughage and convert it into beef.

The distribution of cattle in Malawi is governed mainly by (a) the availability of permanent sources of food and water, (b) prevalence of diseases, especially east coast fever, (c) competitive alternatives and (d) the social values placed upon cattle-keeping. The 1969 Annual Livestock Census reported that there were approximately 494 959 cattle in Malawi, or more than 4·6 head per sq. km. (12 per square mile). The density of cattle in Malawi is approximately one-third higher than the average for the continent of Africa which is about 3·5 cattle per sq. km. (9 per sq. mile). The average density of cattle in the Northern and Central Regions is 5·79 and 6·2 head per sq. km. (15 and 16·6 per sq. mile) respectively which is more than double the 2·47 per sq. km. (6·4 per sq. mile) in the Southern Region.

The number of cattle in Malawi has been increasing at the rate of three to four per cent each year during the period 1963 to 1969 which gives an average annual increase of about 16 500 head. This increase is partly a result of the efforts of the Department of Veterinary Services in disease control and extension work. The greatest increases have taken place in the customary land areas near Blantyre, Mulanje and Nsanje in the Southern Region and in the Mzimba area in the Northern Region.

Only two-and-a-half per cent of Malawi's cattle are kept on estates. These are mostly beef and dairy herds of exotic breeds. More than three-fourths of the estate cattle are found in the Southern Region where there are large concentrations in the Blantyre and Thyolo areas and lesser concentrations near Mulanje, Chiradzulu and Zomba.

The principal diseases of cattle in Malawi are east coast fever, red water fever and gall sickness (anaplasmosis). Tick-transmitted diseases, particularly east coast fever, cause the greatest losses despite long-continued efforts to counteract ticks by dipping. The Department of Veterinary Services maintains 151 dip tanks for tick control throughout the main cattle-raising areas of the country; nevertheless, east coast fever is still rife in the Northern and Central Regions.

The main products derived from cattle in Malawi are beef and hides, for the dairy industry is very small. Cattle markets, holding grounds and trade routes have been established throughout Malawi under the Cattle Marketing Development Programme. The objectives of this programme are to increase the production of beef for Malawi's rapidly expanding domestic market, to eliminate the need for imports and ultimately to establish an export market. The markets and pens on the trade routes are constructed and maintained by the Department of Veterinary Services and may be used free of charge by anyone for the purpose of sale or purchase of cattle. Twenty-five cattle markets were operating in Malawi in 1969 and more were planned.

Organized cattle-marketing, which began in 1960, has brought about a steady increase in the local supply of cattle. While the number of cattle slaughtered in 1959 amounted to 26 240 the figure for 1967 exceeded 50 000. Stall feeding schemes in the Southern Region and subsidies for super,

choice and prime grades of beef have been introduced to encourage and promote the production of top grade cattle in Malawi.

The Cold Storage Company in agreement with the government pays a minimum price for all slaughter cattle offered for sale. A seasonal guaranteed price system enables cattle owners to obtain a fair price for their stock throughout the year.

The Department of Veterinary Services provides facilities at its dip tanks for preparing dried hides and also acts as a buying agent for the Cold Storage Company which arranges export sales. Exported hides number more than 30 000 a year and their value exceeds £20 000.

The dairy industry, which is still very small, is centred in the urban areas of Blantyre and Zomba in the Southern Region and Lilongwe in the Central Region. About two-thirds of the milk sold in the Southern Region is produced on specialized dairy farms while the additional milk requirements are obtained from villagers who keep cows. In several of the urban areas in the Northern Region, where the milk supply comes from local villages, the demand is greater than can be met by local production.

Development planners hope to expand the dairy industry and to improve the quality of milk production in Malawi. A milk pasteurization plant is being constructed by the Malawi Government to serve the Blantyre area. This plant will be particularly useful to the many small producers of low quality milk who are unable to bear the cost of capital improvements necessary for the production of clean, high quality milk.

However, many problems remain to be overcome such as the poor milk yields of the common all-purpose Zebu, inadequate water supply for cleansing purposes and distances from markets.

TABLE 1
GROWTH OF THE NATIONAL HERDS 1963–69

Year	Total cattle
1963	396 145
1964	411 419
1965	432 293
1966	450 128
1967	464 006
1969	494 959

TABLE 2
COMPOSITION OF MALAWI CATTLE 1967

	Numbers	Per cent of total
Cows and heifers	264 947	57·1
Calves	117 394	25·3
Oxen	49 649	10·7
Bulls	32 016	6·9
Total	464 006	100·0

TABLE 3
NATIONAL HERD 1969

Province	Estates	Customary Land	Total
Northern Region	976	156 452	157 428
Central Region	2091	237 675	239 766
Southern Region	10 552	87 213	97 765
Malawi	13 619	481 340	494 959

Source: Veterinary Department: Ministry of Natural Resources, Zomba.

R SCHMIDT

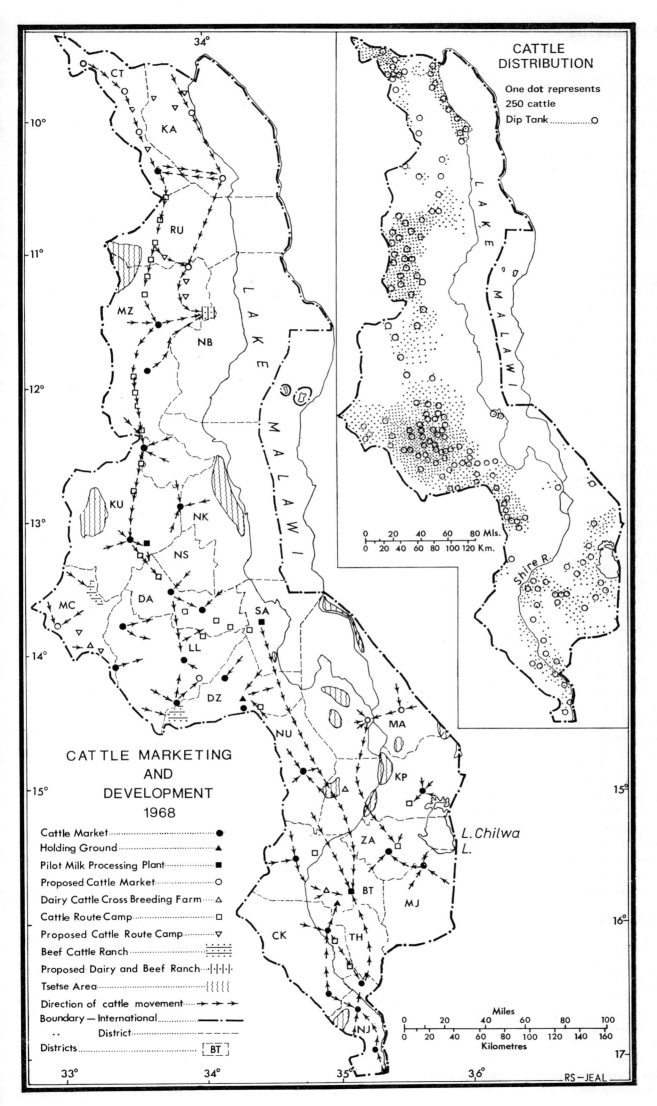

CATTLE DISTRIBUTION

One dot represents
250 cattle
Dip Tank .... O

LAKE MALAWI

0 20 40 60 80 Mls.
0 20 40 60 80 100 120 Km.

Shire R.

CATTLE MARKETING
AND
DEVELOPMENT
1968

Cattle Market·················· ●
Holding Ground·················· ▲
Pilot Milk Processing Plant············· ■
Proposed Cattle Market········· ○
Dairy Cattle Cross Breeding Farm····· △
Cattle Route Camp················ □
Proposed Cattle Route Camp····· ▽
Beef Cattle Ranch················
Proposed Dairy and Beef Ranch···|·|·|·|·|·
Tsetse Area···················
Direction of cattle movement··· → → →
Boundary — International············ ·—·—·—·
        ·· District················· ·—·—·—·
Districts························· BT

L. Chilwa
L.

Miles
0   20   40   60   80   100
0 20 40 60 80 100 120 140 160
Kilometres

RS—JEAL

39 FORESTRY

Forestry activities and potential

Approximately 23% of Malawi's total land area of 95 300 sq. km. (36 800 sq. miles) is under forest. Protected forests amount to 15 993 sq. km. (6175 sq. miles) or 17% of the land area of which some 8000 sq. km. (3000 sq. miles) are state forest reserves. The remaining protected forests include game reserves, local authority forests, village forests and private forests.

A large proportion of the government forest estate is managed with conservation and protection of water supplies as the primary aims. 402 sq. km. (159 sq. miles) of the state forests are productive, including 34 000 ha. (83 000 acres) of plantations in 1969, principally softwood, expanding at a rate of some 1200 ha. (3000 acres) per annum.

In accordance with the government's policy to bring to an end imports of construction timber, there is a timber plantation development project with a target of 29 000 ha. (72 000 acres) by 1990 and an annual planting programme of 800 ha. (2000 acres), mainly softwood. 12 000 ha. (30 000 acres) have been established between 1950 and 1969 under this project, complementary to which is the country's sawmilling development programme. Four state sawmills have been established and are being expanded to convert increasing quantities of softwood logs. The current intake of softwood logs is 22 700 cu. m. (800 000 cu. ft) a year with a sawn timber output of 8500 cu. m. (300 000 cu. ft) per annum. In addition some 14 000 to 28 000 cu. m. (50 000 to 100 000 cu. ft) of indigenous hardwood logs are sawn annually in state sawmills. Total sales from state sawmills amounted to £210 000 in 1968 and are expected to exceed £1 000 000 by 1980, excluding the value of the outturn from the country's future pulp and paper industry. In private sawmills 17 000 to 20 000 cu. m. (600 000 to 700 000 cu. ft) of eucalyptus logs are sawn annually for the tobacco industry.

The other major sphere of development is the Vipya pulpwood project. Planting for pulpwood production began in 1964 after favourable recommendations by consultants. Feasibility surveys were undertaken and by 1969 some 21 500 ha. (53 000 acres) had been established of which 20 600 ha. (51 000 acres) were softwoods, principally pine. Present plans are for a total of 28 000 ha. (69 000 acres) by 1980. It is planned to produce bleached kraft linerboard, fluting and sack paper and to have a mill potential output of 150 tons a day of air-dry kraft pulp in 1977, increasing to 300 tons a day by 1980.

Malawi's forest policy is also to encourage multiple land use. In addition to the protection of water catchments and the supply of forest products, amenities for tourists are being improved. The possibility of subsidiary crops and cattle-ranching in forest reserves is being investigated.

Current expenditure by the Department of Forestry and Game on forest activities, both protection and development, is £460 000 per annum.

Kinds of forests

Malawi is a relatively densely populated country and the natural forest has been modified, to a greater or lesser extent, by man's activity. The indigenous forests can be broadly described as, first, open or closed woodland in which *Brachystegia* species predominate, second, closed evergreen montane forest, and third, streambank forest of mixed species. The natural forest or woodland contains only a very low density of valuable timber trees and fairly extensive areas are, for this reason and also due to inaccessibility, difficult to exploit economically. The natural forest is therefore for the most part of economic importance mainly for its protective value and for the local domestic economy in the supply of traditional building poles and firewood. Only very limited supplies of sawn timber come from the indigenous forests.

The exotic timber plantations are predominantly pines, the major species being *Pinus patula*. Of hardwoods planted the major species are *Gmelina arborea* and *Eucalyptus saligna*. The plantations established for the Vipya pulpwood scheme are almost entirely of *Pinus patula*, though recently the need for a hardwood species to improve pulp quality has led to the establishment of *Eucalyptus saligna*. Current plans aim at 22 000 ha. (54 000 acres) of pines including *Pinus taeda* and 6000 ha. (15 000 acres) of eucalypts by 1976.

The quantities in cubic feet of sawn timber produced in 1968 are as follows:

Hardwoods	
Pterocarpus angolensis	17 800
Afzelia quanzensis	17 800
Entandophragma sp.	8 900
*Eucalyptus saligna	332 000
	376 500
Softwoods	
predominantly *Pinus patula*	
construction grade	78 065
other grades	125 088
	203 153

* Produced by a private company.

In addition 2800 cu. m. (99 100 cu. ft) of pressure-impregnated eucalyptus transmission and telephone poles were produced in 1968. The above figures do not include the production of several minor private sawmills or the production of sawn timber from local pit sawyers who supply the local furniture trade.

Wood-based industries

The main forest industry is sawmilling to produce construction grade timber, but there are secondary woodworking industries, principally box-making and furniture manufacture, based respectively on lower grades of softwood and on high quality hardwoods.

The state owned pressure-impregnation plant at Blantyre, with a potential capacity of 4700 cu. m. (200 000 cu. ft) a year, supplies all the internal requirements of transmission and telephone poles as well as an important export market.

During 1968 the local sawmilling industry provided 66% of the country's requirements of sawn timber of all grades of softwood and hardwood. At present demand is increasing at a higher rate than production, but the gap should begin to close in the mid-1970s.

In the last three years the total production of sawn timber, including that from private mills, has increased from nearly 14 000 cu. m. (500 000 cu. ft.) to almost 17 000 cu. m. (600 000 cu. ft) per annum, and that of creosoted poles from 2220 to 2800 cu. m. (76 000 to 99 000 cu. ft).

All softwood sawn timber supplied from state-owned sawmills is carefully graded, with a rigid specification laid down for all timber sold as construction grade.

Future developments in wood-based industries which are being planned include a *tanalith* impregnation plant integrated with a state sawmill to produce *tanalized* softwood timber. A commercial plywood factory to utilise locally grown eucalyptus logs to produce plywood for tea chests is also under consideration. Other projects under investigation are to produce wood wool slabs, parquet flooring and glue-laminated beams.

A key to forestry resources is given on p. 141.

DIRECTOR OF FORESTRY AND GAME

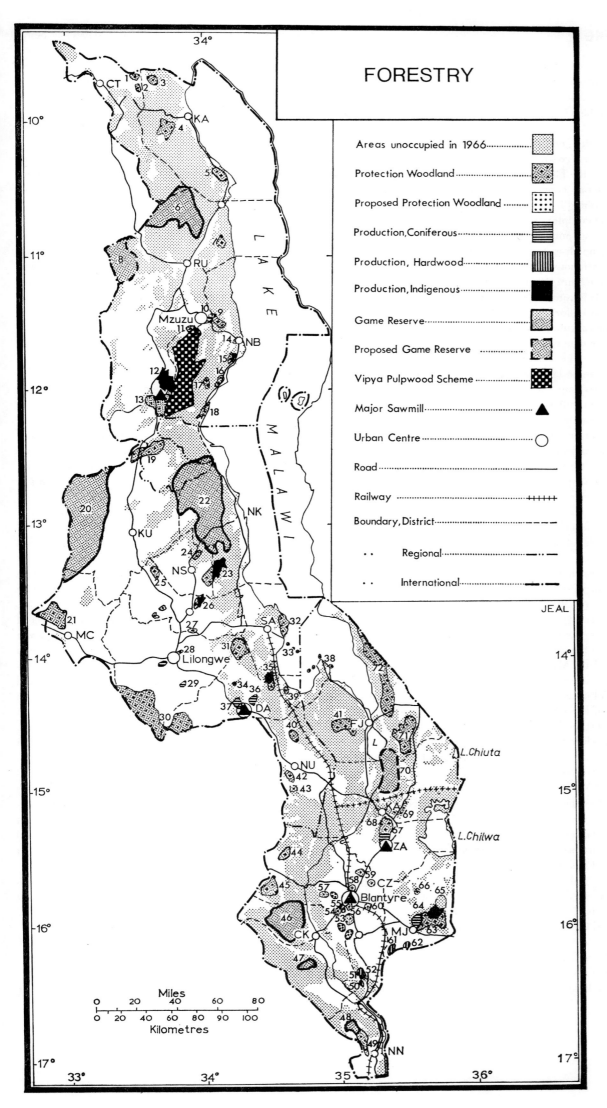

FORESTRY

Areas unoccupied in 1966 ....

Protection Woodland ....

Proposed Protection Woodland ....

Production, Coniferous ....

Production, Hardwood ....

Production, Indigenous ....

Game Reserve ....

Proposed Game Reserve ....

Vipya Pulpwood Scheme ....

Major Sawmill .... ▲

Urban Centre .... ○

Road ....

Railway .... ++++

Boundary, District ....

·· Regional ....

·· International ....

JEAL

40 FISHING

Approximately one-fifth of the surface of Malawi consists of lakes of which Lake Malawi, with an area of 29 060 sq. km. (11 645 sq. miles) is the largest and is shared with Moçambique.

The Rift Valley, containing Lake Malawi, Lake Malombe (388 sq. km. or 150 sq. miles) and the Shire River with its expansion into the Elephant Marsh (518 sq. km. or 200 sq. miles), forms one connected complex on which local and commercial fishing is based.

The second complex, separated from the main rift by the Shire Highlands, comprises those waters lying in or draining a subsidiary, north-east trending trough. The waters here are not a continuous system but drain south to the Ruo which joins the Shire River at Chiromo and also northwards by the Lujenda River to the Indian Ocean. Between the two rivers lies the endorheic basin of Lake Chilwa which, in recent geological time, has been separated from Lake Chiuta and its further extension, Lake Amaramba which is wholly in Moçambique, by a 15-metre (50-foot) sand bar. Sedimentation in these lakes is active and of the 2590 sq. km. (1000 sq. miles) superficial area of Lake Chilwa basin, 699 sq. km. (270 sq. miles) consist of open water and associated lagoons and swamps.

Lake Chilwa, in its present penultimate stage of sedimentation, is subject to fluctuations in water level dependent upon the ratio between the rates of evapo-transpiration and river discharge. In 1967–8 the lake dried up and the catch of fish dwindled from a peak production of 9800 short tons in 1965 to an estimated 100 tons in 1968 but, with the rise in water level that followed adequate rains in subsequent years, the fishing in the lake had completely recovered by 1970.

Not only are there fluctuations in the amount of fishing undertaken depending on the level of water in the basin lakes but there is also a seasonal rhythm in all fishing areas imposed by the migration of fish during the breeding season to sandy beaches and into the bordering marshes and river inlets, or into the deeper water of Lake Malawi.

Generally Lake Malawi shelves rapidly to deep water and consequently fishing, by the methods at present in use, is restricted to limited areas of the lake which are a very small proportion of the whole. The main fishing-grounds are the south-west and south-east arms of the shallow southern end of the lake, while to the north the headlands and bays and the rocky shelves around the islands are good fishing areas.

Two hundred and twenty-five species of fish have been found in Lake Malawi and twelve species in Lake Chilwa. Of these only a few species are of economic value. For instance, during the past few years, only nine species have appeared on the Zomba market. Those of the genus *Tilapia* are of the greatest importance and value. Fish of this genus are very good eating, fillet well and form the principal item of the major commercial fisheries. Shoal fish are also of importance because they can easily be dried in the sun and sold in the inland markets. In 1966 the sardine-like *Barbus paludinosis* formed one-third of the recorded catch from Lake Chilwa. The catfish, *Clarias mossambicus*, which is essentially a riverine and shallow water fish, grows to a size of up to a metre (40 inches) or more in length and its oily flesh makes preservation by smoking easy and it is taken far inland for sale.

At present commercial fishing in Lake Malawi is being undertaken by two licensed firms. Their fishing boats which operate mainly in the southern part of the lake are equipped for ring-netting and trawling and are attended by smaller boats which take the fish to shore bases where the catch is frozen and kept in cold storage until it is collected and transported by refrigerator lorries to the markets and distribution centres.

The chief distribution centre, where there are adequate cold storage facilities, is Limbe. Wholesale and retail dealers collect supplies of fresh fish from Limbe and distribute them to the main markets.

Fishing is also an important occupation of the lakeside and riverine peoples. There are estimated to be six thousand fishermen in the four main fishing areas of Lakes Malawi, Malombe and Chilwa and the Shire River. Three thousand of these combine fishing activities with working a land holding. The remaining three thousand are full-time fishermen most of whom use a variety of nylon nets and long lines set out from dug-out canoes. One hundred and seventy-four full-time fishermen are known to use engine-powered craft equipped with trawl-nets, ring-nets and large gill-nets.

Fish landed at the main beaches is usually sold fresh to traders but much of the catch brought to the smaller beaches or from the more remote fishing grounds is smoked or sun-dried before being sold.

Traders buy as much fish at the landing beaches or from the main wholesalers as their means of transport will allow. The small traders purchase a basket load to hawk by bicycle, but a few large scale entrepreneurs employ buying agents at the beaches and also wholesale and retail agents in the main markets and transport their fish by lorry or by train.

To aid the small traders the Nyasa Fish Transporters' Association was formed in 1965 with a holding of fifteen lorries to transport traders and their fish to the main marketing centres. The lorries run to a time-table and charge graduated fares according to the stages travelled and the size of the fishmongers' baskets.

Between 1964 and 1970 the annual value of exports of fresh and preserved fish increased from £9705 to £133 712 for the first nine months of 1970. The bulk of the increase in export value has been due to two new enterprises, the dispatch of live ornamental fish to Europe (£19 000: 1970) and the development in 1969 of trawling in the south-east arm for *chisawasawa*, a small bottom-living fish which had not previously been exploited by the traditional fishing methods. In 1969 the trawled catch was 1200 tons, and the extension of trawling to other areas is expected to double production.

While commercial fishing is likely to increase, the scattered distribution of the small-scale traditional enterprises make the co-ordination of the industry difficult. To test the possibilities of canning fish a small factory was opened at Senga Bay near Salima, in 1970, which will process local fish and meat produced from the agricultural development project in the immediate hinterland.

The annual consumption of fish per head of population is estimated at 4·8 kg. (10·5 lb.), and the demand at present prices is greater than the production.

Estimates of landings of fish are given on p. 142.

SWANZIE AGNEW

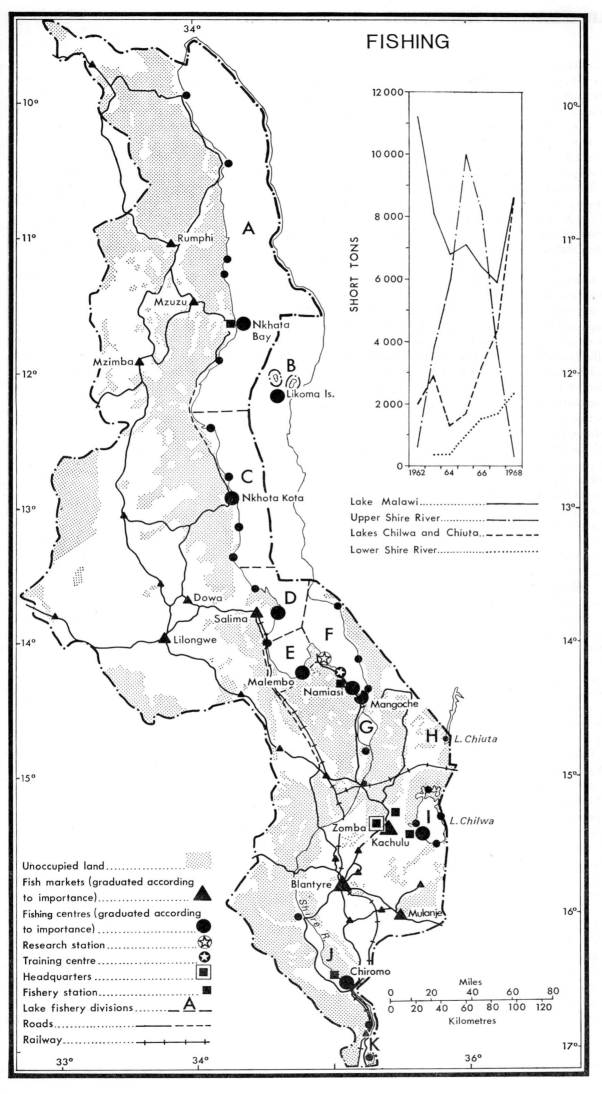

FISHING

SHORT TONS

12 000
10 000
8 000
6 000
4 000
2 000
0

1962   64   66   1968

Lake Malawi.....................
Upper Shire River.............
Lakes Chilwa and Chiuta...
Lower Shire River................

Rumphi

A

Mzuzu

Nkhata
Bay

Mzimba

B

Likoma Is.

C

Nkhota Kota

Dowa

D

Salima

Lilongwe

F

E

Malembo

Namiasi

Mangoche

G

H   L. Chiuta

I   L. Chilwa

Zomba

Kachulu

Blantyre

Mulanje

Shire R.

J

Chiromo

Miles
0   20   40   60   80
0 20 40 60 80 100 120
Kilometres

Unoccupied land.....................
Fish markets (graduated according
to importance).......................
Fishing centres (graduated according
to importance).......................
Research station.....................
Training centre......................
Headquarters........................
Fishery station......................
Lake fishery divisions........ A
Roads................................
Railway..............................

K

41 PUBLIC ELECTRICITY SUPPLY, 1969

In 1950 the total installed generating capacity in the country was only 755 kW, of which 530 kW was installed in a coal-fuelled plant in Blantyre and 255 kW in a hydro-electric plant (with an additional small diesel engine) in Zomba. Outside these two centres there were a few private generating plants, some hydro-electric, the remainder diesel-fuelled. In 1952 a 275 kW generating station, fuelled with diesel oil, was opened in Lilongwe. In 1954 a larger thermal generating plant was installed in Blantyre using coal imported from Wankie, Rhodesia and Moatize in Moçambique. In 1957 the Limbe section of the city was connected with the Blantyre generator, and 11 kW transmission lines reached the Thyolo tea estates. In 1950 the consumption of electricity was only 1 523 000 kWh, but by 1958 this had increased to 19 361 000 kWh, reflecting the growth of several large factories which consumed half the total produced, the connection of many commercial and domestic consumers within Blantyre, and consumption in the Thyolo tea estates. By 1958 installed capacity in the country totalled 8 526 kW, of which the Blantyre station accounted for 7000 kW, Zomba 850 kW and Lilongwe 530 kW. Other public generating plants at district centres, of which the Mzuzu plant was largest accounting for only 136 kW. By 1958 the first step in the construction of a national grid was achieved when a 33 kW transmission line was completed between Blantyre and Zomba, with the object of supplementing the Zomba supply, and making possible supply in 1960 to the Portland cement clinker plant at Changalume.

By June 1958 Blantyre's installed capacity was already inadequate. Previous estimates of future requirements had been too conservative, and consequently capacity of both generators and transmission lines were overtaken shortly after completion. Consideration was given to construction of a new thermal plant in Blantyre, but the existing site, between the railway and Mudi River, could not be expanded. Consideration was given to an alternative site at Luchenza, near to the then major potential consumers, the Mulanje and Thyolo tea estates, and to sources of imported coal. Rapid industrial and commercial expansion in Blantyre during the mid-1950s was made possible by abundant electricity supplies, but expansion in thermal capacity would result in still higher charges, as fuel would have to be imported. Therefore, serious consideration turned to the development of the hydro potential of the middle Shire. In the middle section of its course the Shire falls 308 m. (1260 ft) in 81 km. (50 miles) between Matope and Chikwawa, of which 153 m. (500 ft) of the fall consists of steep rapids and cascades at Matope (Kholombizo), Nachimbeya, Nkula, Tedzani, Mpatamanga and the Murchison (Hamilton) Falls, caused by minor faulting and dyke swarms. Regular water supplies from Lake Malawi, acting as a natural reservoir, removed the negative effect of the eight month dry season. Variations in lake level, and resultant flow in the Shire River (between 1915 and 1935 the Shire was completely dry) were controlled by the construction of a barrage at Liwonde in 1958.

In August 1963, after self-government was attained, responsibility for electricity supply was removed from Federal authority, and loans totalling £2 525 000 were obtained from the Commonwealth Development Corporation of which £1 850 000 was from the Malawi Government, Barclays Overseas Development Corporation, and the Standard Bank. Work began in the same year and in 1966

two 8MW generators were commissioned, followed by a third in 1967, when the Blantyre thermal station closed. These supplies enabled considerable industrial and commercial growth in Blantyre and the establishment of the Nchalo Sugar Estate and Refinery supplied via a 66 kV transmission line. Supply was extended to the Mulanje tea estates area, and the Moçambique town of Milanje. A new 600 kW diesel generating station was constructed in 1967 at Mangoche, from which a 24 km. (15 mile) transmission line along the lakeshore supplied two fish-processing plants and a hotel. In 1965 it had been estimated that demand until 1973 would be met by the total firm capacity (total installed interconnected capacity less the capacity of the largest individual machine) of stations in the Southern Region, but by 1967 it was realized that this date would have to be brought forward to 1971. By December 1968 the system demand in the Southern Region, 19·1 MW, already slightly exceeded safe hydro capacity. In 1968, 80·9 million units were sold in the Southern Region, 3·9 million units in Lilongwe, 0·4 million at Mzuzu and 0·2 million at Mangoche. Development was planned of the remaining potential in the middle Shire, specifically that at Tedzani Falls where potential reaches 120 MW and which would involve the lowest capital cost. In February 1970 an agreement was made with the International Development Association for a loan of £2 187 000 and in March 1970 a further agreement was made with the African Development Bank for a loan of £1 250 000. Internal Electricity Supply Company of Malawi expenditure will total £1 718 000 and the total project will cost £5 155 000. Work at Tedzani will be completed in February 1973 when two 8 MW sets will be operational. However, total demand by 1971 in Lilongwe is estimated to be still greater than firm capacity unless an additional 3 MW plant is added and that centre connected with the Southern Region by a 165 mile long 66 kV transmission line, the second major link in the developing national grid. These were commissioned in 1971. By 1973 total national expected firm capacity will be 46·8 MW, and expected peak demand 36·7 MW.

Although the total estimated potential within the middle Shire area is estimated to be over 600 MW, and this is likely to be developed with the continued growth of the country, particularly that in the southern and central regions, considerable care and careful planning is necessary in the use of this potential. The Shire River is used not only for electricity generation, but is also the main supplier of water to the Blantyre area, and in the future to Liwonde, for industrial and domestic purposes. It is the only reliable supplier of irrigation water for the lower Shire valley, in which very considerable agricultural development is under way, and it is likely also to provide irrigation water in the upper Shire, which is to be developed as a waterway between Lake Malawi and Liwonde. Thus the Shire River system has a delicate balance which might easily be prejudiced by further unco-ordinated development, and a condition of the International Development Association loan was a thorough study of resources of water from Lake Malawi and the Shire River. Major future users of electricity include bauxite mining and processing from Mulanje Mountain, and a pulpwood processing plant at Chinteche. The Cabora Bassa generators in Moçambique might be a supplementary future source of power. Elsewhere the greatest development of consumption is likely to be along the main transmission lines, and the extensions to connect with Liwonde, Mangoche and Salima, proposed for the mid 1970s.

MICHAEL STUBBS

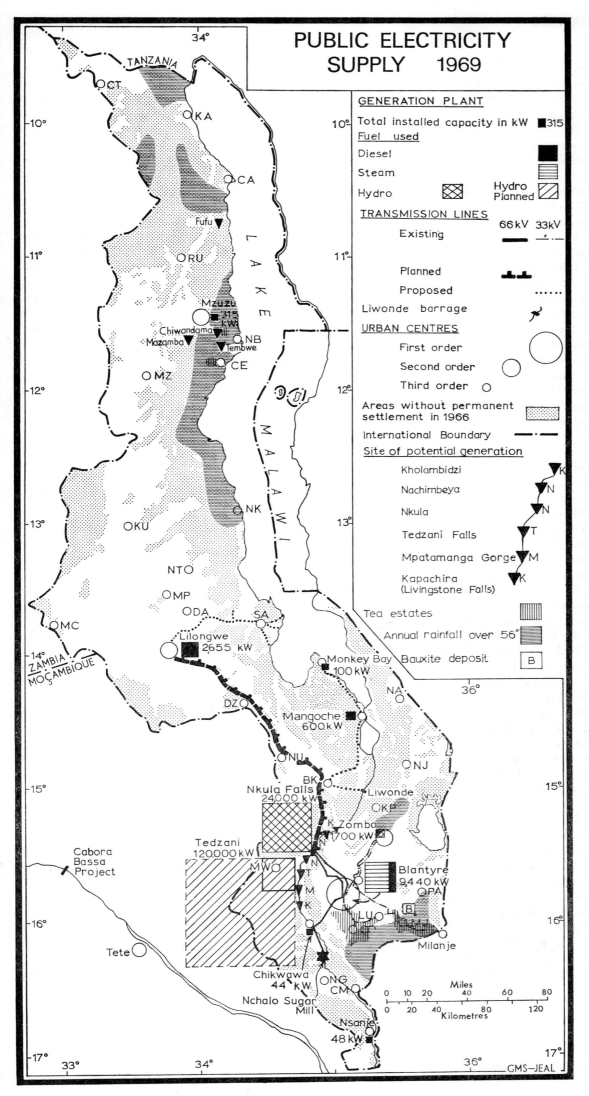

PUBLIC ELECTRICITY
SUPPLY   1969

GENERATION PLANT
Total installed capacity in kW   ■315
Fuel used
Diesel
Steam
Hydro   Hydro
                         Planned
TRANSMISSION LINES
                                66kV 33kV
Existing

Planned
Proposed
Liwonde barrage
URBAN CENTRES
First order
Second order
Third order
Areas without permanent
settlement in 1966
International Boundary
Site of potential generation
Kholambidzi   K
Nachimbeya   N
Nkula   N
Tedzani Falls   T
Mpatamanga Gorge   M
Kapachira   K
(Livingstone Falls)
Tea estates
Annual rainfall over 56″
Bauxite deposit   B

TANZANIA
CT
KA
CA
Fufu
RU
Mzuzu
315 kW
Chiwandama
Mazamba
Tembwe
NB
MZ
CE
LAKE MALAWI
NK
KU
NTO
MP
ODA   SA
MC
Lilongwe
2,655 kW
ZAMBIA
MOÇAMBIQUE
DZ
Mangoche
600kW
Monkey Bay
100 kW
NA
NU
NJ
BK
Nkula Falls
24,000 kW
Liwonde
KP
Tedzani
120 000 kW
K Zomba
1,700 kW
MWO
Blantyre
9,440 kW
PA
Cabora
Bassa
Project
LU   L
B
Tete
Milanje
Chikwawa
44 kW
NG
CM
Nchalo Sugar
Mill
Nsanje
48 kW

Miles
0 10 20   40   60   80
0   20 40   80   120
Kilometres

GMS—JEAL

42 TOURISM, 1970

The natural beauty of Malawi must have given satisfaction to many generations of the country's inhabitants before the arrival of those early Europeans who recorded the deep impression made upon them by the variety and splendour of the landscape. The sites of many European administrative centres were chosen partly in response to the beauty of the landscape and the freshness of a cool and well-watered mountain position, overlooking the often dry plateau surfaces, or the heat of the Rift Valley floor. Zomba, the administrative capital of the Protectorate, was established as an administrative centre as much for these reasons as for its advanced position on the route northwards to the lake. Dowa and Dedza were early administrative centres sited for similar reasons. During the colonial period, Dedza, with its views over the Rift Valley and the southern end of Lake Malawi, became a tourist resort for the European populations of the Central and Northern Regions. Along the lakeshore between Mangoche and Cape Maclear and in the Senga area, private cottages and hotels were constructed. Since Independence emphasis has been placed upon the development of transportation and hotel facilities to meet the growing demand by tourists attracted from southern and central Africa and beyond, and by the growing Malawian middle class, and by foreigners resident in the country.

All regions of the country have a magnificent variety of physical attractions, although those in the centre and south are at present rather more accessible to existing urban populations and visitors. In the northern and north central regions the concentration and variety of the scenery is possibly unsurpassed in Malawi. The Misuku Hills (A) which in the Mughese area (1), contain the *nkharikari* forests and blue monkeys, and the Mafinga Hills (B) (2) are the principal areas of attraction in Chitipa District. Karonga (3) on the lakeshore has historical connections with the slave trade wars, and with the 1914–18 East African campaigns. From the Luromo Peninsula south of Chilumba (C) views across the Lake to the Livingstonia Mountains of Tanzania, and southwards to the Livingstonia Escarpment of the north Vipya and the Nyika Plateau constitute among the most magnificent mountain and lake scenery in central Africa. The latter area also has the attractions of the Manchewe Falls (4) and the Livingstonia Mission (5). Although no hotels exist at present, the Luromo Peninsula site is probably most likely to be developed after the completion of the Lakeshore Highway.

In the north central region there are a number of most attractive areas and sites: the Kasitu Valley (D); the Nyika plateau mountain grasslands at 2134 m. (7000 ft), now the Malawi National Park (E), which offers large herds of zebra and eland, smaller groups of antelopes, and occasional predators, trout fishing, and magnificent views over the Rift Valley; the Vwaza marsh (F) and nearby Lake Kazuni (6); the faulted Ruarwe coastline (G); and the gentler hills and bays and sandy coves of the Nkhata Bay and Chinteche areas (H) which include the site of the Bandawe mission (10); the Likoma Islands (11) and the Anglican St Peter's Cathedral; the still isolated south Chinteche coastline (I), soon to be opened up by the Lakeshore Highway, the Vipya Plateau grasslands (J), afforestation (8) and reservoirs (9); and to the west Hora Mountain (7), associated with the

battles of the Angoni occupation. Existing roads from Lilongwe, Lundazi in Zambia, and soon that along the lakeshore, Mzuzu airport, and the M.V. *Ilala* services on Lake Malawi, offer adequate means of entry, but there are as yet no hotels in the region. Sites likely to be developed shortly are those at Mzuzu, the regional capital, at Nkhata Bay, and on the Nyika Plateau.

In the Central Region Lilongwe with 59 hotel beds affords a well-equipped base for the Nkhota Kota Game Reserve (K); Nkhota Kota itself (12) with its slave trade associations; with the rolling hills and scarps of the Ntchisi, Mwera Hill, and Dowa areas (L) and Ntchisi forest (13); the Chawira hot springs (14) and the Lilongwe River gorge (15); the Kasungu Game Reserve (M); Chitunda Hill cave rock paintings (16); Chonlongwe Falls in the Dzalanyama Forest Reserve; and for the Dedza Mountain (19) and the escarpment area (N) which extends to the Nkhoma Mission area (18) to the north, and southwards to Ncheu and the Kirk Range (O) from which, particularly at Lakeview (20) on the new Zomba-Lilongwe bitumen road, exist magnificent views over the Rift Valley and southern Lake Malawi. The lakeshore east of Salima has 107 beds in two hotels, and is likely to be developed as one of two principal areas of comprehensive tourist facilities beside the lakeshore, the other being that in the Cape Maclear-Monkey Bay area, with which it is soon to be connected by means of the A.I.D. financed Salima-Mua-Monkey Bay and Mua-Balaka roads.

In the south central region the greatest tourist development has occurred along the Mangoche coast particularly in the Cape Maclear and Monkey Bay areas (P), with 4 hotels and 166 beds; opposite Cape Maclear area are the ruins of Fort Maguire (21) while the Cape Maclear area includes the site of the first Livingstonia mission (22). Other places of interest include the Iron Age cemetery at Nkhudzi (23), Mangoche, the early base for anti-slave trade operations around the lake (24) and the hot sulphur springs at Liwonde (25). It is possible that the area north of Liwonde and east of Lake Malombe will be developed as a game reserve. Monkey Bay is the terminus for the weekly M.V. *Ilala II* voyages, on which cars may be transported to Chipoka and Nkhata Bay.

In the Southern Region, the Blantyre area, a watershed site ringed by high residuals between which are views over the Rift Valley and the Palombe plains, and the Thyolo tea-growing area which extends southwards of the city (R), are areas of easy access and great landscape attraction. From the Cholo escarpment, and in particular from Chizunga (29) and Manga (30) tea estates, are magnificent views over the Rift Valley. Blantyre has 342 hotel beds and Zomba 20.

The Zomba plateau with coniferous forests and trout lakes (Q), Mulanje Mountain (S) and the Mwalawolemba rock paintings at Mikolongwe (31), the cascades and pools of the Likabula River (32) and the Chinyama Falls and rapids on the Ruo Valley (33) offer alternative attractions. Adjacent to Blantyre in the Rift Valley the more accessible falls and rapids of the middle Shire include the Mfunda (Murchison) Falls (26) on the Matope Road, Mpatamanga Gorge (27) on the Blantyre-Mwanza Road and the Kapachira (Livingstone) Falls (28) north of Chikwawa. With the lower Shire section of the Rift Valley floor the Matenje (T), Lengwe (U), and Mwabvi Game Reserves (V) and the Malawi Hills (W) constitute the principal areas of attraction.

MICHAEL STUBBS

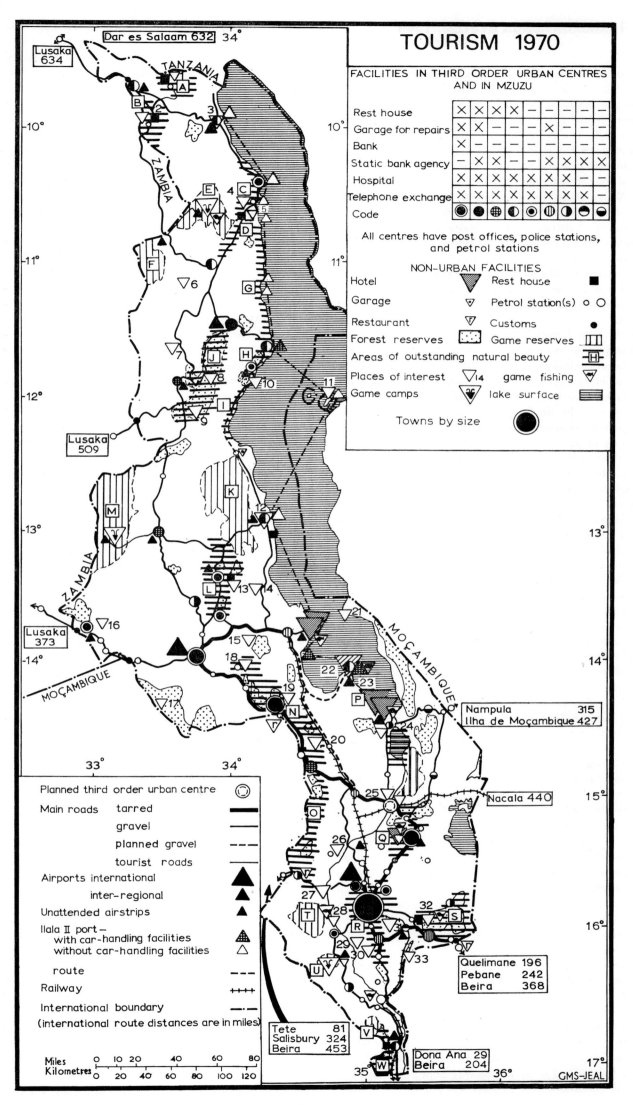

TOURISM 1970

43 TRANSPORTATION SYSTEM, 1969

The 901 km. (560 mile) longitudinal axis of Malawi is constituted by the floor of the East African Rift Valley. Two-thirds are occupied by Lake Malawi, and the remainder followed by the River Shire. Most parts of the country are within 80/85 km. (50/60 miles) of the Rift Valley floor, the farthest point being only 177 km. (110 miles). Types of non-mineral primary production are associated with the several longitudinal and altitudinal/ecological zones – the Rift Valley floor, the escarpment, the middle altitude plateaux surfaces and the higher massifs. The shape of the country, the existence of Lake Malawi, and the potential for inter-regional commodity exchanges suggest as the most efficient transportation system a topological tree in which the diameter would comprise a water transport system with lateral road and rail feeds. However, physical factors and colonial development resulted in a different and less efficient system.

In effect the longitudinal axis requires considerable capital intervention to overcome major problems posed by the physical environment. The Shire River falls at a very low gradient in its Upper and Lower courses, with consequent silting, particularly at its exit from Lake Malawi. This could be improved by dredging, as is now planned between Mangoche and Liwonde. In its middle course it falls 305 m. (1000 ft) in 74 km. (40 miles) providing great potential for hydro-electricity generation but presenting a formidable obstacle to transportation. This could be avoided by means of a rail connection, and currently plans are being prepared for a rail link between Mpimbe, south of Balaka, and Tete via Chikwawa, which might subsequently be further linked to the Chiromo-Beira line thereby completing the longitudinal diameter by the least cost route. Development of transportation on Lake Malawi has also foundered upon the fact that only at Nkhata Bay and Monkey Bay are there harbours on its coast suitable for the protection of any but the smallest vessels from dangerous south-easterly winds. This problem can be overcome only by the construction of artificial harbours, such as that planned for Chinteche with the development of the pulp and board factory there. The limited number of both ports and of low gradient routes from the lakeshore on to the plateau make necessary a complementary road or rail route laterally along the lakeshore, but this faces the difficulty of bridging numerous rivers liable to violent flooding during the wet season. Only since Independence has a lakeshore road been constructed, and this remains to be connected over the Dwangwa and Dwambazi Rivers. A similar problem occurs in the Shire valley where marshes force routes to follow the foot of the escarpments and suffer frequent wash-outs from the many streams issuing from it.

Although requiring considerable investment, these improvements might have been made if modern development had not been of the colonial type, with its emphasis upon the exploitation, under European direction and in restricted locations, of a small selection of natural resources for export. Although most pre-nineteenth century population concentrations in Malawi were in the Rift Valley floor and lakeshore regions, all except that of the Ankhonde in the far north had been dispersed by slave raids and Angoni incursions, and the much reduced population was concentrated in higher plateau and mountain areas. The major European penetration route followed the lower Shire as far as the middle Shire rapids whence it was deflected up the eastern escarpment on to the Shire Highlands, where Blantyre was founded and estate agriculture developed. The direct longitudinal route northwards from Chikwawa was ignored, and routes from Blantyre and Zomba redescended the eastern escarpment to the upper Shire. The early administrative and military network consisted of a longitudinal axis on the upper Shire and Lake Malawi, and lateral feeder tracks westwards on to the plateau. Subsequently, however, a road climbed via Ncheu, Fort Mlangeni and Dedza, to the principal concentration of potential migrant labour in the Angoni highlands. This became the principal national link subsequently with the development in the 1920s of Lilongwe as a tobacco-producing area and its growth to status as the secondary core region. Thus occurred a further distortion from the least cost longitudinal water route. However, the railway later constructed northwards from Blantyre did not attempt to climb to Lilongwe, but remained on the Rift floor and was planned to continue to Domira Bay, but stopped at Salima after a rise in the lake level flooded the former site. A result of this accident was the choice of a very unsatisfactory site on the railway at Chipoka as the principal transfer point between water and rail, while the lake service depot was transferred to Monkey Bay. This seriously prejudiced later growth of the principal transportation axis and the development of the Northern Region. Because of the contemporary high costs of constructing the rail bridge across the Zambezi, and the generally depressed world economy, no further capital was available to rectify the situation. It is now planned to concentrate all terminal and transfer facilities at Liwonde on the new Nacala rail link, after the dredging of the upper Shire to that port. An extension of the railway from Salima to Lilongwe is also under examination.

In the north central region the only area of pre-Independence development was adjacent to the port of Nkhata Bay. Because of the inefficiency of the water route, greater recourse was had to the north-south route on the western plateau surface, but this involved considerable deviations to avoid the dambo and marsh-filled river valleys, and to skirt the major barrier of the Nyika Plateau which added greatly to the circuity of the route and thus effectively isolated the Karonga and Chitipa areas. There was little commodity movement, migrant labour often walked, and administration was carried on through a chain of airstrips.

As long as the greater proportion of commodity flows are international movements with Europe and North America, distance from ocean ports represents the greatest problem to development. Since 1935 the country has had to bear the overwhelming costs of the expensive and unproductive rail link to Beira across the Zambezi, but recently increased congestion in Beira has forced the construction of an alternative rail link to the Vila Cabral-Nacala railway, marking in one sense a return to the pre-colonial west-east routes towards the Indian Ocean. This development, the construction of the lakeshore roads, Salima-Balaka and Mua-Monkey Bay, and the reconstruction of the Zomba-Lilongwe road, represent the major post-Independence developments in the transportation system. Others include replacing the Chikwawa ferry by a road bridge over the lower Shire and improvements to the Liwonde-Mangoche-Monkey Bay road.

Topologically the colonial transportation system had low connectivity, consisting largely of unconnected edges radiating from Blantyre and Lilongwe, including, from the latter, that leading to the north central region, in which Mzuzu had scarcely developed nodality, and the northern region. Post-Independence developments, particularly the lakeshore road, have added very considerably to the connectivity of the system. It is planned that the lakeshore road in the central and northern regions will constitute the major north-south axis between Karonga and Balaka, while the plateau route from Lilongwe to Mzimba will lose its relative importance to the former's lateral feeder routes.

MICHAEL STUBBS

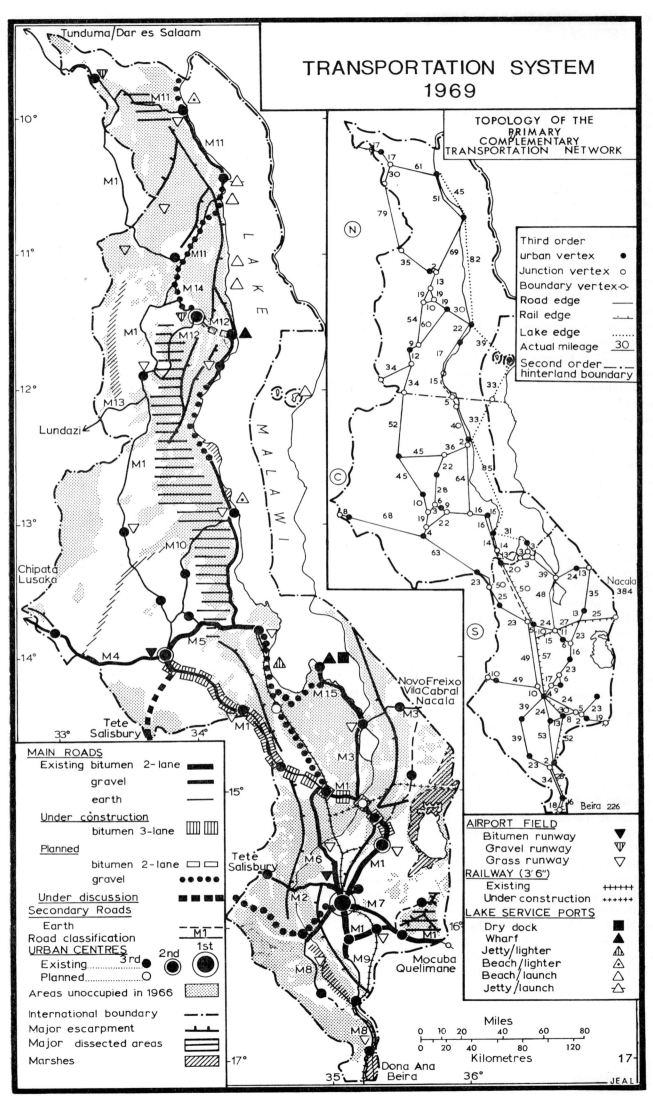

TRANSPORTATION SYSTEM 1969

44 PUBLIC PASSENGER TRANSPORT SERVICES, 1968-9

During 1968 internal public passenger transport carried 14·2 million persons, of which bus services carried the majority (94 per cent), railways 650 000, lake steamer services 104 000 and air services 102 000 (into Chileka Airport).

With the exception of a single privately operated route between Kaporo and Chitimba in Karonga District, the United Transport (Malawi) Ltd operates all bus services. Public services began with 2625 km. (1644 miles) of dry season routes in 1947. By 1964 this mileage had increased to 6983 km. (4340 miles), and by 1969 to 10 882 km. (6695 miles). 34 per cent of this mileage was discontinued during the wet season when many roads become impassable. Disruption was greatest east of Blantyre in the Palombe-Chilwa plain, and around Lilongwe. Almost all southern and central populated areas have at least daily services, but north-central and northern areas have less frequent services. Of the 37 third order urban centres only the three northern-most, Chitipa, Karonga and Chilumba, are not connected with the national system by at least twice-daily services. The northernmost second order centre, Mzuzu, is too small to stimulate local services, and many of the increased frequencies on routes entering Lilongwe, the central order centre, result from the convergence of regional routes and not from a higher level of local services. Only around Blantyre is the impact of the city upon adjacent rural areas reflected in increased frequencies of local services additional to the regional route frequencies.

The table below indicates the rather better services provided in the southern region, which included Blantyre and Zomba. Although having only 13 per cent of the land area and 33 per cent of the population, this region was served by 45 per cent of the dry season journey miles and by 50 per cent of the wet season. The two most peripheral regions have the least developed services. Services are operated by 157 vehicles, most of recent introduction. Operating costs are high because of poor roads, difficult terrain, and small size of depots. Congestion is high on Blantyre's internal services. Cost per mile is 1⅜d. which, although the same fare since 1951, is still high in relation to the average incomes of non-car-owners, the vast majority of the population. The average number of journeys per year is only three per person, and as a high proportion of all journeys are urban, this figure is undoubtedly much lower for the rural population, most of whom travel by bicycle or walk. Taxis supplement buses in Blantyre (39 vehicles), Lilongwe (17), Zomba (9) and Balaka, Salima, and Dowa (1 each). Bus services connect with Tanzania services at Tunduma and with Zambian services at Tunduma, Lundazi and Chipata. Moçambique Railways buses operate from Blantyre to Tete and to Mocuba for Quelimane, and Malawian and Rhodesian services provide a direct route between Blantyre and Salisbury via Tete.

Malawi Railways operates between Beira and Blantyre a weekly diesel rail-car service, which takes twelve hours, and a daily slower service in both directions. Between Blantyre and Nsanje and Blantyre and Balaka additional daily services are operated. Between Blantyre and Salima a daily service is operated. This latter provides the only public service to certain parts of the south-central and central lake regions, and forms part of the major north-south passenger route, which continues by lake steamer to the Northern Region for Chipoka. Costs by this route are much less than by bus, although the latter is preferred if time is important as the difference from the extreme north can be several days. Malawi Railways operates two passenger vessels, the M.V. *Ilala II* which sails weekly from Monkey Bay to Karonga and return, and the M.V. *Chauncy Maples* which sails weekly by alternative routes to Nkhata Bay, calling at smaller ports than its larger sister vessel. The *Ilala* provides the only public service to the Likoma Islands and to the coast between Nkhata Bay and Chitimba, while the *Chauncy Maples* provides the only public service for parts of the Central Lakeshore, and for the Makanjila coast, although regular dhow services connect this with Senga.

Bus, rail and lake services are complementary and the inset map indicates cost of travel from first and second order centres by the cheapest combination of surface routes irrespective of the changes necessary and the time required. The table below indicates the population resident by travel cost zones.

Regular air services connect Blantyre with Zomba, Lilongwe, Mzuzu and Karonga, and small charter planes are used to reach the many air strips which have no scheduled services. Of the 55 external services each week almost half consist of daily flights to Salisbury, the others connecting with adjacent countries, and with South Africa, Mauritius and Kenya, and thence to further destinations. Chileka Airport (Blantyre) handled 104 100 passengers in 1968, and Lilongwe 42 100 passengers, Mzuzu 3700, Karonga 1400 and Salima 500.

POPULATION RESIDENT IN TRAVEL COST ZONES, 1969 (per cent)

Second order hinterland	Population resident in zones of travel cost (in shillings)					
	0–4	5–9	10–14	15–19	20–24	25–29
Mzuzu	2·2	3·4	3·8	1·1	1·2	0·1
Lilongwe	17·6	12·0	3·8	—	—	—
Blantyre	22·7	20·7	9·7	1·5	1·2	0·1

PROVISION OF BUS SERVICES DURING DRY SEASON OPERATION, 1969.
(data in brackets refers to reduced wet season operations)

Data collection region	Route miles	Route miles per 100 sq. miles of occupied area	Journey miles per week	Journey miles per 1000 estimated resident population
Northern	205	62 (41)	2 372	15 (11)
North central	835	59 (52)	10 906	27 (25)
Central	2204	91 (45)	34 671	27 (17)
Central lake	299	82 (64)	4 246	26 (20)
South central	1059	92 (70)	14 365	21 (17)
Southern	1737	115 (81)	59 710	39 (33)
Lower Shire	356	65 (28)	4 984	17 (7)
Total	6695	86 (57)	131 254	29 (23)

MICHAEL STUBBS

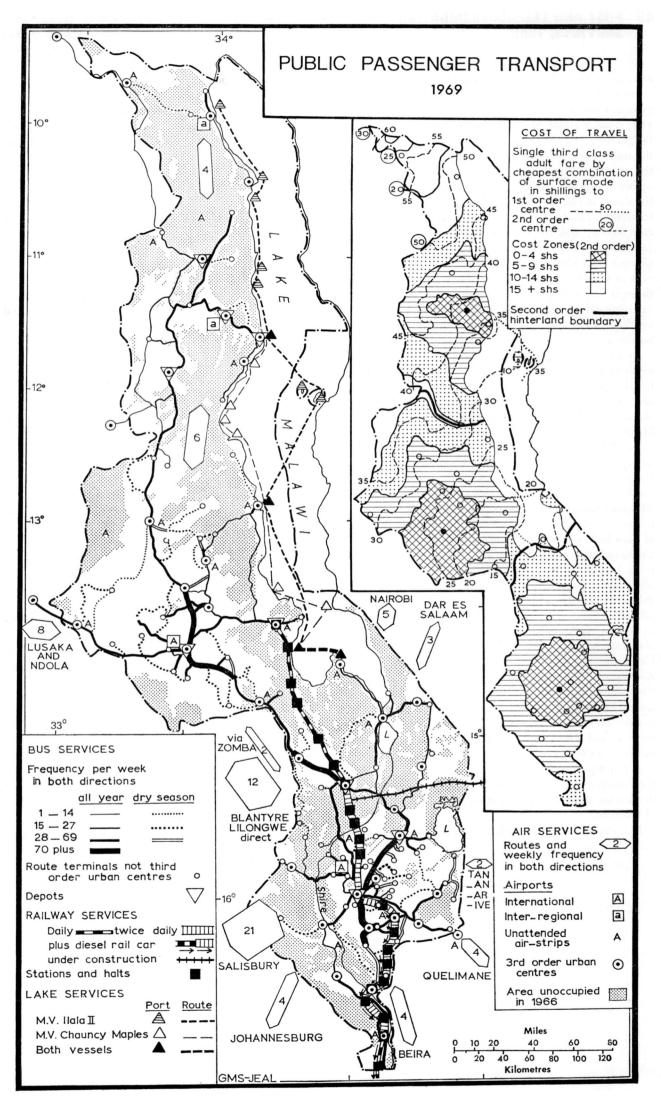

PUBLIC PASSENGER TRANSPORT
1969

COST OF TRAVEL

Single third class adult fare by cheapest combination of surface mode in shillings to

1st order centre ------ 50 ......

2nd order centre ⓩ⓪

Cost Zones (2nd order)
0-4 shs
5-9 shs
10-14 shs
15 + shs

Second order hinterland boundary

LAKE MALAWI

NAIROBI 5

DAR ES SALAAM 3

8 LUSAKA AND NDOLA

via ZOMBA 2

12 BLANTYRE LILONGWE direct

21

SALISBURY

4

JOHANNESBURG

GMS-JEAL

BEIRA

QUELIMANE

TAN -AN -AR -IVE 2

BUS SERVICES

Frequency per week in both directions

	all year	dry season
1 — 14		....
15 — 27		••••••••
28 — 69		
70 plus		

Route terminals not third order urban centres ○

Depots ▽

RAILWAY SERVICES

Daily ▬□▬ twice daily ⅢⅢⅢⅢ

plus diesel rail car ▬▬▶

under construction ┼┼┼┼┼

Stations and halts ■

LAKE SERVICES

	Port	Route
M.V. Ilala II	△	— — —
M.V. Chauncy Maples	△	— · —
Both vessels	▲	— ·· —

AIR SERVICES

Routes and weekly frequency in both directions ⟨2⟩

Airports

International Ⓐ

Inter-regional ⓐ

Unattended air-strips A

3rd order urban centres ⊙

Area unoccupied in 1966 ▦

Miles
0 10   40   60   80
0 20 40 60 80 100 120
Kilometres

45 POST AND TELECOMMUNICATION SERVICES, 1969

In 1894 the first telegraph line in the country was constructed to connect Chikwawa with Blantyre. In 1896 this was extended northwards to Zomba and Fort Johnston, and by 1897 it had reached Nkhota Kota via Mtakataka and Domira Bay, and by 1898 Karonga. The rapidity of construction of the north-south telegraph line was facilitated by the lake, the construction and maintenance teams being able to move by boat along the lakeshore, as the telegraph line followed the shore. In this year branch telegraph lines were extended from Mtakataka to Dedza, up the western escarpment of the Rift Valley, and from Domira Bay to Dowa and Fort Jameson. In 1904, as the railway was constructed between Chiromo and Blantyre, a telegraph line was added, to connect at Chiromo with an earlier constructed line running through Moçambique to Quelimane. In 1920 a further international connection was made with Tanganyika, adding to the earlier international connection with Tete and Salisbury.

By 1950 the telephone system was still restricted to the southern region, with the exception of a line from Zomba to Lilongwe. Limbe and Zomba were connected by a direct line, in addition to one passing through Ntondwe and Namadzi exchanges. From Zomba a line continued to Mangoche and Namwera. From Limbe lines branched via Cholo (Thyolo) and Luchenza to Mlanje (Mulanje), and via Blantyre to Chileka Airport and Chikwawa. The railway company maintained a telephone line from Limbe northwards to Chipoka and southwards to Port Herald (Nsanje). All other parts of the country were served by radio transmitters, mostly at administrative centres. By 1958 a number of lines had been added: between Cholo and Mlanje; from Cholo to Makwasa, from Mlanje to Milanje in Moçambique; from Limbe via Njuli to Chiradzulu; from Namadzi to Magomero, from Limbe, to Bvumbwe; from Kasupe via Balaka to Ncheu and Fort Mlangeni; between Salima and Mbabzi, Namitete, and Likuni; between Dedza and Vila Coutinho; between Fort Jameson (Chipata) and Fort Manning (Mchinji); between Nkhata Bay and Ruarwe and Chinteche; between Mzuzu and Ekwendeni; and between Karonga and Kaporo and Fort Hill (Chitipa). Thus although the nuclei of regional systems had developed by this date around Karonga, Mzuzu, Salima, Lilongwe, and those around Zomba and Blantyre had been extended, inter-regional and some inter-urban connections were still by means of VHF transmitters.

A major problem created by the physical environment is the considerable deterioration of insulation during the long dry season, and consequent serious breakdown at the onset of the rains.

By 1969 and largely since Independence there had been a considerable extension of the telephone network, and of the capacity of exchanges. Much of the Shire Highlands and the Lilongwe areas were served by auto and automanual exchanges open 24 hours per day, and the Mzuzu manual exchange was also open 24 hours per day. The greatest volume of inter-urban telephone traffic was between Zomba and Blantyre, but traffic within Blantyre, with its 4868 direct exchange lines and extensions on private exchanges, probably constituted a considerable proportion of the national total. Zomba and Lilongwe had 1381 and 985 subscribers respectively, Mzuzu 211, Thyolo 187, Dedza 158, Mulanje 111, Bvumbwe 107, Chileka 89, Salima 80, Mangoche 72, Thornwood 64, Luchenza 65, Mzimba 63, and Chikwawa 58. All other centres had fewer than 50 subscribers. Ntaja was the only third order urban centre without a telephone exchange, use being made of the comprehensive police radio service, which was also used to communicate with the vessels of the lake service. 15 exchanges were located in places of lower than third order, including Bvumbwe, Likuni, and Mbabzi which were suburban to Blantyre and Lilongwe, and Chileka, the principal airport 10 miles from Blantyre.

International traffic in 1968 was very largely with Rhodesia, with smaller amounts with Moçambique, largely with Beira concerned with movements between Malawi and that port, with Zambia, and with South Africa. Traffic with East Africa, and international traffic beyond eastern and southern Africa was very small.

Of the 59 post offices at the beginning of 1969 30 were in the Southern Region, 14 in the Central Region and 15 in the Northern Region, while of the 122 postal agencies 36 were in the Southern, 50 in the Central, and 36 in the Northern Regions. Ekwendeni, Champira, Nkhoma and Fort Mlangeni each had post offices (not separately shown on the map) together with their telephone exchanges. Most parts of the country were within relatively easy reach of postal services, and the construction and staffing of post offices and postal agencies was increasing very rapidly as a result of a selfhelp community development programme.

The Malawi Broadcasting Corporation's principal transmitters, totalling 40 kW, recently supplemented by a 100 kW transmitter provided under West German development aid, were at Ngumbe near to the Chileka Airport. Single kilowatt transmitters were located in each of the regions recognized for data collection purposes, that is at Karonga for Karonga and Chitipa, at Mzimba for the rest of the Northern Region, at Nkhota Kota for the central lakeshore and parts of Nkhata Bay, at Lilongwe for the remainder of the Central Region, at Mangoche for the south-central region, and at Bangula for the lower Shire. 50 watt VHF transmitters were located at Chichiri, Mpingwe, Zomba Plateau and Dedza.

MICHAEL STUBBS

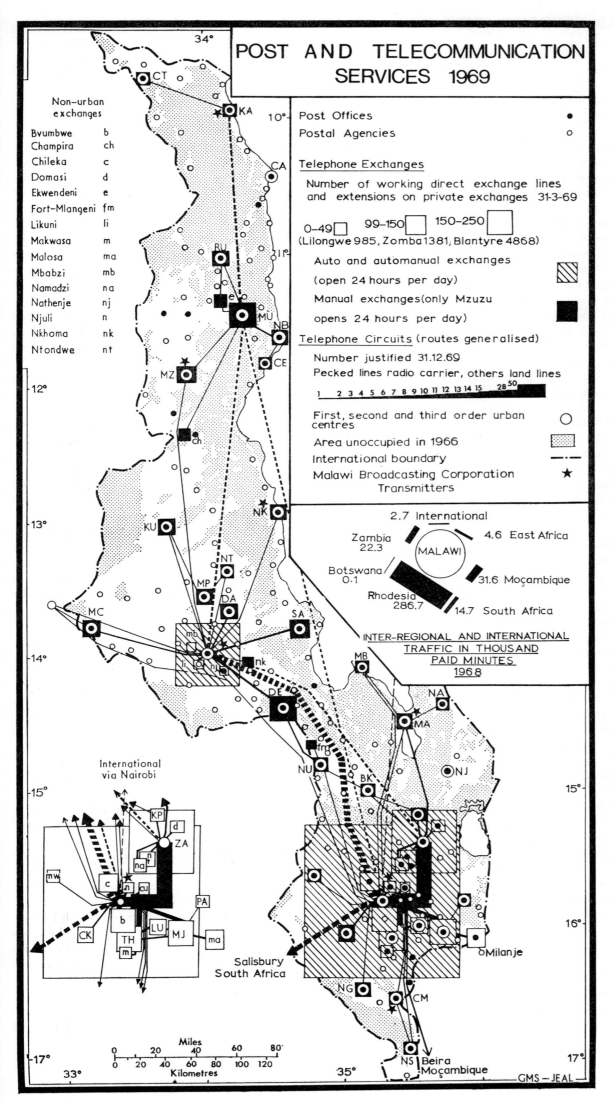

POST AND TELECOMMUNICATION SERVICES 1969

Non-urban exchanges

Bvumbwe	b
Champira	ch
Chileka	c
Domasi	d
Ekwendeni	e
Fort-Mlangeni	fm
Likuni	li
Makwasa	m
Malosa	ma
Mbabzi	mb
Namadzi	na
Nathenje	nj
Njuli	n
Nkhoma	nk
Ntondwe	nt

Post Offices ●
Postal Agencies ○

Telephone Exchanges

Number of working direct exchange lines and extensions on private exchanges 31-3-69

0–49 □   99–150 □   150–250 □
(Lilongwe 985, Zomba 1381, Blantyre 4868)

Auto and automanual exchanges
(open 24 hours per day)

Manual exchanges (only Mzuzu
opens 24 hours per day)

Telephone Circuits (routes generalised)

Number justified 31.12.69
Pecked lines radio carrier, others land lines

1 2 3 4 5 6 7 8 9 10 11 12 13 14 15 28 50

First, second and third order urban centres ○

Area unoccupied in 1966

International boundary

Malawi Broadcasting Corporation Transmitters ★

2.7 International
Zambia 22.3   4.6 East Africa
MALAWI
Botswana 0.1   31.6 Moçambique
Rhodesia 286.7   14.7 South Africa

INTER-REGIONAL AND INTERNATIONAL TRAFFIC IN THOUSAND PAID MINUTES 1968

International via Nairobi

Salisbury
South Africa

Milanje

Beira
Moçambique

Miles
0 20 40 60 80
0 20 40 60 80 100 120
Kilometres

GMS—JEAL

46 GOODS TRANSPORT, 1967-8

Malawi Railways forms the single most important goods transportation system, with lake service vessels and road transport providing feeder services. Between 1964 and 1968 the volume of goods carried on the railways increased from 52 960 000 to 131 400 000 ton miles. The inset map shows for 1967 the volumes carried between the principal transshipment points on the Malawian system. 'Up' traffic, that is traffic moving up the system from the port of Beira and from the Rhodesian and South African railway systems (which connect at Dondo Junction near Beira), totalled 269 000 tons at the southernmost Malawian urban centre, Nsanje. A small amount of internal traffic was added at this point, and a greater amount at Bangula. The greatest tonnage carried over any section of the system was that between Bangula and Luchenza, the section in which the railway climbs 931 m. (3000 ft) into the Shire Highlands. The net tonnage off-loaded at Luchenza was 34 000 tons, and a further net off-loaded 159 000 tons at Blantyre. Northwards from Blantyre that city's manufactured products were carried in addition to imported goods, and there was a progressive off-loading at Mirale for Changalume, and at Balaka, Chipoka and Salima. The goods off-loaded at Chipoka were transferred almost in entirety to the lake-service, largely for Nkhata Bay. Almost all of the 96 000 tons delivered to the railhead at Salima were further distributed over the Central Region, southern parts of the Northern Region, and eastern Zambia. After Rhodesia's declaration of Independence considerable additional goods traffic passed through Salima to and from Zambia, and additional permanent warehousing and transhipment facilities were constructed.

Traffic from Salima increased progressively southwards, being smaller in tonnage than up traffic as far as Mirale, where the addition of cement clinker from Changalume was much greater than the tonnage of coal delivered there. The additional net down traffic generated by Blantyre was much less than the net up traffic, and the net addition at Luchenza, 47 000 tons, was not much less than the 58 000 tons net added at Blantyre. The addition of cotton at Bangula is compensated for by the off-loading of articles from the north. The greatest net addition at any one point is 78 000 tons at Salima, at which the greatest single off-loading also occurred. Only 8000 tons were added at Chipoka.

With the completion of the railway between the Malawian system via Novo Freixo with the Moçambique port of Nacala and its opening to traffic in August 1970 considerable change in the pattern of rail goods traffic is anticipated.

Largely because of the inadequate facilities at Chipoka and the absence of any suitable alternative, the traffic transported by the lake service vessels was very small, principally from Chipoka to Nkhata Bay for distribution to the Mzuzu and Rumphi–northern Mzimba areas. In 1967 the tonnage both loaded and off-loaded at Likoma Island, for which the lake service was the only means of transport, was slightly greater than that at Nkhota Kota. Considering the area and population served, and the relative unimportance of road transport, the volume passing through Kambwe Port for Karonga and Chitipa Districts was very small. In addition to the M.V. *Ilala* and the M.V. *Chauncy Maples*, the former with considerable goods capacity, the fleet included a cargo vessel, the M.V. *Nkhwazi*, and a bulk fuel carrier, the M.V. *Mpasa*, which delivers 28 000 tons of petroleum products to

Nkhata Bay. Both goods traffic and lake vessels capacity are expected to increase very considerably during the 1970s when the proposed new ports at Chinteche and Liwonde are constructed, and the returns from pulpwood transportation assist in making the lake services viable.

Rail and lake services were fed by road transport, the total carrying capacity of goods vehicles in 1968 being 4656 tons, 57 per cent (2658 tons) of which was registered and operational in the central region, almost all in Lilongwe (2239 tons). This resulted partly from the function of road goods transport as feeder to the railhead at Salima, and the transhipment point at Balaka, from all parts of the Central Region and the southern parts of Mzimba District, and partly from the stimulus of the Zambian traffic which followed the Salima-Lilongwe-Mchinji-Chipata route. Although generating much greater volumes of traffic than Lilongwe, only 37 per cent (1627 tons) of registered capacity was located in the Southern Region, with 994 tons in Blantyre and most of the remainder in Thyolo and Mulanje. In contrast the Northern Region contained only 1·6 per cent of registered capacity, the central lakeshore, in which Salima is located, only 0·5 per cent, the south central region 1·6 per cent, and the lower Shire 2·6 per cent.

Between January 1966 and January 1969 the carrying capacity in districts adjacent to the main concentrations more than doubled, indicating a diffusion of goods vehicle ownership into the immediate peripheries, and into the area between Blantyre and Lilongwe (Mangoche, Kasupe, Ncheu, Salima, Dowa, Mchinji and Mzimba).

The location of the depots of the major road transport operators suggests the importance of the railway feeder function of road transport, with depots at the rail-road transhipment points Bangula, Luchenza, Balaka and Salima, and at Nkhata Bay for road-lake service as well as Blantyre and the second order urban centres. In the north central region there were seven small depots (at Mzuzu, Nkhata Bay and at Rumphi and Mzimba) although the total regional licensed carrying capacity was only 54 tons. In part this resulted from the transfer of regional centre functions from Mzimba to Mzuzu, together with the difficult road conditions which make outlying subsidiary depots necessary.

Road traffic volumes in 1968, which also includes passenger vehicles, showed clearly the nodal character of Blantyre and Lilongwe, and the importance of the Blantyre-Zomba connection, while Mzuzu, the northern second order centre, appears at the centre of a linear route connecting Mzimba and Nkhata Bay rather than at the centre of a radial system of higher traffic densities.

Goods traffic carried by air both internally and to and from the international airports increased considerably during the four years after Independence, both as a result of more frequent and faster connections, and of the expansion of the demand in Blantyre for high value goods which could bear the cost.

Importation of goods is reflected to a certain extent by the gross revenue collected at customs stations. Blantyre, Salima (for Zambian traffic), Luchenza and Nsanje (largely for Moçambique traffic) had by far the largest revenues. Moçambique road services cross Malawi extensively between Quelimane and Nampula to the east, and Tete and Angonia in the west, together with some local traffic in the Nsanje area. Little goods traffic crosses the northern international boundaries with Zambia and Tanzania.

MICHAEL STUBBS

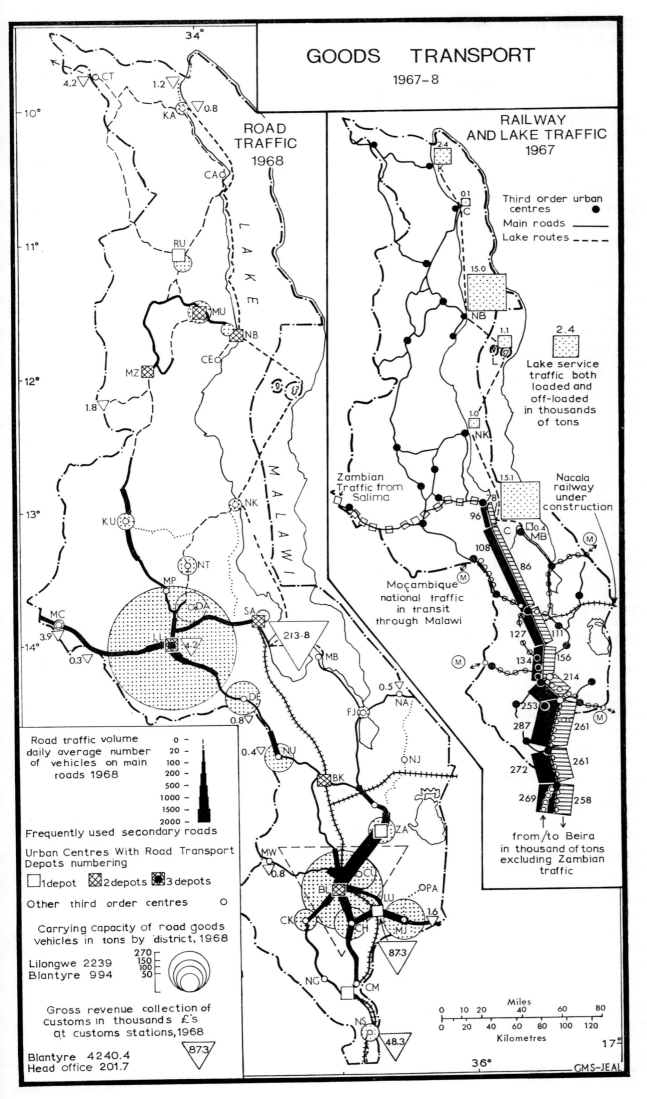

GOODS TRANSPORT
1967–8

ROAD TRAFFIC 1968

RAILWAY AND LAKE TRAFFIC 1967

Third order urban centres ●
Main roads ———
Lake routes – – –

2.4
Lake service traffic both loaded and off-loaded in thousands of tons

Nacala railway under construction

Zambian Traffic from Salima

Moçambique national traffic in transit through Malawi

from/to Beira in thousand of tons excluding Zambian traffic

Road traffic volume daily average number of vehicles on main roads 1968

0	—
20	—
100	—
200	—
500	—
1000	—
1500	—
2000	—

Frequently used secondary roads

Urban Centres With Road Transport Depots numbering

□ 1 depot   ▨ 2 depots   ⊛ 3 depots

Other third order centres ○

Carrying capacity of road goods vehicles in tons by district, 1968

Lilongwe 2239
Blantyre 994

270
150
100
50

Gross revenue collection of customs in thousands £'s at customs stations, 1968

Blantyre 4240.4
Head office 201.7

Miles
0 10 20   40   60   80
0 20 40 60 80 100 120
Kilometres

GMS-JEAL

47 COMMODITY FLOWS, PROCESSING AND MANUFACTURING

A considerable proportion of inter-regional commodity movements consists of removal by road of primary products to transhipment points on the principal longitudinal axis formed by the Beira–Nsanje–Blantyre–Salima railway and its lake service extension to Karonga. Processing and manufacturing within the country is largely carried on in Blantyre, but most products are exported by rail in a raw or semi-processed state. In the reverse direction most imports enter by rail from Beira. Most are consumed finally or in manufacturing in Blantyre, the remainder being further distributed, together with the products of Blantyre's own industries, along the rail-lake axis and its road feeders.

Only five per cent of the value of produce purchased from the 1966–7 crop originated in the Northern Region, production being constrained largely by the high transportation cost from southern sources of production and infrastructural inputs and consumer goods. For example, transport charges per ton of cement delivered within Blantyre were 43$^{d.}$ compared with 320$^{d.}$ at Chipoka, 1048$^{d.}$ at Nkhata Bay, and 1257$^{d.}$ at Karonga. Although the Farmers' Marketing Board equalizes transportation costs for each product across the country, it cannot encourage production in areas where much of the profit on a crop is eliminated by high transport costs within a few miles of its origin. Although costs by lake service to Blantyre are cheaper than by road at Nkhata Bay and Mzuzu, road transport becomes cheaper in the southern Mzimba area and in the whole of the Central Region, and it seems probable that completion of the lakeshore road between Nkhota Kota and Nkhata Bay will push northwards the boundary of effective road competition. A major change in commodity flows may result from the maturing of the Vipya pulpwood plantations and construction of a pulp and board factory at Chinteche in 1975. It is expected that new port facilities at Chinteche and Liwonde will become the principal lake service terminals, and that resultant revenue will make possible a general improvement in facilities and consequent reduction in costs for the Northern Region.

Almost forty-five per cent of the produce purchased from the 1966–7 crop originated in the central and central lakeshore regions. Almost all moved by road to Salima rail terminal. That from the Dedza and Ncheu areas moved to Balaka. Improvement of the Zomba–Lilongwe road is likely to reduce still further costs of road movement in the latter area, and to extend westwards the cost break-even point with movements to Salima. A considerable amount of Moçambique transit traffic originates in the Angonia area, also served by this road.

Industrialization based upon processing primary products is very limited in the Northern and Central Regions. Lilongwe has an FMB tobacco grading and packing plant and an abattoir and cold storage plant, and Mzuzu had a tung factory, now closed. Only Karonga and Nkhota Kota have plants, with a flour and rice mill respectively, out of the fifteen order centres. There are no industries at any of the major transhipment points – Nkhata Bay, Chipoka and Salima – although the latter is particularly well suited for industrial growth. There are government sawmills at Chikangawa on the Vipya and at Dedza, and quarries and brick and tile factories at Mzuzu and Lilongwe. In Lilongwe labour recruitment by the WNLA organization brought into existence in 1953 a clothing factory producing uniforms. Subsequently tyre retreading, cement products, furniture and other clothing plants were established.

Minor flows of food, construction materials and fuel have been stimulated by urban growth in Lilongwe and Mzuzu, largely from within their third order hinterlands. Fish is moved inland from Lake Malawi in both regions.

The south-central region provided 10·2 per cent of the produce purchased from the 1966–7 crop. The railway provides the principal means of commodity movement, except to the Ntaja area, and is fed by road routes, and by a rail spur to the cement clinker quarry at Changalume. Balaka, currently the principal transhipment centre, has no industries. During the 1970s Liwonde will be developed as a rail-road-lake service transhipment centre with storage, processing and assembling plants on the newly completed rail link to Novo Freixo and Nacala.

The Southern Region provided 27 per cent of the produce purchased from the 1966–7 crop, most of which moves to Blantyre and Luchenza. By far the greatest proportion of industrial activity in Malawi is concentrated in Blantyre, the railhead until 1935 and the first commercial and processing centre. The location there of the railway depot and the Imperial Tobacco Company's grading factory in 1908 stimulated industrial growth, but most existing processing and manufacturing has developed since the mid-1950s and particularly since 1964, made possible by utilization of hydroelectric potential of the middle Shire, and construction of industrial sites. Growing inter-dependence between industry and commerce, considerable investment in infrastructure and services, growth of a skilled labour force, attractiveness of social and shopping facilities in Blantyre, and growing dependence upon the market within the city and in the southern region have all added to the momentum of Blantyre's industrial growth.

In the remainder of the region primary products are processed close to their source at fish-cleaning and freezing plants north of Mangoche, sawmills at Zomba, Chigumula and Mulanje, tea factories in the production areas of Thyolo and Mulanje, sugar at Nchalo, and cotton ginneries at Chikwawa and Bangula. Because of congestion in the Limbe railway yards at the height of the marketing season, a tobacco-grading and packing plant at Maleule, 32 km. (20 miles) north of the city, is used to relieve the pressure. At Luchenza fruit and vegetables are canned for both internal and external markets. Tea, sisal and tung also pass through Luchenza for export, and it is a major maize storage and distributing centre. Mattress manufacture at Thyolo and vehicle engineering at Luchenza have been supplemented very recently by bakeries at Namadzi and Mulanje and clothing manufacture at Zomba, possibly the first phase in a decentralization of light industry made possible by the extension of the electricity grid and improved road transport. Luchenza and Bangula, because of their rail and road nodality, appear best suited for further industrial growth.

Petroleum products account for a growing proportion of inward commodity movements, Blantyre absorbing one-third of the total imported. Coal is used by tea factories, and the Changalume clinker plant. Tea chests, sacks and chemicals are imported for the tea and sugar plants. Fertilizers are largely absorbed within the Southern and Central Regions. Half of Blantyre's cement production is absorbed within the city, and a further quarter in Lilongwe. Similarly high proportions of imported manufactured goods, and goods produced in Blantyre, are absorbed within the city itself, the remainder being distributed in the reverse direction to primary products, although there is a greater use of road transport as the commodities have high value per weight.

Small business-men operate over 200 maize mills throughout the country and there are numerous small craft industries. These are usually plants of only two or four workers, with little modern equipment or motive power. A high proportion of the rural population still manufactures most of its requirements.

MICHAEL STUBBS

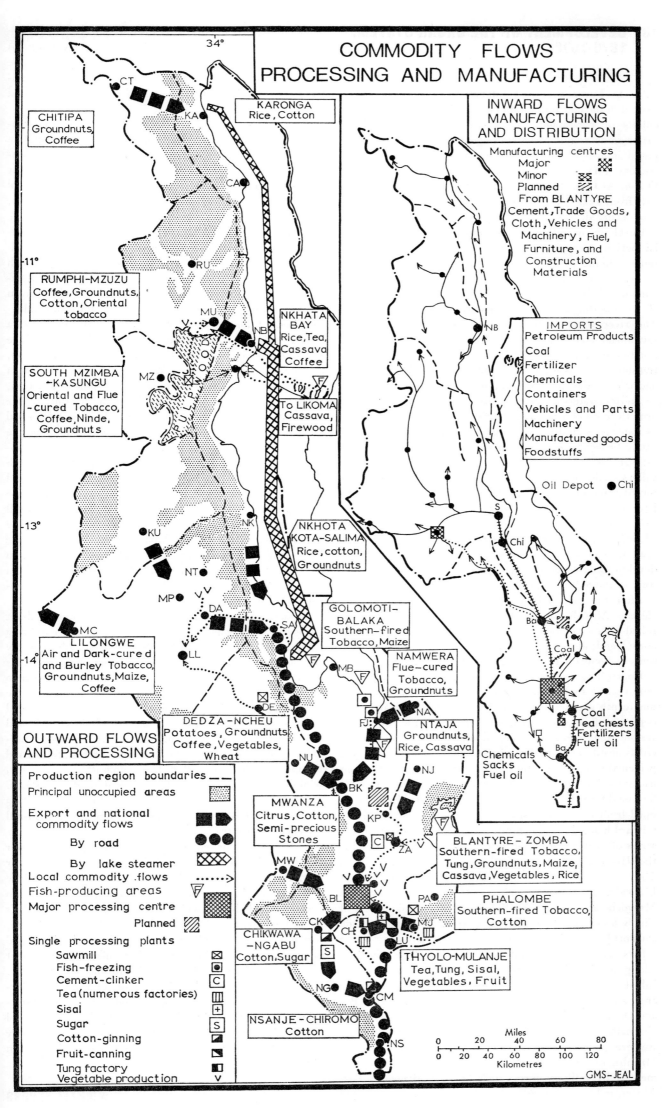

COMMODITY FLOWS PROCESSING AND MANUFACTURING

INWARD FLOWS MANUFACTURING AND DISTRIBUTION

Manufacturing centres
Major
Minor
Planned
From BLANTYRE
Cement, Trade Goods, Cloth, Vehicles and Machinery, Fuel, Furniture, and Construction Materials

IMPORTS
Petroleum Products
Coal
Fertilizer
Chemicals
Containers
Vehicles and Parts
Machinery
Manufactured goods
Foodstuffs

Oil Depot ● Chi

CHITIPA
Groundnuts, Coffee

KARONGA
Rice, Cotton

RUMPHI-MZUZU
Coffee, Groundnuts, Cotton, Oriental tobacco

NKHATA BAY
Rice, Tea, Cassava Coffee

SOUTH MZIMBA –KASUNGU
Oriental and Flue–cured Tobacco, Coffee, Ninde, Groundnuts

To LIKOMA
Cassava, Firewood

NKHOTA KOTA-SALIMA
Rice, cotton, Groundnuts

GOLOMOTI–BALAKA
Southern–fired Tobacco, Maize

NAMWERA
Flue–cured Tobacco, Groundnuts

LILONGWE
Air and Dark-cured and Burley Tobacco, Groundnuts, Maize, Coffee

DEDZA–NCHEU
Potatoes, Groundnuts, Coffee, Vegetables, Wheat

NTAJA
Groundnuts, Rice, Cassava

Coal
Tea chests
Fertilizers
Fuel oil

Chemicals
Sacks
Fuel oil

OUTWARD FLOWS AND PROCESSING

Production region boundaries
Principal unoccupied areas
Export and national commodity flows
   By road
   By lake steamer
Local commodity flows
Fish-producing areas
Major processing centre
   Planned
Single processing plants
   Sawmill
   Fish-freezing
   Cement-clinker
   Tea (numerous factories)
   Sisal
   Sugar
   Cotton-ginning
   Fruit-canning
   Tung factory
   Vegetable production

MWANZA
Citrus, Cotton, Semi-precious Stones

BLANTYRE– ZOMBA
Southern-fired Tobacco, Tung, Groundnuts, Maize, Cassava, Vegetables, Rice

PHALOMBE
Southern-fired Tobacco, Cotton

CHIKWAWA –NGABU
Cotton, Sugar

THYOLO-MULANJE
Tea, Tung, Sisal, Vegetables, Fruit

NSANJE – CHIROMO
Cotton

Miles
0 20 40 60 80
0 20 40 60 80 100 120
Kilometres

GMS-JEAL

48 DEVELOPMENT OF THE URBAN SYSTEM, 1876-1970

Prior to European direct intervention, urban functions existed in the concentration of activities and population at a chief's or paramount chief's court, particularly where major trade routes passed through the society's area. External influences had already stimulated urban growth at Nkhota Kota, on the ivory and slave route to the Indian Ocean. At Chief Mponda's headquarters beside the Shire's exit from Lake Malawi a similar concentration of population occurred.

Development of the urban system during the early colonial period comprised the establishment of transhipment points on the penetration route from the Indian Ocean, Blantyre as the systems nucleus and primate city, and the consequent diffusion from Blantyre of mission, administrative and trading activities and associated urban settlements. The river route of the Zambezi and lower Shire from Quelimane and later from the free port of Chinde on the Zambezi delta was early established. The first transportation transfer point was at Katunga's immediately below the rapids and falls of the middle Shire, whence a route followed a secondary watershed to the site of Blantyre. Before the growth there of a permanent urban centre, however, a fall in water levels in the Shire and an increase in the volume of traffic brought a downstream shift to Chiromo, whence a railway was built to Blantyre following the Ruo and Thuchila valleys. Subsequently, the transhipment point was transferred again downstream to Port Herald (now Nsanje), and later to the Zambezi at Dona Ana, and subsequently to Beira. Redundant as transhipment points, Nsanje became an administrative centre whereas Chiromo did not, and the road to Katunga's from Blantyre made it convenient to develop Chikwawa, on the opposite and higher western bank of the Shire, as an administrative centre.

After the early failure of the Universities Mission to Central Africa's base at Magomero, Blantyre was established as a base for missionary expansion, trade and the Shire Highlands planters. Because of its pleasant climate and scenery Zomba became the administrative capital.

Controlling factors in the diffusion of mission, administrative and trading activities were the location of early nineteenth century concentrations of population and their degree of disruption by the slave trade and the Angoni invasions, the extent of the area dominated by Ayao Moslem chiefs hostile to Christian missions, and the location of the principal slave trade depots and routes. Although missions had some influence upon the growth of the urban system, few modern urban centres above fourth order have developed from the mission sites. From Zomba, its capital and forward base, the Protectorate administration established a series of forts along the Shire-Lake Malawi axis to combat the slave trade and to pacify the Ayao slave-raiding chiefs. The route from Zomba to the lake was guarded by forts at Liwonde, Fort Sharpe and Fort Johnston and by Fort Mangoche and Maguire on the sites of the headquarters of Chiefs Jalasi and Makanjila respectively. Whereas Liwonde and Fort Johnston became district administrative centres, the others became redundant after successful pacification. Along the lakeshore, administrative centres were established at Nkhota Kota, Chinteche, within the Atonga core area, and Karonga, within the Ankhonde core. Nkhata Bay and Domira Bay became important anchorages, the former alternating with Chinteche as administrative centre. On the western plateau early tax collectors were established at Mzimba, Dowa, Dedza and Ncheu, and these were supplemented by military forts, such as Fort Mlangeni, Fort Alston, and Fort Manning, when resistance was encountered

from the Maseko Angoni, Chief Mwase's Achewa, and the Mpezeni Angoni respectively. Fort Alston (now Kasungu) and Fort Manning (now Mchinji) subsequently became administrative centres. Where mission, military, administrative and commercial functions coincided spatially, continued urban growth occurred.

The development of estate agriculture in the Shire Highlands resulted in the development of further administrative centres at Chiradzulu, Cholo (Thyolo) and Mlanje (Mulanje). As the two latter also acted as social centres for European planters, they consequently developed additional facilities and improved equipment, particularly at Mulanje, more distant from competing facilities in Blantyre. The construction of the railway not only encouraged the development of Limbe as its depot but also stimulated the development of stations serving the tea estate areas, of which Luchenza, at the crossing with the Mulanje-Thyolo road, became the most important. Extension of the railway from Blantyre which followed the expansion of tobacco production in the Lilongwe area resulted in the development of a further rail-road transhipment centre at Balaka, and of the railhead at Salima, rail-lake transhipment point at Chipoka, and the lake service depot at Monkey Bay. This dispersal of what should have been a single transhipment function, located at Domira Bay, resulted from the flooding of the latter site when the lake's level rose. Lilongwe, which had been created an early administrative centre, became the commercial centre of the estate and peasant farm tobacco-producing area and Central Province headquarters. In both this area and the Shire Highlands increased populations and increased income stimulated the growth, usually along the principal roads or around markets and estates, of small commercial centres. In the Northern Region after the Second World War the development of tung estates in the Vipya area resulted in the creation of Mzuzu as a base, to which was transferred the provincial administration from Mzimba after the failure of the tung venture, and the expansion of Nkhata Bay as a port.

Expansion of commercial agriculture brought about changes in the size and commercial functions of pre-existing administrative centres, but in spite of the growth of purely commercial transportation centres the former type remains the most numerous. However, Nambuma and Mponela in the Central Region, and Ntaja, Namwera and Ngabu in the Southern Region developed first as important commercial centres which later attracted partial administrative and social service functions, sometimes at the expense of pre-existing administrative centres. Chitipa, Ntchisi, Salima and Kasupe have become full district administration centres, while Palombe and Mwanza have received sub-district status. Agricultural development in the lower Shire is stimulating the growth of Bangula, opposite Chiromo, as a road-rail transhipment centre.

Within the current development programme major changes in the future growth of the urban system are under way. The most important development is the transfer of the national capital from Zomba to Lilongwe, also planned to develop as an industrial and regional service centre. Zomba's physical equipment will be used by the University of Malawi, which will move from Blantyre. Liwonde will be developed as a transportation, processing and manufacturing centre at the crossing-place of primary road, rail and water routes. Chinteche will be developed as the site of a pulpwood factory and new port installation. It is possible that other suitable urban centres will subsequently develop as industrial centres. In all parts of the country development of primary production, tourism and services is resulting in the growth of urban centres of all sizes.

MICHAEL STUBBS

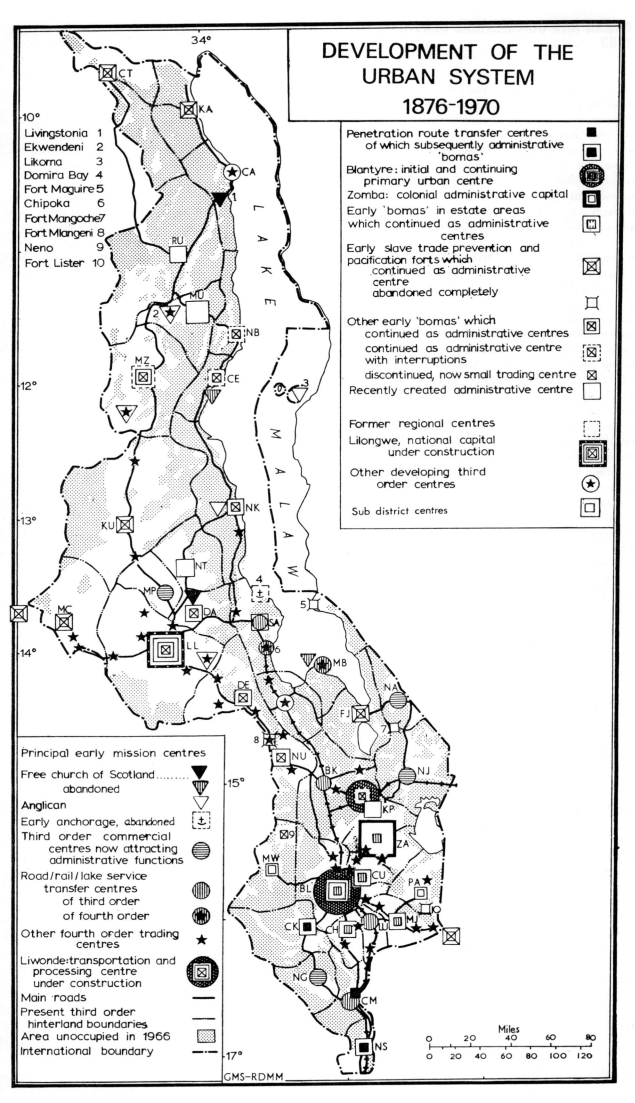

DEVELOPMENT OF THE URBAN SYSTEM 1876-1970

Livingstonia 1
Ekwendeni 2
Likoma 3
Domira Bay 4
Fort Maguire 5
Chipoka 6
Fort Mangoche 7
Fort Mlangeni 8
Neno 9
Fort Lister 10

Penetration route transfer centres
of which subsequently administrative 'bomas'
Blantyre: initial and continuing primary urban centre
Zomba: colonial administrative capital
Early 'bomas' in estate areas which continued as administrative centres
Early slave trade prevention and pacification forts which
continued as administrative centre
abandoned completely

Other early 'bomas' which
continued as administrative centres
continued as administrative centre with interruptions
discontinued, now small trading centre
Recently created administrative centre

Former regional centres
Lilongwe, national capital under construction

Other developing third order centres

Sub district centres

Principal early mission centres
Free church of Scotland..........
abandoned
Anglican
Early anchorage, abandoned
Third order commercial centres now attracting administrative functions
Road/rail/lake service transfer centres
of third order
of fourth order
Other fourth order trading centres
Liwonde: transportation and processing centre under construction
Main roads
Present third order hinterland boundaries
Area unoccupied in 1966
International boundary

Miles

GMS-RDMM

III

49 URBAN AND COMMERCIAL SERVICES, 1969

The first of two complementary maps presents a classification of central places by aggregate order of social and administrative service function, together with an indication of manufacturing and transportation functions, while the second provides information on commercial services.

A division of each non-commercial service function's organizational hierarchy into national, regional, sub-regional and local elements provided the basis for ordering central places. Organizational elements at each spatial level were allocated point scores, basically of 10, 7, 5, and 3, but adjusted to meet slight organizational differences within certain functional hierarchies, particularly at regional and sub-regional levels.

At the national level there was a spatial division between Blantyre – the industrial, commercial, transportation and communication centre, seat of health and educational services and administrative capital of the Southern Region – and Zomba, the national capital and headquarters of many government departments, the Army and the Police. Whereas Zomba, with a population of 20 000 in 1966, grew only slowly up to 1970, Blantyre, with a population of 109 000 in 1966, grew at an estimated rate of 15 per cent per year. Eight per cent of Zomba's population, and seven per cent of Blantyre's were non-African in 1966. Lilongwe, the administrative capital of the Central Region, grew rapidly from a 1966 population of 19 400 (of which only six per cent were non-African). Construction of a new national capital there, which began in 1968, will result in a 1980 population of 125 000. Removal of national administration from Blantyre and particularly from Zomba, will enable the University of Malawi to move to Zomba, which would otherwise revert to third order status. In the Northern Region the administrative capital moved from Mzimba to Mzuzu. These centres had 1966 populations of 4200 and 8500 respectively, of which only two per cent were non-African. These relocations were necessary although expensive adjustments to the inefficient distribution of national and regional functions inherited from the colonial period.

The normal range of scores for third order, sub-regional, centres was between 80 and 120, but older established administrative centres, such as Karonga, Mzimba, Dedza, Mangoche, Thyolo, and Mulanje, were better equipped. Those with scores lower than 80 were non-administrative centres, with limited social services, either serving previously neglected peripheral sub-regions, or on principal transportation routes between administrative centres.

Some fourth order centres, although of low nodality, were better equipped than the lowest scoring third order centres. Nathenje and Namadzi were located on major roads, while Fort Mlangeni consisted largely of the Witwatersrand Native Labour Association depot, and Ekwendeni, Likuni and Malamulo were mission centres with hospitals and educational facilities. The concentration of services at Chileka Airport was a further exceptional case.

The enumerated populations of these centres in August 1966 was very small – 4200 in Mzimba, 2300 in Dedza and Salima, between one and two thousand in 14 others, and under one thousand in the remainder. Only 5.4 per cent of the enumerated population was resident in urban and trading centres in 1966.

There was little spatial coincidence between lower order facilities because of the split between mission and government activities in the fields of health and education, the dichotomy between traditional and modern local administration and judiciary, and little urban physical planning outside the major urban centres.

Although not of second order because they were not regional centres, Karonga, Salima, Balaka and Ngabu occupied an intermediate position between third and second order centres. These were located at some distance from the second order centres, and were nodal to a sub-region largely closed with respect to transportation connections from the regional systems centred on Mzuzu, Lilongwe and Blantyre. In general, transport nodality was much weaker than in the other three regions. Balaka might cede predominance to Liwonde when that centre is developed as a transportation and industrial growth point during the 1970s.

Although no information upon revenue, turnover or taxes for retail, wholesale and other commercial businesses is available, an acceptable alternative for the purpose of quantifying the total functions of trading centres is the schedule of officially designated trading centres prepared by the Ministry of Trade and Industry on the basis of the issue of trading licences (*Government Notice No. 81*, *Business Licensing Act*, *Prescription of Trading Centres*, *Appendix*, Malawi Gazette Supplement, 1st May 1970).

The table on p. 142 indicates for each of the planning Regions the numbers in each category. Two-thirds of the Grade A and Grade B centres are located within the national 'core' regions, the southern and central planning regions, but only slightly more than half of the Grades C and D centres were located here. The following weights were added to centres of each type – Grade A, 10; Grade B, 7; Grade C, 5; and Grade D, 3 and an aggregated obtained for each region and expressed in 'trading centre units'. Additional weights of 100 for Blantyre, 50 for Lilongwe and 25 for Zomba were added in before calculating for each region the estimated August 1970 population per trading centre units.

52 per cent of TCU's were within the two 'core' regions, with the southern planning region having a better population TCU ratio, largely because of the inclusion of Blantyre. If the Blantyre and Lilongwe additions were not included thereby indicating the levels in the surrounding rural areas, the population TCU ratios for southern and central planning regions would be respectively 4849 and 4490, slightly in favour of the latter region. The two small planning regions adjacent to these core regions, the lower Shire and the central lakeshore, had the lowest population/TCU ratio, possibly benefiting from the stimulus of proximity to the cores while having much smaller populations. With its small population the northern planning region also had a favourable population/TCU ratio, although the absence of either Grade A or Grade B centres indicated a much lower level of commercial development. In contrast the south central and north central regions had the highest population/TCU ratios. The explanation of these regional differences appear to lie in the fact that the distribution of trading centres was more closely related with occupied area rather than with the present distribution of population. Most probably if revenue or turnover could be added, and all establishments included, the picture would be very much more favourable in the Southern Region in particular, where small unclassified trading centres and isolated stores serve the dense population. It is possible also that the weight attached to Blantyre does not adequately represent its relative importance in the Southern Region. Furthermore, if population could be weighted by income, then more useful ratios might be available, which might increase the population/income units per trading centre in the Southern Region. Comparison of both the total of TCU's and the number of trading centres of Grades A, B and C with the occupied area (as defined by the area of 'clear field pattern') shows the 'core' regions of the southern and central planning regions at a considerable advantage. The average area of occupied land per trading centre of Grades A, B and C (average size of complementary region) appears as a very sensitive indicator of regional dif-

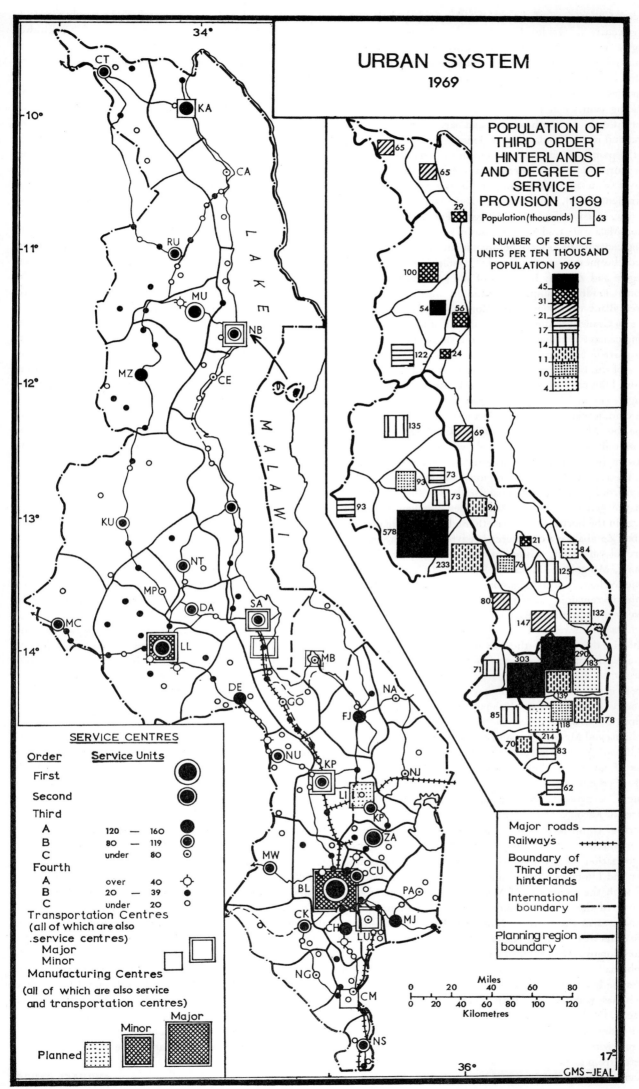

URBAN SYSTEM
1969

POPULATION OF THIRD ORDER HINTERLANDS AND DEGREE OF SERVICE PROVISION 1969

Population (thousands) ☐ 63

NUMBER OF SERVICE UNITS PER TEN THOUSAND POPULATION 1969

45
31
21
17
14
11
10
4

SERVICE CENTRES

Order	Service Units	
First		◉
Second		◉
Third		
A	120 — 160	●
B	80 — 119	◉
C	under 80	⊙
Fourth		
A	over 40	✦
B	20 — 39	●
C	under 20	○

Transportation Centres
(all of which are also service centres)
  Major
  Minor

Manufacturing Centres
(all of which are also service and transportation centres)

     Minor   Major

Planned

Major roads ——————
Railways +++++++
Boundary of Third order hinterlands ——————
International boundary —·—·—·—

Planning region boundary ——————

Miles
0 20 40 60 80
0 20 40 60 80 100 120
Kilometres

LAKE MALAWI

GMS–JEAL

M.M.—8

ferences. Comparison of the estimated 1970 population to trading centre of Grades A, B and C (including Blantyre, Lilongwe and Zomba) shows low ratios in the two core regions, reduced ratios in the two small peripheral planning regions where the multiplication of administrative and transportation systems and centres has increased the number of trading centres in relation to a small population, and higher ratios in the south central, and particularly the north central and northern planning regions.

In the past local demand resulted in the establishment of Asian stores, and their permanent structures and greater turnover stimulated wholesaling and banking, together with government social, administrative and economic services. However, in 1970 the Malawi Government gave notice that all non-Malawian traders with businesses outside certain trading centres had to leave before 1st July 1970. European-owned businesses were largely confined to Blantyre, Lilongwe and Zomba. Branches of the government-owned National Trading Company existed in most third order centres. Blantyre, Lilongwe and Zomba, all of the 11 Grade A and 19 Grade B trading centres, and 41 of the 80 Grade C trading centres remained open to non-Malawian businesses, but no Grade D centre was open.

It is of interest to compare the trading centre hierarchy and the hierarchy of administrative centres. Blantyre and Lilongwe, of the three regional government centres, were large commercial centres outside the trading centre designation, but Mzuzu, regional capital of the Northern Region was of only Grade C status, and was not open to non-Malawian businesses. This unusual situation results partly from the recent move of the regional administrative organization from Mzimba, which has Grade B status, and partly from the generally lower level of development of urban centres in the north. Of the 21 other administrative district centres, Zomba was a commercial centre outside the trading centre classification, while, of the others, only Thyolo, Mulanje, Mangoche, Dedza and Salima had Grade A status, Nsanje, Ncheu, Ntchisi, Mzimba and Nkhota Kota, B status, and the 10 remaining others only C status. This discordance between the administrative centres and the trading centres, which usually developed subsequently, is particularly noticeable in the cases of the lower Shire planning region, where Ngabu and Chiromo are more important as trading centres than the two administrative centres, Chikwawa and Nsanje; in the south central region, where Balaka and Ntaja are more important than Kasupe, the artificially created administrative centre; and in the Central Region where Nambuma and Mponela are more important than the earlier established Dowa. The lower than average trading centre status of northern administrative centres indicates lower levels of commercial development there, as is the failure of Grade C centres to develop other than in the district centres of Karonga and Chitipa.

Further comparison may be made between the commercial hierarchy and the integrated hierarchy used in the categorization of urban centres by order. Blantyre at first order and Lilongwe, Zomba and Mzuzu at second order fit well with the exception of Mzuzu, already discussed. All but one of the Grade A trading centres, Nambuma, was classified as of third order: Nambuma being excluded because of its weak nodal development resulting from proximity to Lilongwe, the absence of a main road, and the fact that Nambuma lies on both sides of a secondary road which marks the boundary between Dowa and Lilongwe Districts, which has resulted in relative neglect by both district councils. Of the 19 Grade B centres 10 were not designated third order, either because they were too near to larger centres with more developed nodality or because they suffered from neglect in social service functions which were concentrated in nearby administrative or mission centres.

Of the 14 third order: centres which had only Grade C trading centre status, two, Chiradzulu and Chikwawa, probably suffered commercial competition from nearby Blantyre. Others: Mwanza, Palombe, Monkey Bay, Namwera in the south, Mchinji, Kasungu in the centre, and all 6 centres – Mzuzu, Nkhata Bay and Chinteche, Rumphi, Karonga and Chitipa – in the north, suffered commercially from being located in peripheral areas of limited commercial activity, but had the moderate range of social and administrative services and transportation route nodality resulting from their administrative status. Of these only Monkey Bay, the headquarters of the Lake Malawi services, and Namwera, were not district or sub-district administrative centres. The situation may be summarized by saying that whereas the provision of district level social and administrative services were relatively uniform over the country, with only the regional services at a higher level (Mzuzu and Mzimba sharing), the level of commercial development decreased very steeply from the Blantyre and Lilongwe 'core' areas. Consequently, in some parts of the country commercial development was relatively more advanced than that of social-administrative service provision, while in other parts of the country the reverse situation occurred. The degree to which commercial development fell behind the minimal social and administrative services formed a useful indicator of the average incomes of the respective hinterlands.

As a final indicator of this situation, analysis will be made of the distribution of banking facilities. Three commercial banks operate within the country. Barclays Bank DCO and the Standard Bank are old-established, while the Commercial Bank of Malawi, partially government controlled, opened its first branches only in 1970. Full branches of all three are located in Blantyre and Lilongwe, and of the two older banks in Zomba. Only one bank operates a full branch in Mzuzu. One full branch of the Commercial Bank of Malawi operates in Dedza. The only third order Grade A status centre with a full branch, Dedza, benefited from the Portuguese associations of both the Commercial Bank of Malawi and the commercial farmers and traders within nearby Moçambique.

The anomalous position of Nambuma again becomes apparent, for of the Grade A trading centres this is the only one without a static agency (that is a permanent building operating at least several days per week) whereas most other such centres have two static agencies. Only a few of the Grade B and Grade C centres had static agencies. Three administrative centres of Grade B status and third order, Nsanje, Ntchisi and Nkhota Kota, were without a static agency. Of the Grade B centres of third order which were not administrative centres, Mponela and Ntaja were in the same position. Eleven other Grade B centres, including the above except for Nkhota Kota and Nsanje, were served only by mobile agencies, as was the Grade A centre Nambuma. Of the Grade C administrative centres of third order, Chikwawa, Chiradzulu, Kasupe, Dowa, Mchinji, and Chitipa were served only by mobile agencies, as were Palombe, Monkey Bay, Chinteche and Mtakataka, which were not administrative centres. One interesting distributional anomaly is the fact that 6 out of 8 of the Grade B and C centres in the north central and Northern Regions had static agencies (all but one agencies of the Standard Bank). This was a very much higher proportion than in the other two regions, where of the total of 90 such centres only 7 had static agencies. This might have related to the traditional labour migration from this area to South Africa (where the Standard Bank had its headquarters), and to the higher levels of education and literacy in the north. Static agencies were located also at Chileka airport and Changalume cement quarry.

MICHAEL STUBBS

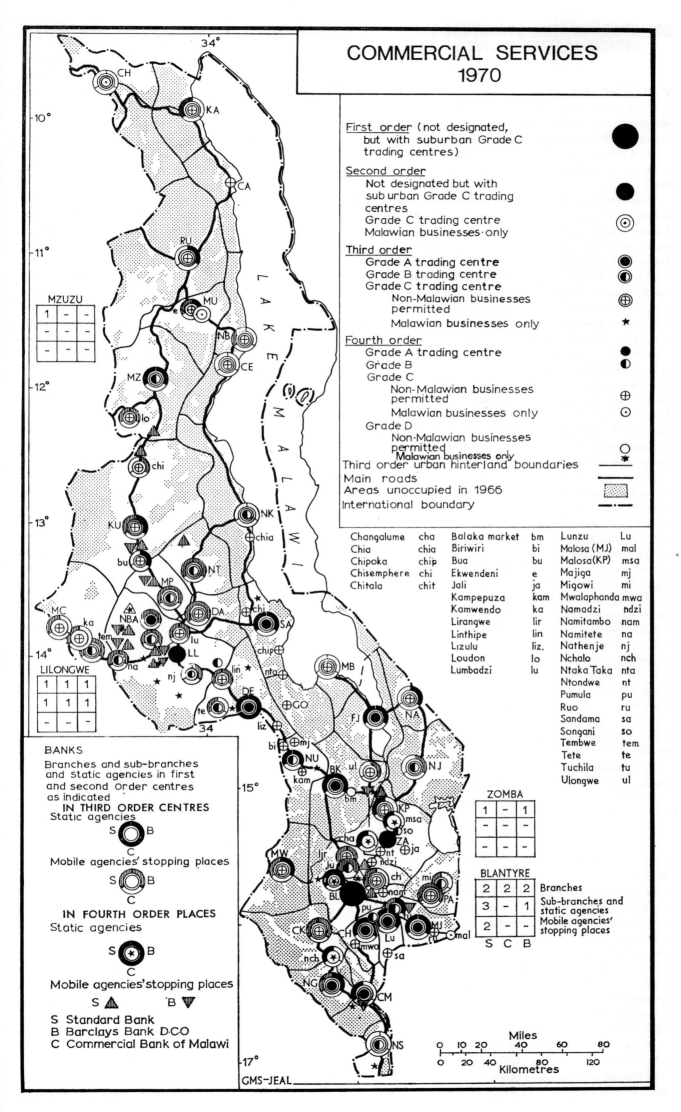

COMMERCIAL SERVICES
1970

First order (not designated, but with suburban Grade C trading centres) ●

Second order
   Not designated but with suburban Grade C trading centres ●
   Grade C trading centre
   Malawian businesses only ◉

Third order
   Grade A trading centre ◉
   Grade B trading centre ◖
   Grade C trading centre
    Non-Malawian businesses permitted ⊕
    Malawian businesses only ★

Fourth order
   Grade A trading centre ●
   Grade B ◖
   Grade C
    Non-Malawian businesses permitted ⊕
    Malawian businesses only ⊙
   Grade D
    Non-Malawian businesses permitted ○
    Malawian businesses only ✳

Third order urban hinterland boundaries ————
Main roads
Areas unoccupied in 1966 ▒
International boundary —·—·—

Changalume	cha	Balaka market	bm	Lunzu	Lu
Chia	chia	Biriwiri	bi	Malosa (MJ)	mal
Chipoka	chip	Bua	bu	Malosa(KP)	msa
Chisemphere	chi	Ekwendeni	e	Majiga	mj
Chitala	chit	Jali	ja	Migowi	mi
		Kampepuza	kam	Mwalaphanda	mwa
		Kamwendo	ka	Namadzi	ndzi
		Lirangwe	lir	Namitambo	nam
		Linthipe	lin	Namitete	na
		Lizulu	liz.	Nathenje	nj
		Loudon	lo	Nchalo	nch
		Lumbadzi	lu	Ntaka Taka	nta
				Ntondwe	nt
				Pumula	pu
				Ruo	ru
				Sandama	sa
				Songani	so
				Tembwe	tem
				Tete	te
				Tuchila	tu
				Ulongwe	ul

MZUZU

1	-	-

LILONGWE

| 1 | 1 | 1 |
1	1	1

ZOMBA

1	-	1

BLANTYRE

2	2	2	Branches
3	-	1	Sub-branches and static agencies
2	-	-	Mobile agencies' stopping places
S	C	B	

BANKS

Branches and sub-branches and static agencies in first and second order centres as indicated

IN THIRD ORDER CENTRES
Static agencies
   S ◎ B
    C

Mobile agencies' stopping places
   S ◉ B
    C

IN FOURTH ORDER PLACES
Static agencies
   S ✳ B
    C

Mobile agencies' stopping places
   S ▲   B ▼

S Standard Bank
B Barclays Bank D·C·O
C Commercial Bank of Malawi

Miles
0 10 20 40 60 80

Kilometres
0 20 40 80 120

GMS-JEAL

115

Thyolo (*Cholo*) was one of the most dispersed settlements, in which an administrative area, including a district hospital, was located in a cul-de-sac south of the main Limbe–Luchenza road. North of a junction between this and a road leading to Chiromo a continuous line of Asian stores along the western side of the road faced a tea estate on the eastern side.

Ncheu grew as both a trading centre for a relatively densely populated area on the main Blantyre and Zomba to Lilongwe road, and the centre providing administrative and social services for the same sub-region. Commercial establishments lay along each side of the main road. To the north-west of the district council food market was the predominantly Asian trading centre, with 26 retail stores, of which 6 were closed and 2 under construction, 4 wholesale establishments, a bank agency, three petrol stations, a number of detached residences and a mosque. To the south-east of the market were several groceries, bars and canteens, a National Wholesale Company depot, a watch repairer, post office, 6 Asian stores, two petrol stations, a football field and community hall and district council low income rest house. Except for the Ministry of Works depot and a tourist rest house on the main road, the central government administrative and social services were located farther to the south-east along a secondary road.

Nkhata Bay was built around a double inlet which provided the only natural harbour along the western coast of Lake Malawi. On the deeper North Bay were located a wharf, jetty and warehouse, and on the small peninsula between the two inlets, the site of early administrative offices, a petroleum depot. Behind the beaches were located a fisheries department research station and Ministry of Agriculture office, warehouses and depots of the Ministry of Works, Farmers' Marketing Board, and road transport and trading companies, and petrol stations. On a small, flat site inland a market occupied part of an open space whose western side was occupied by a Mandala and Asian stores and a post office, and on the northern side by African stores, canteens and bars, adjacent to which were a district council rest house and bus depot. On the slopes around the bay were located a district hospital to the north, administrative offices and a tourist rest house to the west, together with a prison and police barracks, and housing for administrative and police officials to the south.

Chitipa constituted the district administrative centre most distant from Blantyre, and had no Asian trading stores. Administrative functions were concentrated between the airstrip and the main road leading to Zambia and Tanzania, the proximity of whose frontiers made necessary immigration and customs offices, a tourist rest house and petrol station on the western edge of the settlement, together with a Malawi Young Pioneers' base. A district hospital, district council social centre, football field and community development office separated the administrative area from the market, bus stop, maize mill, Kandodo store and the groceries, canteens and shoe repairers at the eastern edge of the settlement. A second, smaller, grouping of groceries, a low income rest house and some housing for secondary school students were located to the north-east, adjacent to a full primary school, district education office, government day secondary school, correspondence college, Roman Catholic church and Farmers' Marketing Board depot.

Mangoche (*Fort Johnston*) was one of the largest district administrative centres, established in a partially-developed grid-iron plan on a site opposite to the earlier military stockade and fort, which was on the east bank of the Shire River. Adjacent to the ferry landing a number of blocks were occupied by administrative and social activities, the area involved attesting to the importance of these functions. Two blocks on the northern side of the main street were occupied by the District Commissioner's, magistrate's and labour offices. The next two blocks inland were occupied to the north by the police station and a bank agency and were backed by residences of senior staff. Those to the south were occupied by the post office and Gymkhana Club and by the Farmers' Marketing Board depot and a second bank agency. South of these were a brick works, and three Ministry of Public Works depots, that adjacent to the Shire being its principal marine depot, and farther south was the district hospital. West of these blocks were located Roman Catholic and Anglican churches, a full primary school, day secondary school and football field. At the junction of the main street with the Monkey Bay–Zomba road were two garages and petrol stations, a tourist restaurant, a number of bars and canteens and groceries, together with a meteorological station and Church of Central Africa Presbyterian church. To the north of the administrative area one block contained the district council and Malawi Congress Party office, and a prison, north of which two further blocks were occupied by 33 Asian stores, a wholesaler, and three petrol stations. This was one of the few towns in Malawi where the banks were separated from the Asian commercial centre. Adjacent to the west was the Electricity Supply Company of Malawi's generator, a water tower, and a European wholesale company's depot. Police lines separated this area from the district council permanent market, bus depot, canteens and radio and bicycle repairers.

Karonga was constructed around the small airstrip, originally built to the south of the district administrative offices and residences which overlooked the beach. A tourist rest house and a district hospital were added subsequently to complete the northern side of the airstrip. To the east, between airstrip and beach, were located separately a Kandodo store and several Asian stores, a district council food market and adjacent groceries, bars and craftsmen. A Ministry of Public Works depot and a police and immigration station and housing occupied the southern edge of the airstrip.

Nkhota Kota had been the centre of an 'East Coast' slave trader and had attracted a considerable population before the colonial period, and subsequently became a mission and district administrative centre. Many of the modern functions were embedded within a matrix of traditional villages. Port installations consisted of older and more recent jetties on a beach protected by a sand spit, and near to the jetties were located a rice mill and tourist rest house. On the road leading from the jetty were located a Farmers' Marketing Board depot, two maize mills, a petrol station, two Kandodo stores, 11 groceries and bars, and the district council food market. An Anglican mission comprising convent, maternity hospital, primary school and offices separated this commercial area from the Asian trading area to the south, which consisted of 10 retail and three wholesale stores, and, farther south, a mosque. To the south of the Asian trading area was the district council office, rest house, and prison. Adjacent to the mission was the Malawi Congress Party office and two groceries. Between the mission and the western edge of the settlement, bounded by an airstrip, was the central government's administrative area, post office, a district hospital, day secondary school, while the police station and housing lay to the south. At the western road junction were grouped petrol stations, Farmers' Marketing Board and Ministry of Public Works depots, Baptist church, groceries and a shoe shop.

MICHAEL STUBBS

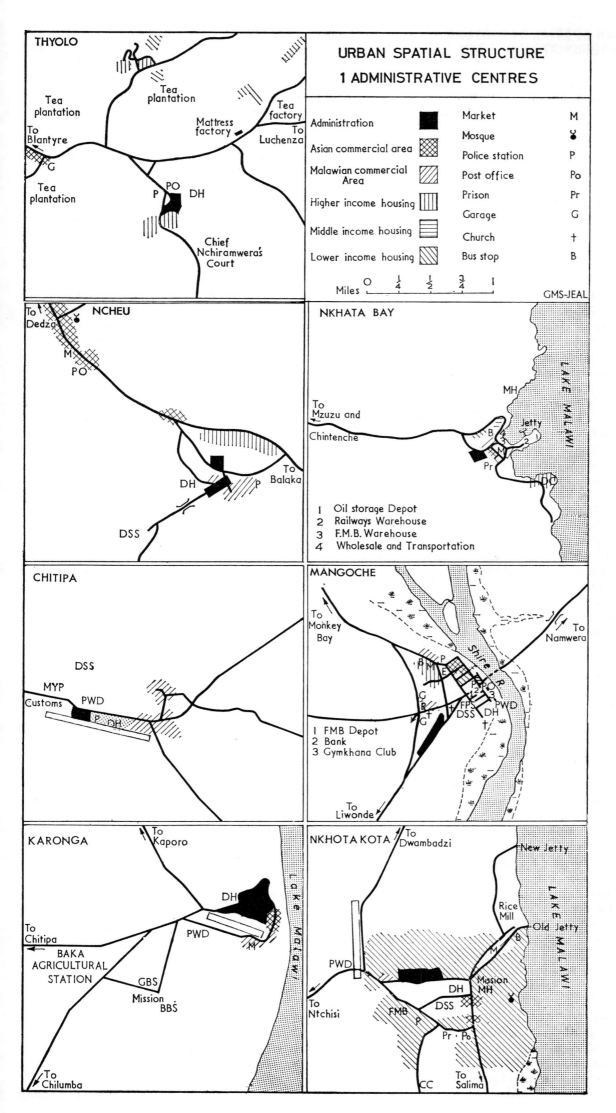

THYOLO

Tea plantation
Tea plantation
Tea plantation

Tea factory
Tea factory

Mattress factory

To Blantyre
G
To Luchenza

P PO DH

Chief Nchiramwera's Court

URBAN SPATIAL STRUCTURE

1 ADMINISTRATIVE CENTRES

Administration	Market	M
Asian commercial area	Mosque	☿
Malawian commercial Area	Police station	P
Higher income housing	Post office	Po
Middle income housing	Prison	Pr
Lower income housing	Garage	G
	Church	+
	Bus stop	B

Miles 0 ¼ ½ ¾ 1

GMS-JEAL

NCHEU

To Dedza
M
PO

DH P
To Balaka
DSS

NKHATA BAY

LAKE MALAWI

MH

To Mzuzu and Chintenche

B
Jetty
2
M
Pr
+ PO

1 Oil storage Depot
2 Railways Warehouse
3 F.M.B. Warehouse
4 Wholesale and Transportation

CHITIPA

DSS
MYP
Customs PWD
P DH

MANGOCHE

To Monkey Bay

To Namwera

Shire R.

P
M
P PO
G R
G R PWD
+ FPS
+ DSS DH
G +

1 FMB Depot
2 Bank
3 Gymkhana Club

To Liwonde

KARONGA

To Kaporo

DH

To Chitipa
PWD
M
BAKA AGRICULTURAL STATION
GBS
Mission
BBS

To Chilumba

LAKE MALAWI

NKHOTA KOTA

To Dwambadzi

New Jetty

LAKE MALAWI

Rice Mill

Old Jetty
B

PWD
M
DH
Mission MH
To Ntchisi
FMB
DSS
P
Pr · Po
CC
To Salima

51 URBAN SPATIAL STRUCTURE 2: NON-ADMINISTRATIVE CENTRES

Mponela, situated halfway along the main Lilongwe–Kasungu road, has grown to equal Dowa, the district administrative centre, in function. Most buildings line the main road, and consisted of several clearly defined functional groups. To the south, on both sides of the road, a Kandodo store, 17 Asian retail stores, and one Asian wholesaler, Dowa Co-operative Society's store, stopping places for Barclays and Standard Bank mobile agencies, three petrol stations, a mosque and primary school constituted the main business area. To the north, and on the eastern side of the main road, were grouped six groceries, eight bars and canteens, a Malawi Congress Party local headquarters, a National Wholesale Company depot, an Adventist church and an open market containing a butchery but without permanent buildings. This latter was located away from the main road. Beside the Kasungu River was a cattle market, Veterinary Department office and dip tank. On the western side of the main road was a district council area containing a rest house, social centre, women's vocational training centre, and football ground. Adjacent was the post office, police station, area agricultural supervisor's office and rural training centre, and the Farmers' Marketing Board depot. On the edge of the town to the north were located a Church of Central Africa Presbyterian church and primary school, and to the south Church of Christ and Adventist churches and a recently constructed day secondary school.

Ntaja grew within the last decade to form the largest central place in the moderately densely populated Kawinga area which formed part of the eastern periphery of the Southern Region. At the junction of the Zomba–Namwera road and a secondary road, the nucleus of the settlement was formed by Asian stores, of which there were thirteen in 1970, one closed, and one also functioning as a wholesale depot. A mosque, established at the road junction, served not only the urban Asian population, but also the Moslem Ayao villagers. Opposite the Asian stores were the district council permanent market with associated maize mill and butchery, and a post office. To this nucleus have been added a Farmers' Marketing Board market, the Area agricultural supervisor's office and rural farmer's training centre, a full primary school and Church of Central African Presbyterian church, a local court's office, a police station, a district council social centre and a Ministry of Works depot.

Balaka grew at the junction of the Zomba–Lilongwe road with the Blantyre–Salima railway, and with a secondary road to Ulongwe and Fort Johnston. East of the railway, 18 Asian retail stores, two wholesalers and a Standard Bank static agency lined the junction of the two roads. On the south side of the main road the district council permanent market, which included a butchery and rest house, formed a square surrounded on three sides by 16 groceries, bars and canteens. A police station, rural hospital and Assistant District Commissioner's Office represented administrative and social functions, not yet at a district level, added after the centre's commercial development. Opposite them are located day secondary and full primary schools. Along the Zomba road was located the depot of an African transportation contractor. Between the Fort Johnston road and the railway was a large Farmers' Marketing Board depot and Oilcom petrol station, while opposite was the Area Labour Office. To the west of the railway was the station and bus depot, an Asian wholesaler and National Wholesale Company depot, an Asian store and the post office. Farther westwards along the road were located petrol stations, two garages with mechanics, a rest house, social centre, football ground, three churches, and veterinary and agricultural offices.

Chiromo and *Bangula*. Chiromo developed as a rail-river transfer point after the completion of the Chiromo–Blantyre railway in 1907, and after the latter's extension across the Shire to Nsanje its development was arrested. Because the greater part of agricultural production came from the west bank, and there was no road bridge across the Shire, Bangula on the western bank of the Shire developed as a depot and trading centre. Chiromo occupied a site along the main road and between the railway and the Ruo River. It consisted of three separate areas: the first comprised Asian stores, the Lower Shire Co-operative Society store, bank mobile agency stopping places, and a petrol station. The second comprised the post office and telephone exchange, located adjacent to the railway station and the Farmers' Marketing Board depot. The third group comprised groceries, a carpenter and shoe, bicycle, watch and radio repairers around a district council food market and a bus depot. Separated from this area by a brick works was the police station and rural hospital, nearest to the road ferry connecting to Bangula. Bangula included a large Farmers' Marketing Board depot and cotton ginnery, an oil depot, an electricity generator near to the railway station; a group of five Asian stores and a maize mill, grocery and bar along the Ngabu road; and a district council food market and maize mill, groceries, canteens, bars, a private low-income rest house, a carpenter and watch and shoe repairers and a bus depot around the junction of the Chiromo, Nsanje and Ngabu roads. The Malawi Broadcasting Corporation's Lower Shire transmitter was also located here.

Lizulu was representative not only of many small trading centres without administrative and social services, but also in particular of several centres on the main Lilongwe–Zomba road which, between Dedza and Ncheu, runs within a few feet of the Moçambique boundary. Malawian and Moçambican buildings face each other across this road. In Lizulu a district council market, a grocery, canteen and carpenter's shop were complemented by five Asian stores, one recently closed, while on the Moçambiquian side were located a bar and four Portuguese stores, one then under construction.

Monkey Bay, located on the only natural harbour on the southern coast of Lake Malawi, developed as the depot and terminal of the lake services. The Malawi Railways' depot, which includes an electricity generator, floating dock, jetty and training school, a tourist hotel, and a Fisheries Research Institute, occupied the southern coast of the small bay, on the western hilly slopes of which were the residences of the lake service's higher income staff. A Kandodo store, Anglican church, government dispensary and maternity clinic, post office and police station were located south of these buildings, and an airstrip to the south-east. Along the road leading southwards to Mangoche were located a district council rest house, four Asian stores and a mosque, a district council market without permanent buildings, a maize mill, carpenters and bicycle repairers, groceries and canteens, and a Roman Catholic church.

Luchenza performs transhipment functions between the main Blantyre–Quelimane road and the Blantyre–Beira railway, serving neighbouring parts of Moçambique as well as the Malawian tea producing districts of Thyolo and Mulanje. Accordingly warehousing and transportation activities are prominent. Although not an administrative centre, Luchenza performs central place functions for a densely populated sub-region, and the original Indian stores are being supplemented rapidly by African entrepreneurs in retail and service activities. Most probably the centre will attract further service and manufacturing activities, and will further improve its regional and local transportation nodality.

MICHAEL STUBBS

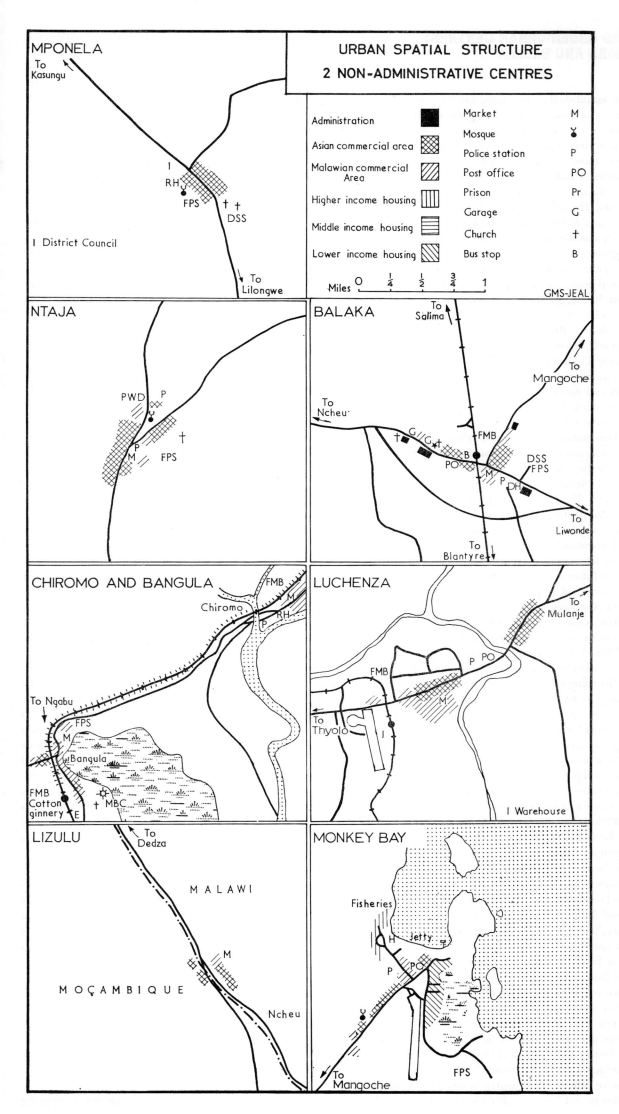

MPONELA

To Kasungu

RH
FPS
† †
DSS

l District Council

To Lilongwe

URBAN SPATIAL STRUCTURE
2 NON-ADMINISTRATIVE CENTRES

Administration	■	Market	M
Asian commercial area	▨	Mosque	☾
Malawian commercial Area	▨	Police station	P
Higher income housing	▥	Post office	PO
Middle income housing	▤	Prison	Pr
Lower income housing	▨	Garage	G
		Church	†
		Bus stop	B

Miles 0 ¼ ½ ¾ 1

GMS-JEAL

NTAJA

PWD P
P
M FPS
†

BALAKA

To Salima

To Mangoche

To Ncheu

G G † FMB
† ■
B
PO DSS FPS
M P DH
To Liwonde

To Blantyre

CHIROMO AND BANGULA

FMB
M
Chiromo RH
P

To Ngabu
FPS
M
Bangula
FMB
Cotton
ginnery
† MBC

LUCHENZA

To Mulanje

P PO

FMB

M

To Thyolo
l

l Warehouse

LIZULU

To Dedza

M A L A W I

M

M O Ç A M B I Q U E

Ncheu

MONKEY BAY

Fisheries

Jetty
H
P PO

☾

FPS

To Mangoche

119

52 THIRD ORDER URBAN CENTRES: MZIMBA AND SALIMA

Mzimba was established as an administrative centre for the area within the jurisdiction of the Angoni chiefs. Although later the seat of the Northern Provincial Commissioner it has declined in importance during the last twenty years. In 1950 Rumpi (now Rumphi) District was detached from northern Mzimba and later the provincial administration moved to Mzuzu accompanied by several commercial establishments. The District Council is located at the head-quarters of Chief M'mbelwa at Edingeni. Rural population declined with a movement towards more fertile soils to the west. The government administrative area is centred on the District Commissioner's offices and consists of a magistrate's and traditional courts, a prison, police station and lines, an official guest house, football field and golf course. Subsequent additions were District Labour and Education Offices, a Malawi Broadcasting Corporation transmitter (MBC), and offices for Air Malawi, adjacent to the airstrip, and the Farmers' Marketing Board. Close to, but separate from the administrative area, is the commercial centre. Asian stores and residential compounds and a mosque and two bank agencies are separated by the District Council permanent market (M) from African-owned and managed groceries, bars and canteens. Near to the market is a maize mill (m), bus depot and garage, and the District Council's public rest house. Between this part of the commercial centre and the Mzimba River is a high density housing area and a cemetery. The District Hospital and clinic lie within the commercial centre, adjacent to the bus depot and market. This is a normal locational relationship, partly because relatives of in-patients normally live in a special area and prepare food for them, and therefore prefer proximity to the market and stores, and partly because the hospital, being a central government responsibility, was established near to the District Commissioner's offices. Farthest from the administrative centre, overlooking the junction of the Kavikura Stream with the Mzimba River, is the Church of Central Africa Presbyterian church and full primary school (FP), on the road to which has been built a government secondary boarding school (DS). Other church and education buildings lie to the north of the Mzimba River on the main road to Mzuzu. At the junction of the main road and the Edingeni road which leads through the town a transport-oriented group has developed, with a garage and petrol station (P), a second tourist guest house, the telephone exchange (t) and post office, and veterinary, agriculture and forestry department offices. The Road Motor Services depot (RMS) is located on the main road to Kasungu and Lilongwe, and the Witwatersrand Native Labour Association offices and depot lie farther from the centre of the town.

Salima originated later than most principal urban centres in Malawi, becoming the railhead for the Beira–Blantyre–central Malawi line upon its completion from Blantyre in 1935. This line had been intended originally to continue to a railhead and lake port site immediately to the north at Domira Bay, but this site was flooded by a rise in the level of Lake Malawi. The present site was chosen as having adequate water from the Linthipe River and sufficiently non-marshy flat land for the railway facilities.

The town centre was planned and laid out in a grid-iron pattern west of the railway tracks and installations. After Independence the lakeshore section of the former Dowa District was detached to form Salima District, with the centre of district administration in the town. Subsequently the town achieved the legal status of 'township' with its own administrative offices. The greatly increased movement of commodities to and from Zambia after the Rhodesian Uni-

lateral Declaration of Independence, and the continued development of the Central Region, particularly Lilongwe, stimulated an expansion of the terminal facilities. The Zambian Government constructed a warehouse for its copper exports, and the petroleum companies expanded their depots. A West German Technical Assistance team is currently directing an intensive integrated agricultural development scheme in Salima District and a permanent administration building has recently been completed in Salima. Increased primary production will possibly bring about the development of processing industries. To the east the lakeshore coast is being developed as a tourist centre which is likely to expand considerably when Lilongwe becomes the national capital.

Zambia Government (2), Farmers' Marketing Board (12, 13, 14, 15), Road Motor Services (6) and Malawi Railways warehouses (4), the depots of five oil companies (7, 8, 10, 11, 16) and the Customs offices (5) are located adjacent to the railway sidings, in which there is a small power station. Access at the northern end is available to the cattle-holding area at Kuti, and the associated Veterinary Department centre (17) and for coal loading (1). Houses for both lower and higher income personnel of these concerns are all located adjacent to the respective functional areas. A double lane avenue leading west from the station (3) separates the central government, district and town administrative buildings to the north from the Asian commercial centre, also separated by a tree-covered open space. The commercial centre is undergoing extensive improvement and expansion, with several new and reconstructed stores. Asian traders still live within their store compounds or in adjacent houses, and the mosque (19) is located centrally. Although there is open land adjacent to the Asian commercial centre, the district council market (M), recently reconstructed, is located on the opposite side of the Lilongwe main road. Shoe and cycle repairers, barbers, and a small tannery are adjacent. Beyond the market is the Malimba location with several groceries and a bar. A community centre (20) football ground, and housing for government workers and police, line the western side of the Lilongwe road, adjacent to the central areas. On the periphery a Roman Catholic school and church, a more recent government day secondary school (DS) with teacher housing, and a seventh Day Adventist Mission are located within the township boundary. Close to the rail/road crossing on the through road to the lakeshore hotels and weekend bungalows, and close to the petroleum companies depots are petrol stations and a garage. A District Council rest house (18) is located opposite the small United Transport Company's bus terminal (9). The Witwatersrand Native Labour Association's depot and housing is located close to the market. An airstrip with regular weekly flights lies some 8 miles to the east. Within the town the one-storey buildings are spaced at a very low density, there is considerable unused land, and large areas are used for agriculture on the periphery. Available land within the railways area is still sufficient for expansion of terminal facilities and the possible introduction of light industries. Almost all streets are tree-lined and some are bitumen-surfaced. Whereas police and other government housing is of a high standard, the unplanned Malimba suburb has buildings of much lower quality.

Key to map notation

1 Government offices	6 Villages
2 Asian commercial area	7 Low income housing
3 African commercial area	8 Rail terminal area
4 High income residences	9 District hospital
5 Police and government 'lines'	

MICHAEL STUBBS

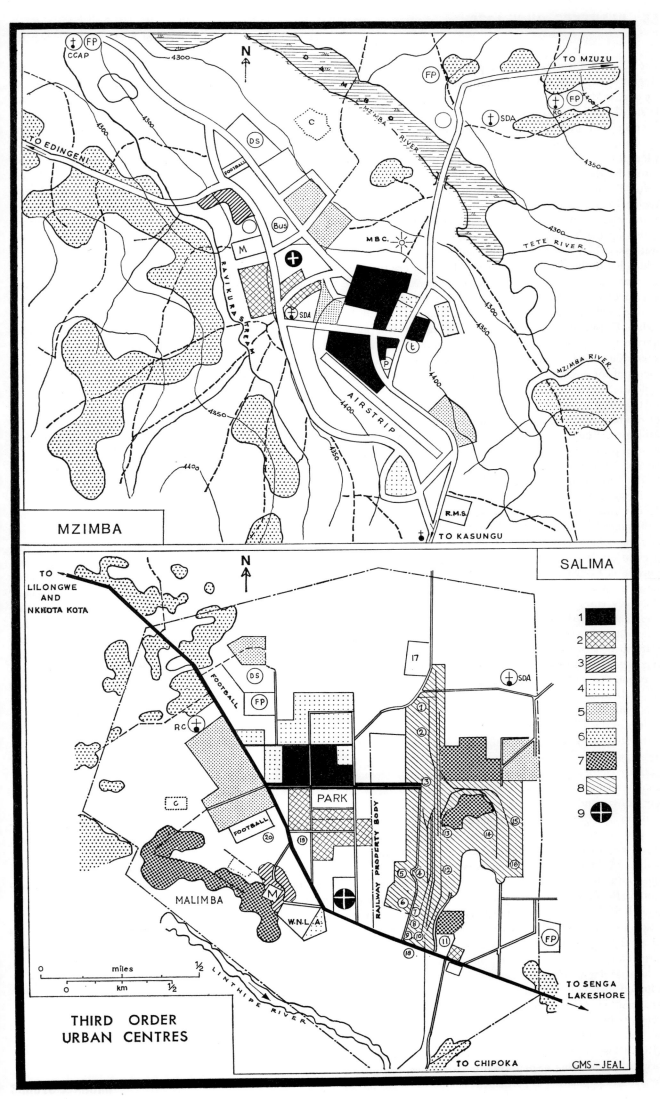

MZIMBA

SALIMA

1
2
3
4
5
6
7
8
9

TO MZUZU

TO EDINGENI

CCAP
FP
DS
FOOTBALL
Bus
M
SDA
MBC
RAVIKURA STREAM
P
AIR STRIP
R.M.S.
TO KASUNGU

MZIMBA RIVER
TETE RIVER
SDA
RC
FP
FP

TO LILONGWE AND NKHOTA KOTA

FOOTBALL
DS
FP
RC
C
FOOTBALL
M
MALIMBA
W.N.L.A.
PARK
RAILWAY PROPERTY BODY
SDA
17

TO CHIPOKA

TO SENGA LAKESHORE

FP

LINTHIPE RIVER

miles   ½
km   ½

THIRD ORDER
URBAN CENTRES

GMS–JEAL

The City of Blantyre, with a population of 109 000 in August 1966, and a subsequent estimated annual increase of 15 000, is Malawi's primate city, containing almost all professional, commercial and social services and most manufacturing and processing establishments.

The city originated with the establishment of the Free Church of Scotland's Blantyre Mission (BM) in 1876, followed by the African Lakes Company depot (ALC), individual European traders and a British consul. Choice of the regional site was decided partly by the need to leave the Shire River route at Chikwawa and the opportunity of access up the Thyolo Escarpment afforded by a secondary watershed between the Likabula and Mwampanzi Rivers, which led to the site area. Additional factors were the need to establish a base in the healthier conditions of the Shire Highlands rather than in the Rift Valley floor, the need to remain as close as possible to river communication with the Indian Ocean after the failure of the earlier and more northerly Magomero Mission, and the favourable attitude of Chief Kapeni whose area included the site. The initial elements of the town each occupied a relatively easily defensible site, above the Mudi River, and protected to the north by the steep watershed boundary of the Likabula. The ring of residual hills – Michiru, Nyambadwe, Ndirande, Mzedi, Mpingwe, Bangwe and Soche – afforded opportunities for refuge, previously utilized by the resident population in the face of Ayao and Angoni raids.

The first Asian traders established their stores during the mid-1890s. A higher income residential area developed in Mount Pleasant, along the Chikwawa Road, and a club and golf course were built in the Mudi River valley between this and the commercial centre. Much of the remainder of the present city's area either remained as village land, or was purchased from Chiefs Kapeni and Matope and developed into European estates, which first grew coffee, and later, in the early years of the present century, tobacco. Between 1904 and 1907 the railway from Chiromo was constructed following the valley of the Luchenza River, crossing the watershed between this and the Mudi River and following the latter to Blantyre, where a small station was built between the commercial centre and the steep slopes of the Likabula watershed. As this site was too constricted a depot was built in a former estate in the Limbe area, 8 km. (5 miles) to the east. The Imperial Tobacco Company became interested in the tobacco produced in local estates, and in 1908 purchased a second estate and built their grading and packing factory (ITG) adjacent to the railway's depot. A commercial centre rapidly developed to the west, between the railway and Limbe River, and housing for the railway company's higher and middle income workers was constructed to the east. Very considerable amounts of timber were required for packing purposes, and the Imperial Tobacco Company planted large areas in *Eucalyptus saligna* to the south along the Thyolo Road, and to the north along Zomba Road. Within these plantations it established compounds for lower income and seasonal workers which in the 1950s were reconstructed to form a model workers' suburb of a very high standard. The railway company established large compounds for its lower paid workers on the further side of Mpingwe Hill. Around Limbe station, warehouses, tobacco auction floors, and small factories developed, many financed by Asian businessmen who had commenced as retailers in the Limbe and Blantyre commercial areas. The Roman Catholic cathedral complex was added to the north (RC). Closer to Blantyre, the Ndirande low-income suburb, originally consisting of nine traditional villages, had grown in size and population as permanent labour was attracted to the town. Other similar villages occupied the areas between Blantyre and Limbe and north of Soche Hill. During the period of Malawi's incorporation within the Federation of Rhodesia and Nyasaland, considerable extensions in the built-up area and modifications in the spatial structure occurred. Sunnyside was established as a high income government residential area. Beside the early electricity generating station (E) other factories and oil depots were built. Along the Mudi River and its tributaries first a series of small dams, the Hynde Dams, was constructed, and finally the larger Coronation Dam. The southern pediment of Ndirande Mountain between Ndirande and Matenje suburbs was cleared of existing villages and designated a protected water catchment, as was an area immediately north of Soche Hill. Between Blantyre and Limbe, particularly in the Chichiri area, other villages and suburbs were cleared, and the Queen Elizabeth Central Hospital, a secondary and primary school and other public buildings were constructed. In the Newlands and Namiwawa areas and through the area then within municipal limits, all villages and African suburbs were cleared. The residents had to move beyond the boundary, and concentrated in densely built-up areas wherever a convenient access road existed, thus originating the present low and lower middle income suburbs of Chilomoni, Zingwangwa, Bangwe and Matenje. In Soche housing was constructed for middle income residents. Since Independence and an extension of the city boundaries, there has been considerable building activity, with the construction of a new high income suburb in Namiwawa, extension of the government suburbs of Sunnyside and Nyambadwe, of middle and lower middle income housing in the Soche and Kanjedza areas, and of lower income 'site and service' housing in the Chimwankhunda and Chilobwe areas. The light and heavy industrial estates have been almost filled. Within the Blantyre, but not the Limbe, commercial area, new multi-storey office buildings have appeared, and considerable improvement in the urban physical equipment has been achieved. As a key component in the country's spatial development considerable further investment in Blantyre is planned. The provision of low income houses, improvement of suburban service centres and the mass transit system, and the extension of water, electricity and sewerage supplies remain major problems. The duality of the urban structure, with centres in both Blantyre and Limbe, which has added to the cost of providing services, the constricting circle of steep residual hills, and the large forest plantations all make difficult the achievement of an efficient urban spatial system.

Key to map notation

1	High income housing	14	Religious activities
2	Middle income housing	15	Heavy industry
3	High and middle income flats	16	Light industry, construction and road transport
4	Institutional 'lines'	17	Railways
5	Imperial Tobacco Group model village	18	Utilities
6	Low and lower middle income 'site and service' and squatter housing	19	Reservoir catchment protected forest
7	Unplanned suburbs	20	Forest reserve
8	Villages	21	Imperial Tobacco Group *Eucalyptus saligna* plantations
9	Commercial areas	22	Unforested reservoir catchment protected area
10	Government offices		
11	Education activities	23	Reservoirs
12	Health activities	24	Steep slopes
13	Recreation activities		

MICHAEL STUBBS

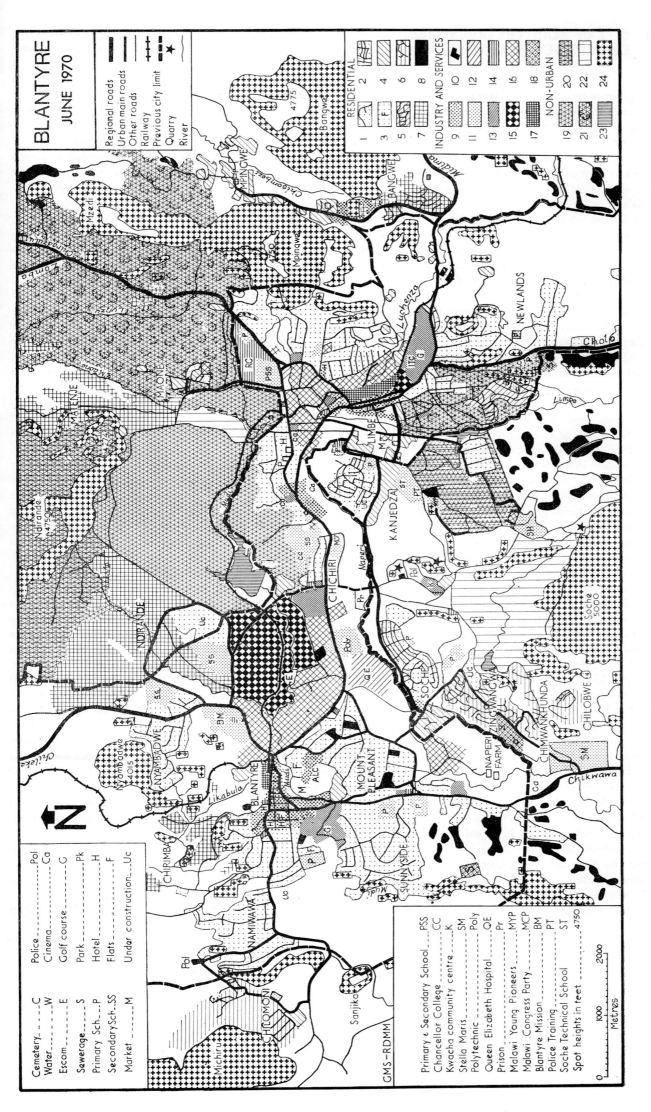

BLANTYRE
JUNE 1970

Regional roads
Urban main roads
Other roads
Railway
Previous city limit
Quarry
★ River

RESIDENTIAL
1 2
3 4
5 6
7 8

INDUSTRY AND SERVICES
9 10
11 12
13 14
15 16
17 18

NON-URBAN
19 20
21 22
23 24

Cemetery — C   Police — Pol
Water — W   Cinema — Ca
Escom — E   Golf course — G
Sewerage — S   Park — Pk
Primary Sch. — P   Hotel — H
Secondary Sch. — SS   Flats — F
Market — M   Under construction — Uc

Primary & Secondary School — PSS
Chancellor College — CC
Kwacha community centre — K
Stella Maris — SM
Polytechnic — Poly
Queen Elizabeth Hospital — QE
Prison — Pr
Malawi Young Pioneers — MYP
Malawi Congress Party — MCP
Blantyre Mission — BM
Police Training — PT
Soche Technical School — ST
Spot heights in feet — 4750

0   1000   2000
Metres

123

54 CITY OF BLANTYRE INDUSTRIAL ENTERPRISES, JUNE 1970

A large proportion of the primary production entering the commercial economy is processed or utilized in manufacturing in the Blantyre area, either for export by rail to Beira, or for use within Blantyre, or for redistribution to the rural areas. Most imported commodities are transported to Blantyre for break-of-bulk or re-assembly. Those not consumed in Blantyre are then reshipped to other parts of Malawi.

By far the greatest share of both processing and manufacturing in Malawi is concentrated within the City of Blantyre. The following factors appeared to have been largely responsible for this: the early establishment of commerce and processing because of Blantyre's position, until 1935, as the railhead and centre of the major commercial agricultural area in the country: the location of the major maintenance base of the Blantyre–Beira railway at Limbe, in which most engineering work was done and which was largely responsible for the early training of a skilled and semi-skilled labour force; the development of hydro-electric power at Nkula Falls on the middle Shire; the provision of fully serviced industrial sites; the growing inter-dependence between industries and commercial undertakings in the city which made it difficult to establish industries outside the centre; the stimulus afforded to the smaller-scale industries by capital and managerial efforts provided by the Asian and Portuguese entrepreneurs; the attraction of shopping and entertainment facilities in Blantyre; and the large local market for consumer goods.

Industries in Blantyre which involve the processing of primary products, and hence manufacture products for both internal consumption and for export include: the grading and sorting of tobacco and the manufacture of cigarettes; the grading and sorting of groundnuts and manufacture of groundnut confectionery and of edible oils, groundnut cattle meal, and soap; the manufacture of cotton seed oil and cake; the manufacture of cotton yarn, which is then woven, bleached, dyed and finished within an integrated textile plant; maize flour; milled rice; coffee products; the processing of hides and skins and manufacture of leather goods and footwear; furniture; wooden boxes for tobacco packing; Portland cement and cement products, which include railway sleepers; bricks, tiles, crushed stones and aggregates; gem cutting and polishing; beer and gin.

Such industries require small quantities of imported materials as well as the local products, but the following industries require very considerable quantities of imported raw materials: confectionery and bakery products based upon wheat; soft drinks; cosmetics and medicines; mattresses; matches; candles; paper bags and stationery; polishes; ropes, twines, and fishing nets; hoes, ploughs and farm carts; two lorry assembly plants and a lorry body plant; batteries; bicycle parts and assembly; fencing and wiring; nails, steel doors, window frames and beds; structural steel tubes and sections; industrial and medical oxygen; refrigeration and air conditioning equipment; glass and hardware; radios and gramophones; enamelled and aluminium hardware; canvas goods and knitwear.

Permits have been granted to firms to begin production of fertilizers, paper products, piping and clothing.

Most industries in the City of Blantyre are located in either the Heavy or the Light Industrial Estates which are situated to the east of the Blantyre Central Business District. The former is crossed by the Beira–Blantyre–Salima–Nacala railway, and by the Mudi River, on which stands the Mudi Dam, the major internal source of water supply. The industrial area grew from a nucleus provided by the coal-burning electricity generating station, which was later replaced by the Nkula Falls hydro-generating station. It was first laid out during the period of the Central African Federation, after clearing the sites of the low income suburbs and scattered villages which then occupied the area. Since Independence in 1964 the City of Blantyre and the Malawi Government have further extended the industrial area and provided rail spurs, roads, electricity, water and sewerage. Only a few sites remained unoccupied. For this reason plans were prepared for the delimitation of an additional site for Blantyre's industrial development, but little land remained available within the central area of the city, and it is probable that sites farther away, most probably along the major road or rail routes from the city, will be chosen. Such decentralization of processing industries along the railway occurred at an earlier date, for Malawi Railways maintained a tobacco storage warehouse some 32 km. (20 miles) north of Blantyre at Maleule; and other tobacco-grading factories and warehouses, one used by a firm of furniture removers, were located beside the railway east of Limbe. A brick and tile factory was situated on the main road from Blantyre to Chileka Airport and Ncheu, a small complex of factories was located near the city boundary along the Zomba road, and a sawmill stood at Chigamula on the Thyolo road. The Imperial Tobacco Group maintained a grading factory within their eucalyptus plantations at Maone. The depots of construction and transportation companies and of petroleum products distributors were also located within the light industry estate, as were a few office buildings.

A number of factories and warehouses were situated in Limbe, although, as there was no industrial estate there, the distribution was rather more dispersed than was the case in the Blantyre industrial estates. Adjacent to Limbe station were a number of tobacco auction floors and warehouses together with the Imperial Tobacco Group's principal factory. Along the Limbe–Blantyre road, and between it and the Zomba road, were a number of factories, of which the largest was Lever Brothers' soap and edible oils factory, construction depots, and warehouses, between which are cinemas, social clubs, sports grounds and residences.

The completion of the Nacala rail link, and the development of Liwonde as a major processing and transportation centre, are likely to attract to the latter industries which might have otherwise been located in Blantyre.

J AMER

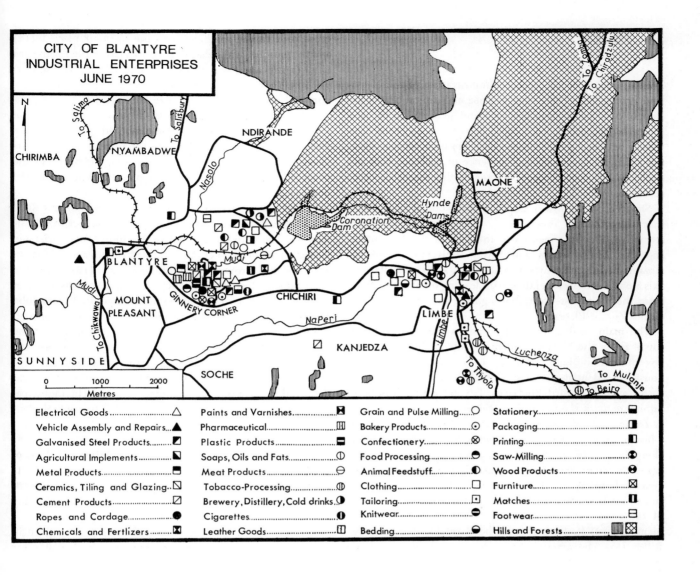

CITY OF BLANTYRE
INDUSTRIAL ENTERPRISES
JUNE 1970

CHIRIMBA

NYAMBADWE

NDIRANDE

MAONE

Hynde Dams

Coronation Dam

BLANTYRE

Mudi

MOUNT PLEASANT

GINNERY CORNER

CHICHIRI

NaPeri

LIMBE

Limbe

Luchenza

SUNNYSIDE

KANJEDZA

SOCHE

To Salima

To Salisbury

Nasolo

To Zomba

To Chiradzulu

To Chikwawa

Mudi

To Thyolo

To Mulanje

To Beira

0   1000   2000
Metres

Electrical Goods............△	Paints and Varnishes..........⊠	Grain and Pulse Milling.....○	Stationery..............⊟
Vehicle Assembly and Repairs...▲	Pharmaceutical...........⊞	Bakery Products.........⊙	Packaging.............◧
Galvanised Steel Products........◪	Plastic Products............⊟	Confectionery..........⊗	Printing...............◨
Agricultural Implements.........◥	Soaps, Oils and Fats........◑	Food Processing.........◓	Saw-Milling...........⊛
Metal Products..............⊟	Meat Products............⊖	Animal Feedstuff.........◐	Wood Products.........⊝
Ceramics, Tiling and Glazing..◩	Tobacco-Processing........⊕	Clothing...............□	Furniture.............⊠
Cement Products...........◪	Brewery, Distillery, Cold drinks.◕	Tailoring..............⊡	Matches..............◧
Ropes and Cordage.............●	Cigarettes.................◑	Knitwear..............⊖	Footwear.............⊟
Chemicals and Fertlizers.........⊠	Leather Goods............⊞	Bedding..............⊖	Hills and Forests.............▦⊠

125

55 ZOMBA

Zomba, centre of the British administration of the Nyasaland Protectorate from 1891 to 1964 and capital city of the Republic of Malawi, will lose its premier role when the new capital is established in Lilongwe in 1975. In 1973 the University will occupy Chirunga estate (1) on a terrace above the Likangala River, and the presence of academic staff and students will change the character of this essentially civil service town.

Situated on the lower slopes of the wooded talus slopes that skirt Zomba escarpment, the town is scenically attractive. Deep ravines score the face of the 'mountain' and the sloping spurs and flatter shelves between the streams divide the town into sections, each with its own axis along a steeply ascending road leading off at right angles from the main east–west thoroughfare and main road that circles Zomba Plateau.

The main road conveniently divides the 'Government' town from the Asian residential and trading area (2), government housing for Africans (3) and other high density housing residential quarters. The lower town is laid out on flatter ground towards the river, beyond which clusters of hutments mark the peri-urban fringe (4).

Zomba, 64 km. (40 miles) north of Blantyre is entered by a bridge over the perennial Likangala River which, running along the foot of the escarpment, gives a convenient boundary to the municipal area. Immediately across the bridge the general hospital (5) lies to the right, the state prison (6) and the only mental hospital (7) in the country, to the left of the road. A road branching at the clock tower war-memorial (8) leads to the Cobbe Barracks of the Malawi Rifles (9). The army *boma* or fort guards the southerly approach to the town and is sited on a shelf strategically placed astride the early route down the rift valley escarpment to the Shire River landing stage used in the pioneer period of water transport.

Police and Security Headquarters (10) and training establishment guard the approaches to the town from the east and south-east. While there is no clearly demarcated city centre, the focus may be said to be the crossroads where the Town Council and District Offices along with the Provincial Commissioners Court (11) front the main road opposite the commercial area of banks and main departmental stores. The cross road to the south leads to the open-air market (12) and the mosque, while that to the north passes the Gymkhana Club (1925) and leads into the gardens of State House (13) 1006 m. (3300 ft), the residence of thirteen former Governors and now the seat of the President of the Republic.

Below and to the east of State House lie the houses of senior civil servants set in large timbered gardens. Above State House the road continues to the plateau where forests of exotic and indigenous trees, cascading streams and the town reservoir offer amenities exploited by a residential hotel (14).

From the entrance to State House, Commissioner's Road branches eastwards along the contour to connect the President's Lodge with the Legislative Assembly, Secretariat and Government Press (15). Government offices and ministries are clustered around the Old Residency (16) (now the Government Rest House) which was built by Consul Hawes in 1886, on 40 ha. (100 acres) of land acquired from John Buchanan, horticulturist to the Scottish Mission in Blantyre. Below the Old Residency land could be irrigated from the Mulunguzi stream, and this land once used for crops was later developed into a Botanical Garden and Park.

In 1900, Zomba was proclaimed a township which was dissolved in 1932 but reconstituted in 1934. The municipal area has been recently enlarged the better to control planning within the township area.

The population in 1966 was 19 616 of whom 18 013 were Africans, 939 Europeans and 664 Asians and those of mixed race. The smallness of the town is a reflection on the restricted opportunities for employment outside government service, the army and the police and the one clothing factory (60 persons).

An estimate of growth by natural increase was given in May 1971 as 4%; and while no figures were available for growth by immigration, it is believed that such growth within the township is negligible, since no municipal housing has been added since 1966.

Influx associated with urban drift is likely therefore to be confined to the peri-urban fringe where small enterprises and market gardeners seek support from the salaried classes. Nevertheless pressure of population is mounting annually in Zomba district where, despite much wasteland, the overall density in 1966 was 110 persons per sq. km. (284 persons per sq. mile).

SWANZIE AGNEW

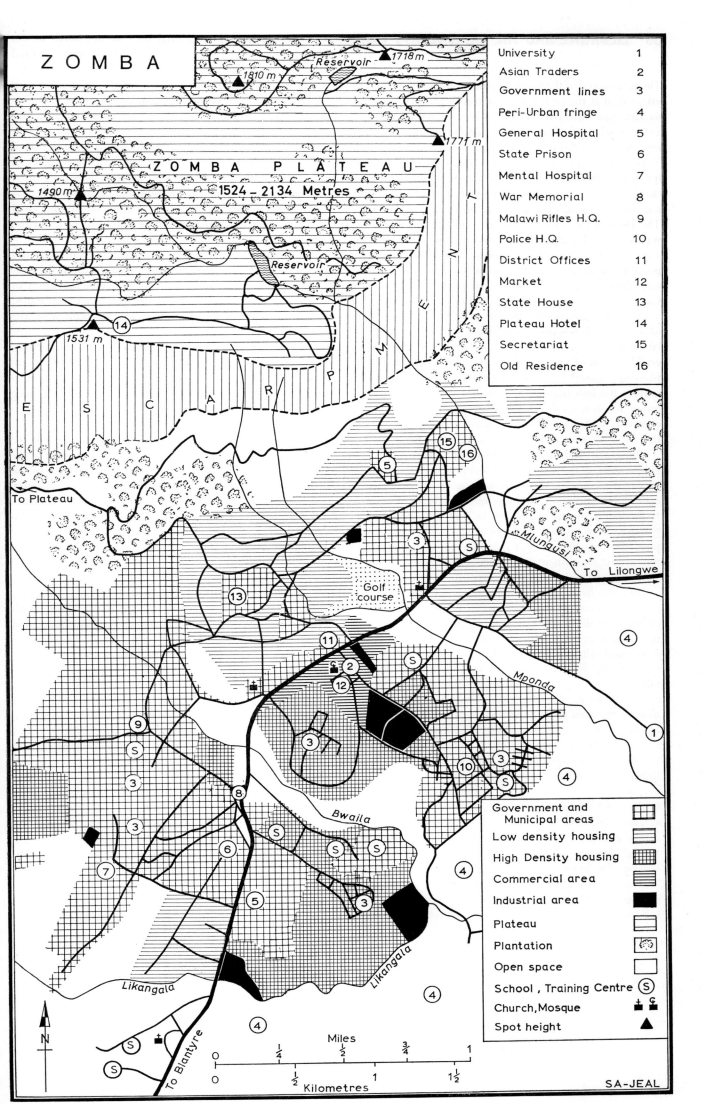

ZOMBA

University	1
Asian Traders	2
Government lines	3
Peri-Urban fringe	4
General Hospital	5
State Prison	6
Mental Hospital	7
War Memorial	8
Malawi Rifles H.Q.	9
Police H.Q.	10
District Offices	11
Market	12
State House	13
Plateau Hotel	14
Secretariat	15
Old Residence	16

Government and Municipal areas
Low density housing
High Density housing
Commercial area
Industrial area
Plateau
Plantation
Open space
School, Training Centre
Church, Mosque
Spot height

Miles
0   ¼   ½   ¾   1
0   ½   1   1½
Kilometres

SA-JEAL

56 LILONGWE AND THE CAPITAL CITY PLAN

The first capital of the former Protectorate of Nyasaland was established at the end of the nineteenth century at Zomba, 64 km. (40 miles) from the main commercial centre of Blantyre where the majority of business interests developed, especially after the railway opened in 1907.

The isolation of Zomba and its restricted site raised frequent discussion on the subject of a move of the capital to Blantyre and in 1946, after a cyclone had devastated Zomba, a commission was set up to advise on a move of the capital. The issue of the Central African Federation shortly afterwards caused the report to be shelved and it was not until 1964 that the then Prime Minister, Dr H K Banda, proposed to parliament that the capital should move to Lilongwe. This was finally substantiated by the passing of the Capital City Development Corporation Act in 1968.

Lilongwe was chosen as the site of the new capital because of its central position in Malawi situated between the Northern and Southern Provinces. It was considered that the establishment of a new capital city at this point, along with planned industrial and commercial centres, would help correct the imbalance in economic development which has arisen for historical reasons whereby the southern areas centred on Blantyre and Zomba are more developed than the two provinces to the north of the Shire River valley.

The gently undulating Lilongwe Plain, with deep ferruginous soils, is the largest and most productive agricultural area in the country. Here 404 700 ha. (1 000 000 acres) of agricultural and ranch land are presently being reorganized to increase crop and animal production. It is expected that the rise in agricultural production and the increase in urban population engendered by the capital as a new growth point will attract investment and assure an expansion within the city's commercial, business and industrial enterprises.

Lilongwe has long been the chief service and distributary centre for much of the northern part of the country. This customary role is to be enhanced by its association with the new capital and the improvements in the transport system. Lilongwe is already connected by a bitumenized road to the railhead and lake ship services at Chipoka, 97 km. (60 miles) to the east. A modern highway connects the town to the Southern Region and it is planned to extend this first class motor road to the Zambian border in the west and the frontier to the north. A route for a railway from Salima to the new capital is projected which will give direct access to the Indian Ocean port of Nacala. From Lilongwe the rail link may be eventually extended westwards to Zambia. A new airport will be sited near Lumbadzi, 20 km. (12 miles) to the north of the new capital, which will replace Chileka and receive aircraft from the major international airlines.

The area for the new capital city is 5 km. (3 miles) from the existing town, but it is not intended that there shall be separate development. The city will have four main centres. The first is the already established core of Lilongwe; the second is the Capital Hill area where the government buildings and the main shopping areas are to be sited; the third is an industrial and residential area to the north in the vicinity of Kanengo Hill; and the fourth is another industrial area in the neighbourhood of Nchesi Hill.

The plan divides the 'Designated Area' into sections each of which fulfils a particular function in relation to the needs of the city. Each section is to be served by roads which will change the existing system of communication.

Residential areas are planned according to a specified housing density; low density housing will have plots of three-quarters of an acre or more; medium density housing, half an acre and high density housing will have plots between an eighth and a quarter of an acre. 'Traditional housing' will cover the largest area which will be fully serviced, but the plot holders will build their own houses.

The existing commercial area of Lilongwe is divided into two parts by the river. and contains offices, banks, the general hospital and an hotel. These will become subsidiary to the New City Centre where, besides head offices and shops, hotels and entertainment centres will be built near the government buildings.

The plan envisages a new industrial area to the north of the new capital served by road and later by rail. Workers are to be accommodated within walking distance of the factories. The southern industrial area will be developed along similar lines as expansion takes place.

Among the 'special areas', the Master Plan provides for the Presidential residence or State House; an ornamental lake 146 ha. (360 acres); a national park surrounding the new ministry buildings; areas for the headquarters of the Police, Army and Young Pioneers; an area for cultural buildings, overlooking the lake; and an area for the stadium. There is also liberal provision in 'undetermined' areas for unforeseen needs of the future. Within the greatly enlarged municipal bounds ample room remains for controlled growth.

The present thermal electricity supply of the town is to be superseded by a 66 kV high tension line connected to the hydro-electric stations on the Shire River. This ample power supply will do much to encourage industrial enterprise. A branch line of 33 kV will transmit power from Lilongwe to Salima which will thus share the benefits accruing to the Capital City.

Water is already supplied to Lilongwe from the Lilongwe River below the Kamuzu Dam. The dam is located 24 km. (15 miles) to the west of the town where a wall across the headwater of the Lilongwe River has created a lake 18 km. (11 miles) in length. Ultimately the dam storage capacity will be raised to assure 9 million litres (2 million gallons) a day.

According to the 1966 Census figures, there were 18 256 Africans in Lilongwe town, 742 Asians and 426 Europeans. The population of the Designated Area of Lilongwe, i.e. covering the new municipal area, is now estimated at 40 000; it is expected that the population of the new city will be 125 000 in 1980 and 500 000 by the end of the century.

SWANZIE AGNEW

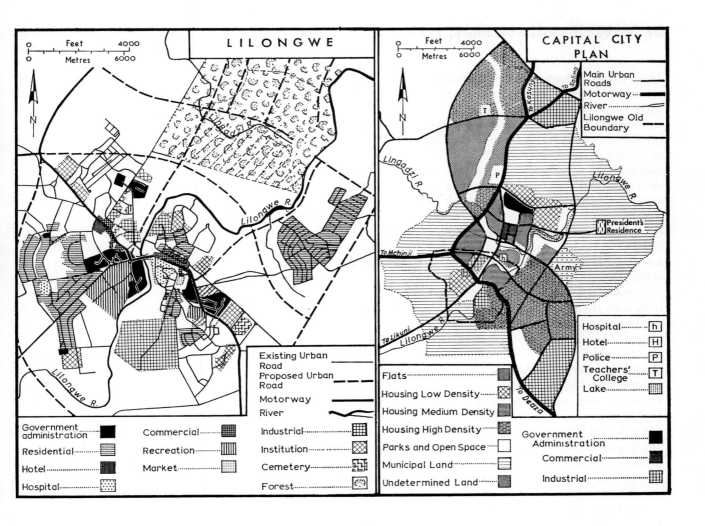

LILONGWE

Feet 4000
Metres 6000

Existing Urban
Road
Proposed Urban
Road
Motorway
River

Government
administration
Residential
Hotel
Hospital

Commercial
Recreation
Market

Industrial
Institution
Cemetery
Forest

CAPITAL CITY
PLAN

Feet 4000
Metres 6000

Main Urban
Roads
Motorway
River
Lilongwe Old
Boundary

Flats
Housing Low Density
Housing Medium Density
Housing High Density
Parks and Open Space
Municipal Land
Undetermined Land

Hospital   h
Hotel   H
Police   P
Teachers'   T
College
Lake

Government
Administration
Commercial
Industrial

President's
Residence

Army

To Salima
To Kasungu
Lingadzi R.
Lilongwe R.
To Mchinji
To Likuni
Lilongwe R.
To Dedza

57 DEVELOPMENT SUMMARY, 1970

At the time of Independence only the small proportion of the natural resources of the country located within the Shire Highlands and Lilongwe 'core' areas had been even partially developed. Their development had resulted in considerable population movements, and in the former at least had resulted in high densities and congestion without compensating improvements in techniques and income. As a complement most other areas had been deprived of their healthy active male labour force, with subsequent stultifying effects upon their development. The transportation system was inadequate in that the single external rail link, connected to an increasingly congested and costly port, Beira, and the internal system, were inadequate both with respect to the capacity of the existing network, and the fact that many areas of high potential were not served by the single axis which connected Beira with the two 'core' areas and a few minor areas of commercial production. The urban system was only partially developed, and the range of internal processing and manufacturing limited. Since Independence, considerable development has been achieved.

In the Shire Highlands 'core' area emphasis has been upon the development of manufacturing industries and the expansion of services in Blantyre itself, and this has stimulated vegetable and milk production within a radius of 24 to 32 km. (15 to 20 miles), and banana and pineapple production in the wetter and warmer areas south of the Thyolo and Mulanje tea estates. There has been considerable success through normal extension efforts in the adoption of small scale conservation methods and the application of fertilizers, but increasing population densities have made comprehensive conservation and provision of domestic water critically important needs in the area. The tea estates in the Thyolo and Mulanje areas have greatly increased their acreages and production, using irrigation during the dry season, and some form nuclei for a Smallholder Tea Authority development project which has successfully diffused tea production to adjacent peasant farmers. Increased tobacco and cotton production by peasant farmers has occurred on the eastern periphery of the most densely populated crescent, using normal extension methods and improved infrastructure. The greatest potential for future production appears to be intensive irrigated rice and vegetable production and fish-farming on alluvial and marsh soils around Lake Chilwa, together with commercial fisheries on that lake itself. The possible development of bauxite mining and processing on Mulanje Mountain will stimulate very considerable infrastructure investment and add to employment and regional incomes. Much of the growth of the Blantyre region resulted from the utilization of the hydro-electricity potential of the middle Shire area and this will be further expanded by the development of the Tedzani site, which will supply also the central and south central regions.

Because of its proximity to Blantyre, accessibility to the railway and relatively low population, the very high potential of the Lower Shire section of the Rift Valley floor in Chikwawa District, adjacent to the Shire Highlands, has been very considerably developed since Independence. This area now includes the Nchalo Sugar Estate, the Lower Shire Rainfed Cotton Project, the Kasindula Irrigated Rice and Cotton Estate, and settlement schemes of which that at Chikonje near Chiromo included both cotton and irrigated rice production under Taiwanese direction, fisheries improvement in the Elephant Marsh, and the development of the Lengwe game reserve. There has been considerable migration into the area from the higher densities of both Nsanje and the Shire Highlands. Nsanje District, which occupied the most southerly part of the Rift Valley floor within Malawi, has a much denser population and although cotton and groundnut production has increased there, it has not yet been the site of comprehensive development.

In the Central Region post-Independence emphasis has been upon the comprehensive Lilongwe Development Project, involving intensive extension efforts, rural credit, conservation works and infrastructure, and land tenure registration, all designed to secure a tenfold increase in maize production and a doubling of groundnut production. Lilongwe is to become the new national capital and its growth is expected to further stimulate agricultural development in the region. To the north, outside the zone of ferruginous soils, the Kasungu flue-cured tobacco growers scheme provides a nuclear estate system for the training of peasant farmers. A greatly improved road between the Lilongwe and Shire Highlands 'cores' has been completed, and a main electricity transmission line will connect Lilongwe with Tedzani Falls. Lilongwe airport is to be expanded to international standards, and surveys are being made for the connection of Lilongwe by rail to the present railhead at Salima.

In the central lakeshore region a comprehensive project is being developed in Salima District, with the principal objective of greatly increasing cotton production. To the north, in Nkhota Kota District, the construction of the lakeshore road has made it possible to plan the development of irrigated rice production at several marsh and delta sites. An integrated tourist facility development will take place at Senga on the lakeshore near Salima.

The south central region lies between the Lilongwe and Blantyre development cores, and is crossed by the principal national road and rail routes. In the future, electricity transmission lines and the dredged upper Shire will provide further improved transportation. Liwonde is to be developed as an industrial and transportation centre. Fisheries and tourist development in the southern lakeshore area are major fields of development. The potential for cotton and irrigated rice projects is very great. It is possible that a rail link from the Balaka–Blantyre line to Moatize and Tete in western Moçambique will be constructed.

In the Northern and north-central regions development has been limited because of the high cost of transportation to and from Blantyre and Beira. Pre-Independence development was restricted to the rubber, and later, the tea estates near Nkhata Bay, and the Colonial Development Corporation's tung estates around Mzuzu. Peasant farmers supplied some cattle, but principally only migrant labour for Zambia, Tanzania and South Africa. Post-Independence emphasis has been upon increased production of such high value export products as Turkish tobacco, tea and coffee, and rice and cotton in the lakeshore and Rumphi areas, together with the improvement of cattle production. Recently, attention was given to intensive rice cultivation in the Kaporo, Hara and Limphasa lakeshore areas and to the planning of a comprehensive land development project in the potentially very productive Karonga lakeshore, and an integrated rural development project in the high rainfall area around Nkhata Bay. The largest development project was the pulpwood afforestation on the Vipya Plateau, which will provide the raw material for the development of a pulp and board industry at Chinteche, which will then become an industrial growth pole for the north central region. The area has very considerable tourist attraction, hitherto scarcely developed, and considerable attention is being given to this form of development. Transportation has been improved with the construction of the lakeshore road, and it is planned to improve lake services with new ports at Chinteche and on the Karonga lakeshore.

MICHAEL STUBBS

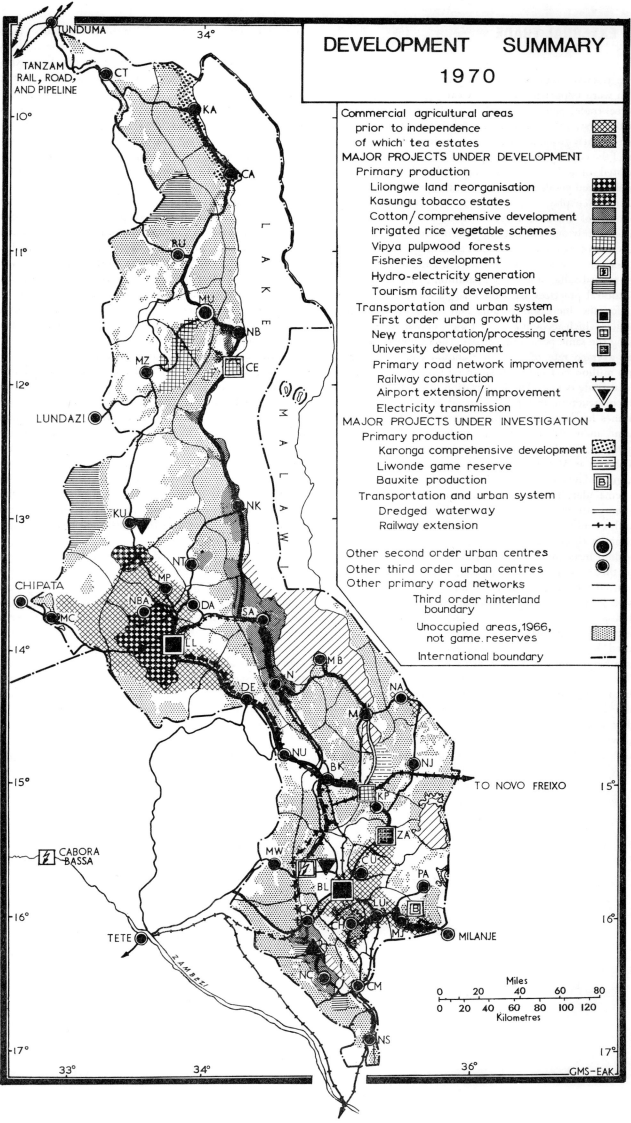

DEVELOPMENT SUMMARY
1970

Commercial agricultural areas
    prior to independence
    of which tea estates
MAJOR PROJECTS UNDER DEVELOPMENT
    Primary production
        Lilongwe land reorganisation
        Kasungu tobacco estates
        Cotton/comprehensive development
        Irrigated rice vegetable schemes
        Vipya pulpwood forests
        Fisheries development
        Hydro-electricity generation
        Tourism facility development
    Transportation and urban system
        First order urban growth poles
        New transportation/processing centres
        University development
        Primary road network improvement
        Railway construction
        Airport extension/improvement
        Electricity transmission
MAJOR PROJECTS UNDER INVESTIGATION
    Primary production
        Karonga comprehensive development
        Liwonde game reserve
        Bauxite production
    Transportation and urban system
        Dredged waterway
        Railway extension

Other second order urban centres
Other third order urban centres
Other primary road networks
        Third order hinterland
        boundary
        Unoccupied areas, 1966,
        not game reserves
        International boundary

The extractive commodities of elephant ivory and rubber, which were important in the very early period of Malawi's external trade, gave way to cultivated crops of which coffee was the first, followed later by tobacco, cotton and tea. More recently groundnuts have become important. Since the turn of the century the greater part of Malawi's exports have consisted of a few important agricultural commodities. Manufactured goods have long been the principal imports.

Commerce plays an increasingly important role in the economy of Malawi. Import duties are the source of approximately one-third of the government's total revenue. The value of exports increased at an average rate of almost ten per cent per annum for the period 1964 to 1968 reaching a record value of nearly £17 million in 1968. Improved agricultural practices with their larger yields are responsible for the increased volume and value of agricultural products which account for about 99% of Malawi's exports. During the same period of 1964 to 1968 imports increased at an average rate of 20% per annum and amounted to £25·9 million in 1968. This situation has resulted in a substantial trade deficit. The importation of capital equipment and construction materials financed by various aid programmes has been one of the main causes of the deficit. Recent industrial and manufacturing developments are helping to restrain this imbalance of trade.

Tobacco is Malawi's principal export commodity with tea, groundnuts and edible legumes making up the bulk of the remainder. This indicates the extent to which Malawi's economy still depends on agricultural resources. Commonwealth countries, South Africa and the Republic of Ireland take about three-quarters of Malawi's exports. The United Kingdom buys about a half of the exports and takes more than three-quarters of the cotton, groundnuts and maize produced for sale abroad. The United Kingdom is also the largest importer of Malawi tea and from there it is redistributed and Britain takes also the largest proportion of the tobacco crop. Exports of tea to other countries besides the United Kingdom are increasing and tobacco exports to Sierra Leone and the Netherlands are now important.

The only major export commodities for which the United Kingdom is not an important market are cassava, edible legumes and tung oil. West Germany buys nearly eighty per cent of the cassava which is exported from Malawi. More than one-half of the grain legumes (peas and beans) are taken by Ceylon, Japan and Kenya. Tung oil is

exported to India, Poland and South Africa. Since 1966 Malawi's exports to Rhodesia have decreased considerably but during the same period the value of imports from Rhodesia has remained approximately the same from year to year.

The agricultural commodities produced for export can be divided into estate grown crops and smallholder crops. The estates produce tea, tung oil, flue-cured and burley tobaccos. Cassava, cotton, groundnuts, legumes, maize and dark-fired, sun-cured and Turkish tobaccos are grown by smallholders.

The goods imported into Malawi are broadly speaking the same as before independence except that there have been substantial increases in the amounts of materials and machinery imported for industry and construction. The principal imports are beer, cotton and rayon fabrics, motor cars and lorries, the most important of these being cotton fabrics. Recently a brewery and a factory for the production of cotton fabrics have been set up in Blantyre and will have the effect of reducing or putting an end to further importation of these commodities.

Malawi obtains about a half of her imported goods from the United Kingdom and Rhodesia. The United Kingdom is the principal source of imports supplying nearly one-third of the goods imported. The most important of these are motor vehicles and parts, cotton fabrics and ammonium sulphate. Rhodesia, which is the second largest source of Malawi's imports, supplies chiefly consumer goods such as beer, clothing, dairy produce, paper products, tyres and tubes. A large proportion of the fabrics and clothing imported come from Hongkong and Japan. Tyres and tubes and motor vehicles are also important items imported from Japan. Iran supplies most of the motor spirit requirements of Malawi.

The pattern of imports and exports has been changing in recent years. The United Kingdom, the United States of America, South Africa, West Germany and the Republic of Ireland have all increased their share of Malawi's external trade. Nevertheless, a comparison of Malawi's external trade in 1968 with that of the previous four years shows that very few countries are buying larger proportions of the export commodities while more countries are entering the market and selling goods to Malawi. The United Kingdom is now the only country with which Malawi generally maintains a favourable trade balance.

Tables of imports and exports are given on p. 142.

R SCHMIDT

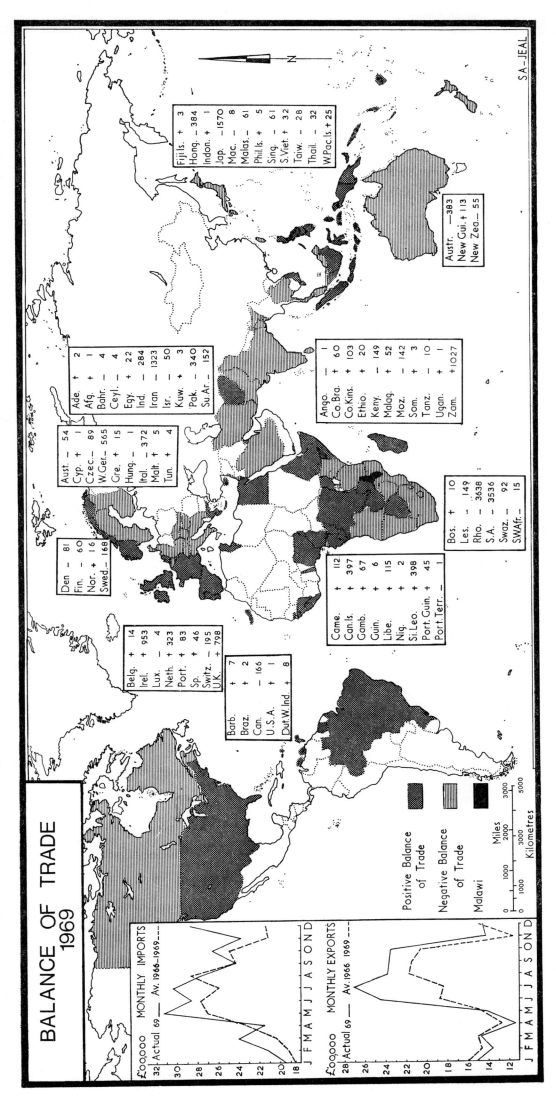

BALANCE OF TRADE 1969

MONTHLY IMPORTS
£00000 Actual 69 —— Av. 1966-1969 ---

32
30
28
26
24
22
20
18

J F M A M J J A S O N D

MONTHLY EXPORTS
£00000 Actual 69 —— Av. 1966 1969 ---

28
26
24
22
20
18
16
14
12

J F M A M J J A S O N D

Positive Balance of Trade

Negative Balance of Trade

Malawi

Miles
0   1000   2000   3000
0 1000 2000 3000 5000
Kilometres

N

SA-JEAL

Den	–	81
Fin.	–	60
Nor.	+	16
Swed.	–	168

Aust.	–	54
Cyp.	+	1
Czec.	–	89
W.Ger.	–	565
Gre.	+	15
Hung.	–	
Ital.	–	372
Malt.	+	5
Tun.	+	4

Ade.	+	2
Afg.	+	1
Bahr.	–	4
Ceyl.	–	4
Egy.	+	22
Ind.	–	284
Iran	–	1323
Isr.	–	50
Kuw.	+	3
Pak.	–	340
Su.Ar.	–	152

Fiji Is.	+	3
Hong.	–	384
Indon.	+	1
Jap.	–	1570
Mac.	–	8
Malas.	–	61
Phil.Is.	+	5
Sing.	–	61
S.Viet.	+	32
Taiw.	–	28
Thail.	–	32
W.Pac.Is.	+	25

Austr.	–	383
New Gui.	+	113
New Zea.	–	55

Ango.	–	1
Co.Bra.	+	60
Co.Kins.	+	103
Ethio.	+	20
Keny.	–	149
Malag.	+	52
Moz.	–	142
Som.	+	3
Tanz.	–	10
Ugan.	+	1
Zam.	+	1027

Bos.	+	10
Les.	–	149
Rho.	–	3638
S.A.	–	3536
Swaz.	–	92
SWAfr.	–	15

Came.	+	112
Can.Is.	+	397
Gamb.	+	67
Guin.	+	6
Libe.	+	115
Nig.	+	2
Si.Leo.	+	398
Port.Guin.	+	45
Port.Terr.	–	1

Belg.	+	14
Irel.	+	953
Lux.	–	4
Neth.	+	323
Port.	+	83
Sp.	+	46
Switz.	–	195
U.K.	+	798

Barb.	+	7
Braz.	+	2
Can.	–	166
U.S.A.	+	1
Dut.W.Ind	+	8

133

BIBLIOGRAPHY

This bibliography is far from exhaustive. It includes works referred to in the preparation of this book, along with others of value to geographers, geologists, biologists and those interested in the economy of Malawi.

A. General Geographies

PIKE, J G and RIMMINGTON, G T *Malawi: A Geographical Study*, Oxford University Press, London, 1965

YOUNG, A *A Geography of Malawi*, Dent, London, 1964

B. Natural Resources, General

BROWN, P and STOBBS, A *The Physical Environment of Southern Malawi with special reference to Soils and Agriculture*, Government Printer, Zomba, 1970

BROWN, P and YOUNG, A *The Physical Environment of Northern Nyasaland with special reference to Soils and Agriculture*, Government Printer, Zomba, 1962

—— *The Physical Environment of Central Malawi with special reference to Soils and Agriculture*, Government Printer, Zomba, 1965

C. Geology and Geomorphology

BLOOMFIELD, K *Geological Map of Malawi*, Malawi Geological Survey, 1966

—— 'The Pre-Karroo geology of Malawi', Malawi Geological Survey Department Mem. 5, 1968

BLOOMFIELD, K and YOUNG, A 'The Geology and Geomorphology of Zomba Mountain', *Nyasaland Journal*, Vol. 14, 1961, pp. 54–80

CAHEN, L and SNELLING, J *The geochronology of Equatorial Africa*, North-Holland, 1966, p. 195

CANNON, R T, HOPKINS, D A, THATCHER, E C, PETERS, E R, KEMP, J, GASKELL, J L, and RAY, G E 'Polyphase deformation in the Moçambique belt, northern Malawi', Bulletin of the Geological Society of America, 1969

DIXEY, F 'The Nyasaland Section of the Great Rift Valley', *Geographical Journal*, Vol. 68, 1926, pp. 117–40,

—— 'Mlanje Mountains of Nyasaland', *Geographical Review*, Vol. 17, 1927, pp. 611–26

—— 'Early Cretaceous and Miocene Peneplains of Nyasaland and their Relation to the Rift Valley', *Geological Magazine*, Vol. 74, 1937, pp. 49–67

—— 'The Early Cretaceous Valley-floor Peneplain of the Lake Nyasa Region and its Relation to Tertiary Rift Structure', *Quarterly Journal of the Geological Society*, Vol. 95, 1938, pp. 75–108,

—— 'Some Observations on the Physiographical Development of Central and Southern Africa', *Transactions of the Geological Society of South Africa*, Vol. 41, 1938, pp. 113–71

—— 'Geomorphic Development of the Shire Valley, Nyasaland', *Journal of Geomorphology*, Vol. 4, 1941, pp. 97–116

—— 'Erosion Cycles in Southern and Central Africa.' *Transactions of the Geological Society of South Africa*, Vol. 45, 1942, pp. 151–81

—— 'The Relation of the Main Peneplain of Central Africa to Sediments of Lower Miocene Age', *Quarterly Journal of the Geological Society*, Vol. 101, 1946, pp. 243–53

—— 'Erosion and Tectonics in the East African Rift System', *Quarterly Journal of the Geological Society*, Vol. 102, 1946, pp. 339–58

—— 'Erosion Surfaces in Africa; some Considerations of Age and Origin', *Transactions of the Geological Society of South Africa*, Vol. 58, 1955, pp. 265–80

—— 'Some Aspects of the Geomorphology of Central and Southern Africa' (Du Toit Memorial Lecture), *Transactions of the Geological Society of South Africa*, Vol. 58, 1955

—— 'Vertical tectonics in the East African Rift System.' *Compte Rendu of the 20th International Geological Congress*, Mexico, 1956.

—— 'The East African Rift System', *Overseas Geology Mineral Resources Bulletin*, Supplement, 1957

FITCHES, W R, 'The Mafingi group', *Proceedings of the Geological Society*, London, Vol. 1642, 1967, p. 215

GARSON, M S 'The Geology of the Lake Chilwa Area', *Geological Survey Bulletin, Malawi*, No. 12, 1960, pp. 1–67

HARKIN, D A 'The Rungwe Volcanics at the Northern End of Lake Nyasa', *Geological Survey of Tanganyika*, Dar es Salaam, n.d.

MAIR, A and STEPHEN, I 'The Superficial Deposits of the Lower Shire Valley, Nyasaland', *Colonial Geology and Mineral Resources*, Vol. 6, No. 4, 1956, pp. 391–406

MALAWI GOVERNMENT *Bulletins, Memoirs and Records of the Geological Survey of Malawi*, Government Printer, Zomba

MOREL, S W 'Pre-Cambrian Perthosites in Nyasaland', *Geological Magazine*, Vol. 108, No. 3, 1961

PIKE, J. G 'A Brief Note on the Upper Pleistocene Raised Beach', *Nyasaland Journal*, Vol. 11, 1958, pp. 57–9

SMITH, W C 'Carbonites of the Chilwa Series of Southern Nyasaland', *Bulletin of the British Museum (Natural History) Mineralogy*, Vol. 1, No. 4, 1953

STRINGER, K V 'New Province of Igneous Ring-Complexes in Southern Nyasaland.' *Nature*, Vol. 170, 11 October 1952, p. 630

STRINGER, K V, HOLT, D N and GROVERS, A W 'The Chambe Plateau Ring Complex of Nyasaland', *Colonial Geology and Mineral Resources*, Vol. 6, No. 1, 1956, pp. 3–18

TILLEY, C E 'The Nepheline Rocks of the Port Herald Hills, Southern Nyasaland', *Overseas Geology and Mineral Resources*, Vol. 8, No. 3, 1961, pp. 255–9

WILLIAM, R G M 'Mud Flow in the Chelinda Valley, Nyika Plateau', *Nyasaland Journal*, Vol. 15, 1962, pp. 30–31

D. Climate

HOWE, G M 'Climates of the Rhodesias and Nyasaland according to the Thornthwaite Classification', *The Geological Review*, Vol. 43, 1953, pp. 525–39

JOHNSTON, H C J 'The Weather', *Nyasaland Journal*, Vol. 2, 1949, pp. 30–34

LAYCOCK, D H 'Rainfall in the Nyasaland Tea Areas', *Nyasaland Farming and Forestry*, Vol. 2, No. 2, 1958

RHODESIA AND NYASALAND METEOROLOGICAL SERVICE *Sunrise and Sunset Tables for the Federation of Rhodesia and Nyasaland*, Department of Printing and Stationery, Salisbury, Rhodesia, 1959

—— *Totals of monthly and annual rainfall in Nyasaland*, Department of Printing and Stationery, Salisbury, Rhodesia

—— *Mean annual rainfall map of Rhodesia and Nyasaland*, Department of Printing and Stationery, Salisbury, Rhodesia

—— *Mean Upper Winds over the Federation of Rhodesia and Nyasaland*, Department of Printing and Stationery, Salisbury, Rhodesia, 1958

—— *Mean Surface Winds over the Federation*, Department of Printing and Stationery, Salisbury, Rhodesia, 1960

—— *Notes on the Rainy Season in Northern Rhodesia and Nyasaland* by S. Lineham, Department of Printing and Stationery, Salisbury, Rhodesia, 1961

TETLEY, A E 'Rainfall characteristics in Nyasaland', *Professional Paper No. 1, Water Development Department*, Zomba, Malawi, 1959

E. Soils

CUTTING, C V 'Nyasaland Tea Soils', *Nyasaland Farming and Forestry*, Vol. 3, No. 2, 1958

CUTTING C V, WOOD, R A, BROWN, P and AMBROSE, H B 'Assessment of fertility status and the maintenance of productivity of Soils in Nyasaland', *Comptes rendus, Conférence Interafricaine des Sols (3ᵉ)*, Dalba, November 1959

YOUNG, A *Preliminary Soil Map of Nyasaland*, Government Printer, Zomba, 1960

YOUNG, A and STEPHEN I 'Rock Weathering and Soil Formation on High-Altitude Plateaux of Malawi', *Journal of Soil Science*, Vol. 16, No. 2, 1965, pp. 322–33

F. Vegetation

BINNS, B *A First Checklist of the Herbaceous Flora of Malawi*, Government Printer, Zomba, 1968

BRASS C, J 'The Vegetation of Nyasaland', *Memoir of the New York Botanical Gardens*, Vol. 8, 1953

BURTT-DAVY, J and HOYLE, A C revised by Topham, P *Checklist of the Forest Trees and Shrubs of Nyasaland*, Government Printer, Zomba, 1958

CHAPMAN, J D 'Some Notes on the Taxonomy, Distribution, Ecology and Economic Importance of *Widdringtonia*, with particular reference to *W. whytei*', *Kirkia* (Salisbury), Vol. 1, 1961, pp. 138–54

—— *The Vegetation of the Mlanje Mountains, Nyasaland: a Preliminary Account with Particular Reference to Widdringtonia Forests*, Government Printer, Zomba, 1962

CLEMENTS, J B 'Nyasaland Indigenous Timbers', *Nyasaland Agricultural Quarterly Journal*, Vol. 2, 1942, pp. 6–19

—— 'Pines in Nyasaland', *Nyasaland Agricultural Quarterly Journal*, Vol. 5, 1945, pp. 44–5

EXELL, A W and WILD, H *Flora Zambesiaca: Moçambique, Federation of Rhodesia and Nyasaland, Bechuanaland Protectorate*, Vol. I, Part I, Crown Agents for Overseas Governments and Administrations, London, 1960

HURSH, C R *The Dry Woodlands of Nyasaland*, Part I General Forestry Problems. Part II Silviculture, Management and Research', International Co-operation Administrations, Salisbury, Rhodesia, 1960

JACKSON, G 'Preliminary Ecological Survey of Nyasaland', *Proceedings of the Second Inter-African Soils Conference*, Leopoldville, Vol. 1, 1954, pp. 679–90

JACKSON, R G and WIEHE, P *An Annotated Checklist of Nyasaland Grasses*, Government Printer, Zomba, 1958

PALGRAVE, OLIVE, H C 'Trees of Central Africa', *National Publications Trust*, Salisbury, 1957

RATTRAY, J M and WILD, H 'Vegetation Map of the Federation of Rhodesia and Nyasaland', *Kirkia*, (Salisbury), Vol. 1961/62, pp. 94–104

TOPHAM, P 'Nyasaland Trees and Shrubs', *Nyasaland Journal*, Vol. 12, 1952, pp. 11–17

WILD, H and FERNANDES, G *Vegetation Map of the Flora Zambesiaca area*, H.M. Stationery Office, London, 1968

WILLAN, R G 'Notes on the Vegetation of Northern Nyasaland', *Empire Forestry Journal*, Vol. 19, No. 1, 1940, pp. 48–61

—— 'Indigenous Trees of Nyasaland', *Nyasaland Journal*, Vol. 12, 1959, pp. 50–56

WILLIAMSON, J *Useful Plants of Nyasaland*, Government Printer, Zomba, 1956

G. Hydrology and Water Resources

ARNOLD, C W B 'Lake Nyasa's Varying Level', *Nyasaland Journal*, Vol. 5, 1952, pp. 7–17

BAILEY, R T 'Hydrographic Survey of Lake Nyasa (1955–1959)', *International Hydrographic Review*, Vol. 37, 1960, pp. 53–5

BEAUCHAMP, R S A 'Chemistry and Hydrography of Lakes Tanganyika and Nyasa', *Nature*, Vol. 146, No. 3659, 24 August 1940, pp. 253–6

—— 'Hydrological Data from Lake Nyasa', *The Journal of Ecology*, Vol. 41, No. 2, 1953, pp. 226–39

COCHRANE, N J 'The Cyclic Behaviour of Lakes Victoria and Nyasa', *Colonial Geology and Mineral Resources* (London), Vol. 6, No. 2, 1956, pp. 169–275.

—— 'Lake Nyasa and the Shire River', *Proceedings of the Journal of Civil Engineering*, Vol. 8, Paper No. 6178, 1957, pp. 363–82

DAY, SIR ARCHBALD 'Lake Nyasa Hydrographic Survey', *Nyasaland Journal*, Vol. 9, 1956, pp. 57–64

DIXEY, F 'Variations in lake level and sunspots', *Colonial Geological and Mining Resources*, Vol. 3, No. 3, 1953, pp. 213–18

FEDERATION OF RHODESIA AND NYASALAND, *Report to Specialist Meeting on Physical Hydrology at Bukavu, July 1958*, Department of Water Development, Zomba, Malawi

HALCROW, SIR WILLIAM and PARTNERS *The Shire valley project. A report on the control and development of Lake Nyasa and the Shire River*, London, 1954

HOLT, D N 'Location of Underground Water Supplies in Nyasaland', *Overseas Geological Mining Resources*, Vol. 5, (4), 1955, pp. 438–40

JOLLYMAN, W H 'Tides and Seiches in Lake Nyasa', *Nyasaland Journal*, Vol. 8, No. 2, 1955, pp. 31–5

KANTHACK, F E 'The Fluctuations of Lake Nyasa', *Geographical Journal*, Vol. 98, No. 1, 1941, pp. 20–33

—— 'The Hydrology of the Nyasa Rift Valley', *South African Geographical Journal*, Vol. 24, 1942

LATHAM, E W 'Flooding at Chiromo as a result of cyclone "Edith" ', *Nyasaland Journal*, Vol. 10, No. 1, 1957

—— 'Some Points of Interest in the Hydrology of the Shire River', *Proceedings of the Fifth Informal Conference of Hydrology*, Blantyre, 1960

—— 'Water Resources and Water Development in Nyasaland', *Nyasaland Journal*, Vol. 17, 1964, pp. 57–70

MAXWELL, W A 'The Shire Valley Project', *Nyasaland Journal*, Vol. 7, 1955, pp. 39–45

MOSS, B and MOSS, J 'Aspects of the Limnology of an Endorheic African Lake (L. Chilwa, Malawi)', *Ecology*, Vol. 50, No. 1, 1969, pp. 109–18

PIKE, J G 'The movement of water in Lake Nyasa', *Nyasaland Journal*, Vol. 10, No. 2, 1957

—— 'The Sunspot/Lake Level Relationship and the Control of Lake Nyasa', *Journal of the Institution of Water Engineers* (London), Vol. 29, No. 3, 1965

—— 'The Hydrology of Lake Nyasa', *Journal of the Institution of Water Engineers* (London), Vol. 28, No. 7, 1964

RICHARDS, E V 'The Shire Valley Project', *Nyasaland Journal*, Vol. 7, 1954, pp. 7–18

STARMANS, G A N 'Note on the surface water resources of the Protectorate', *Nyasaland Journal*, Vol. 9, No. 1, 1957, pp. 22–4

H. Fisheries

JACKSON, P B N, HARDING, D, FRYERM, G and ILES, T D *Report on the fish and fisheries of northern Lake Nyasa*, Government Printer, Zomba, 1962

KALK, M (ed.) *Lake Chilwa Co-ordinated Research Project, 1966–1970*, University of Malawi, Limbe, 1970

KIRK, R 'The Fishes of Lake Chilwa', *Society of Malawi Journal*, Vol. 20, 1967, pp. 1–14

LOWE, R H 'Report on the *Tilapia* and Other Fish and Fisheries of Lake Nyasa, 1945–1947', *Fishery Publications*, Vol. 1, No. 2, 1952, H.M. Stationery Office, London

MZUMARA, A J P 'The Lake Chilwa Fisheries', *Society of Malawi Journal*, Vol. 20, 1967, pp. 58–68

RENSON, H L F *Fish Marketing*, Ministry of Agriculture, Zomba, Malawi, 1969

I. Mineral Resources and Mining

COOPER, W G G 'Nyasaland's Resources', *South Africa Mining Engineering Journal*, Vol. 59, No. 1, 1950, pp. 433–9

MALAWI GOVERNMENT, MINISTRY OF NATURAL RESOURCES *Mineral Resources of Nyasaland*, Government Printer, Zomba, 1961

PELLETIER, R A *Mineral Resources in South-Central Africa*, Oxford University Press, Cape Town, 1964

J. History, General

DEBENHAM, F *Nyasaland: The Land of the Lake*, H M. Stationery Office, London, 1955

HANNA, A J *The Beginnings of Nyasaland and North-Eastern Rhodesia, 1859–1895*. Oxford, Clarendon Press, London, 1956

—— *The Story of the Rhodesias and Nyasaland*, Faber and Faber, London, 1960

JONES, G *Britain and Nyasaland*, George Allen and Unwin, London, 1964

MAUGHAM, R C F *Nyasaland in the Nineties*, Lincoln, Williams, London, 1935

MORRIS, M J *A Brief History of Nyasaland*, Longmans Green, London, 1952

OLIVER, R *Sir Harry Johnston and the Scramble for Africa*, Chatto and Windus, London, 1964

PACHAI, B, SMITH, G W and TANGRI, R (ed.) 'Malawi Past and Present', selected papers from The University of Malawi History Conference, 1967, Blantyre, 1971

PIKE, J G *Malawi: A Political and Economic History*, Pall Mall Press, London, 1968

RANSFORD, O *Livingstone's Lake*, John Murray, London, 1966

WILLS, A J *An Introduction to the History of Central Africa*, Oxford University Press, London, 1964

K. Administration and Local Government

JOLLY, H G G 'The Progress of Local Government in Nyasaland', *Journal of African Administration* (London), Vol. 6, 1960

MAIR, L 'Native Administration in Central Nyasaland' *Colonial Research Studies*, H.M. Stationery Office, London, 1952

L. History of Education

'African Education in Nyasaland', *The Times Educational Supplement* (London), No. 1356, 1941

AMERICAN COUNCIL ON EDUCATION 'Education for Development', *Report of a Survey Team on Education in Malawi*, United States Agency for International Development, New York, 1964

BENEDICT, B *Preliminary Survey on the needs of youth in Nyasaland*, Zomba, 1963

BLAIR, A P, WALKER, E and WILLIAMS, D O *Report of the Survey Team on Technical Education and Training in Malawi*, Ministry of Overseas Development, London, 1969

CHIWONA, P H M 'The Costing of Primary Educational Development with Special Reference to Malawi', International Institute for Educational Planning, I.I.E.P./INT/NO 13 (mimeograph), Paris, 1969

DAVIDSON, B 'African Education in British Central and Southern Africa *Présence Africaine*, N.S., No. 6, 1956, pp. 106–12

MALAWI GOVERNMENT Ministry of Development and Planning, *Report on Survey of requirements for trained manpower in Malawi*, Government Printer, Zomba, 1967

NYASALAND GOVERNMENT *Report of the Committee of Enquiry into African Education*, Zomba, 1962

PHELPS-STOKES *Reports on Education in Africa*, 1922 and 1924 abridged with an introduction by L G Lewis, Oxford University Press, London, 1962

RIMMINGTON, G T 'From Church to State to District: The

Developing Educational System of Nyasaland', *Journal of Education* (Nova Scotia), Series 5, Vol. 13, 1964
—— 'Education for Independence. A Study of Changing Educational Administration in Malawi', *Comparative Education*, Vol. 2, No. 3, 1966, pp. 217–23

M. Ethnology, Anthropology, Pre-colonial African History
BLACK, C *The Lands and Peoples of Rhodesia and Nyasaland*, A and C Black, London, 1960
BRUWER, J 'The composition of a Cewa village (Mudzi)', *African Studies*, Vol. 8, 1949, pp. 191–8, Witwatersrand University Press, Johannesburg, South Africa
CLARK, J D 'Prehistory in Nyasaland', *Nyasaland Journal*, Vol. 9, 1956, pp. 92–119
MITCHELL, J C *The Yao Village*, Manchester University Press, 1956
NYIRENDA, S 'History of the Tumbuka-Henga people', Translated and edited by T Cullen Young, *Bantu Studies*, Vol. 4/5, Johannesburg, South Africa
——*Nyasaland Journal*, Vol. 16, 1963, No. 2
—— 'The Yao,' *Nyasaland Journal*, Vol. 16, No. 1, 1963
—— 'The Arabs', *Nyasaland Journal*, Vol. 16, No. 2, 1963
—— 'The Portuguese', *Nyasaland Journal*, Vol. 17, No. 1, 1964
READ, M *The Ngoni of Nyasaland*, Oxford University Press, London, 1956
ROBINSON, K R *The early iron age in Malawi: an appraisal*, Government Printer, Zomba, Malawi, 1969
TEW, M *Peoples of the Lake Nyasa Region*, Oxford University Press, London, 1950
VAN VELSEN, J 'Notes on the history of the lakeside Tonga of Nyasaland', *African Studies* (London), Vol. 18, No. 3, 1959
—— 'Labour migration as a positive factor in the continuity of Tonga tribal society', *Rhodes-Livingstone Journal*, Vol. 26, 1961, Lusaka
WILSON, G 'The constitution of the Ngonde', *Rhodes-Livingstone Papers*, Vol. 3, 1939, Lusaka
—— 'An introduction to Nyakyusa Society', *Bantu Studies*, Vol. 11, No. 2, 1952
YOUNG, T CULLEN (ed.) *Notes on the History of the Tumbuka-Kamanga Peoples*. Livingstonia Mission Press, Livingstonia, Malawi, 1932

N. Demography
ATKINS, G 'The Nyanja-speaking population of Nyasaland and Northern Rhodesia (a statistical estimate)', *African Studies*, Vol. 9, 1950, pp. 35–9, Witwatersrand University Press, Johannesburg, South Africa
BAKER, C A 'Blantyre District: A Geographical Appreciation of the Growth, Distribution and Composition of its Population', *Nyasaland Journal* Vol. 12, 1959, pp. 7–35
—— 'A note on Nguru Immigration to Nyasaland', *Nyasaland Journal*, Vol. 14, 1961 pp. 41–2
BETTISON, D G 'The demographic structures of seventeen villages, Blantyre, Nyasaland', *Rhodes-Livingstone Communications*, No. 11, 1958, Lusaka
DIXEY, F 'The Distribution of Population in Nyasaland', *Geographical Review*, Vol. XVIII, No. 2, April 1928, New York
MALAWI GOVERNMENT *Malawi Population Census 1966 Preliminary Report*, Government Printer, Zomba, 1966
—— *Malawi Population Census 1966. Village Population by sex, age, race and education, by districts*, Government Printer, Zomba, 1968
—— *Malawi Population Census 1966 Final Report*, Government Printer, Zomba, 1969
RIMMINGTON, G T 'Population growth in the Dedza District of Nyasaland', *Nyasaland Journal*, Vol. 16, No. 2, 1963
STUBBS, G M *Spatial, Demographic, Social, and Economic characteristics of the population of Malawi, 1966: an analysis of the results of the 1966 census for information areas of third and fourth order*, University of Malawi, Department of Geography, Blantyre (mimeo), 1970

O. Agriculture, Forestry and Electricity Generation
AMER, J and HUTCHESON, A M *The Nchalo Sugar Estate: A Major Agricultural Development in Malawi*, Malawi Information Department, Zomba, 1966
—— *The Nkula Falls Hydro-Electric Scheme: a Key to development in Southern Malawi*, Zomba, 1966
ANON Production in Malawi', *Nyasaland Farmer and Forester*, Vol. 5, No. 4, 1961, pp. 18–34
BROWN, P 'Maize Growing in Nyasaland: 1. Distribution and Cultivation', *Empire Journal of Experimental Agriculture*, Vol. 31, No. 121, 1963, pp. 71–82

DAVIES, W T *Fifty years of Progress. An Account of the African Organisation of the Imperial Tobacco Company, 1907–1957*, Imperial Tobacco Company, Bristol, 1958
ELECTRICITY SUPPLY COMMISSION OF MALAWI *Annual Reports for the year ending 31st December 1964–1969*, Blantyre, 1965–1970
FOSTER, L J and CRASKE G 'Coffee Growing in Nyasaland', *Nyasaland Farming and Forestry*, Vol. 3, No. 2, 1958
GORDON, J G *Compendium of Agricultural Statistics of Malawi* (interim draft), Ministry of Economic Affairs, Zomba, 1968
HADLOW, G G S 'The History of Tea in Nyasaland', *Nyasaland Journal*, Vol. 13, No. 1, 1960
HOFFMAN, H K F *Case Studies of Progressive Farming in Central Malawi. Report on a Social-Economic Survey conducted in areas of the Lilongwe Plateau*, Government Printer, Zomba, 1967
KAUFFMAN, I H *A Study of Agricultural Co-operative Societies in Nyasaland*, Agency for International Development, Washington, 1963
KETTLEWELL, R W 'Agricultural Change in Nyasaland 1945–1960', *Food Research Institute Studies*, Stanford University, Vol. 5, No. 3, 1965, pp. 229–85
MALAWI GOVERNMENT *Annual Reports of the Department of Veterinary Services and Animal Husbandry*, Government Printer, Zomba
—— *Annual Reports of the Department of Agriculture and, since 1969, the Ministry of Agriculture*, Government Printer, Zomba
—— *An Outline of Agrarian Problems and Policy in Nyasaland*, Government Printer, Zomba, 1955
—— *A Sample Survey of Agricultural Small-holdings in the Southern Region of Malawi*, National Statistical Office, Zomba, 1965
—— *A Sample Survey of Agricultural Small-holdings in the Central Region of Malawi*, National Statistical Office, Zomba, 1966
—— *A Sample Survey of Agricultural Small-holdings in the Lower Shire Valley, Malawi*, Department of Census and Statistics, Zomba, 1967
—— Ministry of Natural Resources, *A guide to Agricultural Production in Malawi 1968–1969*, Government Printer, Zomba
MASON I L and MAULE, J P *The Indigenous Livestock of Eastern and Southern Africa*, Royal Commonwealth Agricultural Bureaux, Farnham, 1960
MCLOUGHLIN, P F M 'Some Aspects of Land Reorganisation in Malawi, 1950–1960', *Ekistics*, Vol. 24, No. 141, 1967, pp. 193–200
MORGAN, W B 'The Lower Shire Valley of Nyasaland: A changing system of Agriculture', *Geographical Journal* (London), Vol. 199, 1953
RANGELEY, W H J *A Brief History of the Tobacco Industry in Nyasaland*, *Nyasaland Journal*, Vol. 10, 1957, pp. 62–83
—— 'A Brief History of the Tobacco Industry in Nyasaland – Additional Notes', *Nyasaland Journal*, Vol. 11, 1958, pp. 24–7
RIMMINGTON, G T 'Agricultural Development in the Dedza District of Nyasaland', *Nyasaland Journal*, Vol. 16, 1963, pp. 28–48
TERRY, P T 'African Agriculture in Nyasaland 1858–1864', *Nyasaland Journal*, Vol. 14, No. 2, 1961
—— The rise of the African cotton industry in Nyasaland, *Nyasaland Journal*, Vol. 14, No. 1, 1962

P. Transport and Communications
MALAWI GOVERNMENT *Annual Report of the Road Traffic Commissioner from the 1st January 1966 to 31st December 1966 and for the year ended 31st December 1967*, Government Printer, Zomba, 1967, 1968
—— *Annual Report of the Ministry of Works and Supplies for the year ended 31st December 1967*, Government Printer, Zomba, 1968
—— *Annual Reports of the Controller of Customs and Excise, for the year ended 31st December 1967*, 1968, Zomba, Government Printer, 1968, 1969
—— *Annual Report of the Department of Civil Aviation for the year ended 31st December 1968*, Zomba, Government Printer, 1969
TALBOT, W D 'Some notes on the dhows of Fort Johnston District', *Nyasaland Journal*, Vol. 15, No. 2, 1962
TWYNAN, C D 'The telegraph in British Central Africa', *Nyasaland Journal*,' Vol. 6, No. 2, 1953

Q. Urban System
BETTISON, D G 'Cash wages and occupational structure, Blantyre, Nyasaland', *Rhodes-Livingstone Communications*, No. 9, Lusaka, 1958
BETTISON, D G and APTHORPE R J 'Authority and residence in peri-urban social structure, Nyasaland', *Nyasaland Journal*, Vol. 14, No. 1, 1961

CARDEW, C A 'Nyasaland in 1894–95', *Nyasaland Journal*, Vol. 1, No. 1, 1948

GERKE, W J C and VILJOEN, C J *Master Plan for Lilongwe, the capital city of Malawi*, Johannesburg, 1968

KADZOMBE, E D *Structure of manufacturing industries in the City of Blantyre, Malawi*, University of Nigeria, Nsukka (dissertation), 1967

RANGELEY, W H G 'Early Blantyre', *Nyasaland Journal*, Vol. 7, No. 1, 1954

WILLIAMS, S G 'The old police posts of Nyasaland', *Nyasaland Journal*, Vol. 12, No. 2, 1957

R. Social Services

GELFAND, M *Lakeside Pioneers: Socio-Medical Study of Nyasaland* (1875–1920), Basil Blackwell, Oxford, 1964

MALAWI GOVERNMENT *Annual Report of the Ministry of Education for the year* 1965, Government Printer, Zomba, 1966

—— *Annual report on the work of the Nyasaland/Malawi Ministry of Health for the year* 1964, Government Printer, Zomba, 1967

—— *Annual Report of the Malawi Police Force* 1967, Government Printer, Zomba, 1968

—— *Medical institutions and facilities in Malawi*, Government Printer, Zomba, 1968

STUBBS, G M *The spatial distribution of health services in relation to population distribution and regional spatial systems, Malawi* 1969, University of Malawi (mimeo.), 1970

S. Development

FEDERATION OF RHODESIA AND NYASALAND *Report on an Economic Survey of Nyasaland, 1958–1959 (the Jack Report)*, Government Printer, Salisbury, 1959

MALAWI GOVERNMENT *Development Plan* 1965–1969 Government Printer, Zomba, 1964

—— 'Background Information to the Budget 1966', *Treasury Document No. 5*, Government Printer, Zomba, 1966

—— *Prospects for Industrial Development*, Government Printer, Zomba, 1966

—— *Economic Report*, Government Printer, Zomba, 1967

—— *Economic Report*, Government Printer, Zomba, 1968

—— *Development Programme 1968–1970* Government Printer, Zomba, 1969

—— *Development Programme 1970–1972/73*, Government Printer, Zomba, 1970

NYASALAND PROTECTORATE *Report of the Post-War Development Committee*, Government Printer, Zomba, 1946

—— *Report of the Nyasaland Land Commission (The Abrahams Report)*, Government Printer, Zomba, 1946

—— *Capital Development Plan 1957/61* Government Printer, Zomba, 1957

—— *Development Plan 1962–1965*, Government Printer, Zomba, 1962

APPENDIX

RAINFALL CHARACTERISTICS OF MALAWI* (Chapter 10)

Rainfall district	Average rainfall (inches) Wet	Dry	Ann.	Driest year %	Wettest year %	Coefficient of variation Wet	Dry	Ann.	Nov. to Mar.	April and May	June to Aug.	Sept. and Oct.
Mulanje	73·2	11·0	84·2	60	146	0·21	0·45	0·20	75	12	8	5
Cholo Highlands	48·7	6·1	54·8	59	144	0·27	0·39	0·22	79	10	7	4
Shire Highlands	46·1	3·2	49·3	53	154	0·23	0·48	0·23	88	7	3	2
Palombe	37·0	0·9	37·9	50	164	0·31	—	0·31	92	5	1	2
Lower Shire	30·1	3·0	33·1	42	167	0·29	0·46	0·30	85	8	5	2
Upper Shire	29·4	1·1	30·5	55	150	0·24	—	0·24	91	6	1	2
Nsanje Hills	53·0	10·1	63·1	47	154	0·27	0·44	0·28	77	10	10	3
Namweras	39·4	1·0	40·4	51	165	0·23	—	0·23	92	5	1	3
Kirk Range	39·1	2·1	41·2	53	150	0·24	0·35	0·21	90	6	2	2
S.W. Lake	44·5	1·2	45·7	58	184	0·26	—	0·25	90	8	0	2
Central Province	34·9	0·7	35·6	58	144	0·21	—	0·21	94	5	0	1
Mzimba	33·5	0·5	34·0	64	142	0·17	—	0·15	94	5	0	1
Vipya	38·6	20·4	59·0	60	166	0·23	0·65	0·24	73	25	1	1
W. Lake	67·4	4·2	71·6	60	165	0·25	0·75	0·26	66	28	5	1
Nyika	49·6	3·6	53·2	66	157	0·24	0·55	0·25	74	21	4	1
N. Lake	38·9	1·9	40·8	62	161	0·20	0·56	0·20	90	8	1	1
Chitipa	33·6	2·9	36·5	60	158	0·19	—	0·19	98	1	0	1

Season rainfall in % of mean of district

* Taken with permission from J G Pike and G T Rimmington *Malawi: a geographical study*, Oxford, 1965

SHIRE RIVER, MEAN ANNUAL FLOW IN CUSECS, 1948–69 (Chapter 11)

Year	Liwonde	Matope	Chikwawa	Chiromo	Nsanje*
1948–49	10 557	10 265	—	10 798	9 459
1949–50	10 392	10 804	—	11 480	9 677
1950–51	10 474	10 754	—	11 089	9 534
1951–52	12 090	12 808	14 243	14 743	11 022
1952–53	10 468	10 754	11 165	11 545	10 023
1953–54	7 855	8 179	8 215	7 729	7 349
1954–55	7 179	7 828	8 309	9 108	8 529
1955–56	8 106	8 616	9 493	9 633	8 475
1956–57†	2 667	2 810	3 424	3 091	4 932
1957–58	14 070	14 317	14 674	15 168	10 875
1958–59	11 422	11 497	11 644	12 300	10 106
1959–60	9 942	10 064	10 186	9 983	9 819
1960–61	9 342	9 613	10 388	10 374	10 191
1961–62	12 702	12 835	13 665	13 576	11 615
1962–63	15 067	17 085	18 622	20 836	13 815
1963–64	17 691	18 364	19 573	19 738	15 086
1964–65	12 758	13 585	13 470	14 271	no data
1965–66	8 700	8 911	10 558	7 049	no data
1966–67	11 953	12 392	12 201	11 071	13 986
1967–68	14 122	14 717	14 244	14 409	14 874
1968–69	10 003	9 903	10 178	12 708	no data

Source: Water Resources Division, Ministry of Agriculture and Natural Resources, Zomba.

* Drop in the flow at Nsanje may be accounted for by the spread of the waters through Dinde Marsh. The flow at Chiromo is affected by the Elephant marsh and by back flow from the Ruo River at flood.

† During this year the flow of the Shire River was restricted by the construction of a barrage at Liwonde. The barrage was breached in August 1957.

LEGEND AND KEY TO VEGETATION (Chapter 13)

1 Montane grasslands, scrubs and forests — Evergreen Forest relics; *Exotheca; Andropogon; Monocymbium; Loudetia* Grasslands, *Protea* Shrub-Grasslands; Montane Evergreen Scrub. *Acacia abyssinica.*

1A Moist semi-deciduous forest — *Burttdavya nyasica; Chlorophora excelsa; Piptadeniastrum buchananii.*

2 *Brachystegia* woodlands and scrubs — *Brachystegia spiciformis; B. manga; B. floribunda; B. boehmii; B. longifolia; B. allenii; B. tamarindoides; B. taxifolia* woodlands and scrubs. *Julbernardia globiflora; J. paniculata; Isoberlinia angolensis; I. tomentosa* woodlands and scrubs. *Burkea africana. Uapaca kirkiana* woodlands and scrubs. *Hyparrhenia* and *Arundinelleae* swamps and seasonal swamps.

2A *Brachystegia* and evergreens — *Brachystegia spiciformis, Erythrophloeum maraviense, Saba* woodland. *Brachystegia longifolia, Uapaca* spp. woodland. *Piptadeniastrum buchananii.*

3 *Combretum; Acacia; Piliostigma* woodlands and scrubs — *Combretum* spp.; *Piliostigma thonningii; Acacia polycantha* var. *campylacantha; Pterocarpus angolensis; P. rotundifolius; Erythrina tomentosa* woodlands. *Markhamia; Securinega virosa; Royena sericea* scrubs. *Hyparrhenia* and *Arundinelleae* swamps and seasonal swamps.

4 Escarpment and foothill woodlands, scrubs and thickets — *Grewia* spp.; *Hymenocardia; Capparis; Popowia obovata* thickets. *Adansonia digitata; Sclerocarya birrea; Kirkia acuminata; Sterculia quinquiloba* standards and thicket. *Oxytenanthera abyssinica* brakes. *Brachystegia boehmii; Julbernardia globiflora; Bauhinia petersiana; Pterocarpus angolensis* woodlands.

5 Lowland, lake and river plains, woodlands, thickets, scrubs and parklands — *Adansonia digitata; Sterculia appendiculata; S. africana; Sclerocarya birrea; Ostryoderris stuhlmannii; Cordyla africana* parklands. *Hyphaene ventricosa; Ricinodendron rautanenii; Terminalia sericea; Albizia harveyi; Delbergia melanoxylon; Acacia polyacantha* var. *campylacantha; A. spirocarpa A. xanthophloea; Dichrostachys cinerea* woodlands and thickets. *Pterocarpus atunesii; Fagara* sp.; *Grewia* spp.; *Acacia pennata; Acanthaceae* thickets and standards. *Euphorbia ingens; Commiphora* sp. thickets.

6 Mopane woodland — *Colophospermum* mopane woodland with glades.

7 Alluvia parkland — *Acacia albida; Cordyla africana* standards with cultivations.

8 *Terminalia* woodlands — *Terminalia sericea* semi-swamp woodlands. *Terminalia sericea, Brachystegia boehmii* woodland. *Terminalia sericea* on sandbars.

9 Swamp and swamp grasslands — *Typha australis; Vossia cuspidata; Phragmites mauritianus; Pennisetum purpureum; Echinochloa pyramidalis* swamps. *Chloris gayana; Hyparrhenia. rufa; Setaria palustris; Bothriochloa; Cynodon* spp.; *Panicum* spp. grasslands

PRINCIPAL DEMOGRAPHIC INDICES FOR POPULATIONS IN INFORMATION AREAS CLASSIFIED BY DEMOGRAPHIC STRUCTURE TYPES, 1966 (Chapter 28)

Type	Proportion of total population aged under 5	Child-woman ratio	Sex rate specific to age 15–64	Sex rate specific to age 15–29	Dependency rate	Population Number	Population Per cent	Information Areas Rural	Information Areas Urban
A	19·4	878	1473	1246	730	14 624	0·4	—	14
B	17·6	772	1390	1265	696	215 246	5·3	3	8
C	17·0	747	1457	1300	668	33 664	0·8	2	6
D	19·9	821	818	806	1007	647 582	16·0	35	—
E	18·6	746	829	843	936	1 801 166	44·6	62	3
F	17·0	630	788	718	814	612 499	15·2	26	3
G	20·8	838	675	669	1084	50 638	1·3	4	—
H	18·9	769	705	667	1017	524 658	13·0	28	—
I	17·6	626	635	594	908	139 506	3·5	9	1
MALAWI	18·6	740	827	809	921	4 039 583	100·0	169	35

PROPORTION OF AFRICAN POPULATION 5–24 YEARS OLD ATTENDING SCHOOL, MALAWI, 1966 (Chapter 30)

	5	6	7	8	9	10	11	12	13	14
Males	2·7	6·3	13·7	19·7	26·5	29·1	35·3	35·8	39·6	40·4
Females	2·2	5·1	10·8	15·6	20·9	22·8	29·3	28·4	27·9	26·1

	15	16	17	18	19	20	21	22	23	24
Males	40·5	35·0	31·0	29·8	27·2	20·2	15·3	10·3	7·2	4·4
Females	23·3	15·2	9·1	7·3	4·4	2·2	1·5	1·0	0·7	0·6

AGRICULTURAL RESEARCH AND TRAINING FACILITIES AND MALAWI YOUNG PIONEERS (Chapter 33)

1 Misuku
2 Chitipa
3 Kaporo
4 Baka (Karonga)
5 Chilumba
6 Nchenanchena
7 Bolero
8 Kacheche
9 Mpherembe
10 Euthini
11 M'mbelwa
12 Mbawa
13 Emfeni
14 Mzuzu
15 Chinteche
16 Kaluluma
17 Chulu
18 Lisasadzi
19 Santhe
20 Ntchisi
21 Madisi
22 Mponela
23 Chisepo
24 Nambuma
25 Dowa
26 Mchinji
27 Tembwe
28 Kasiya
29 Namitete
30 Nsaru
31 Lumbadzi
32 Mpingu
33 Sinyala
34 Mkwinda
35 Kampini
36 Nathenje
37 Chimutu
38 Lobi
39 Dedza
40 Mtakataka
41 Nkhota Kota
42 Benga
43 Chitala
44 Nkhande
45 Nsipe
46 Sharpevale
47 Nankhumba
48 Mangoche
49 Namwera
50 Ntaja
51 Balaka
52 Malosa
53 Zomba
54 Chingale
55 Makoka
56 Chiradzulu
57 Lunzu
58 Symon
59 Mwanza
60 Thyolo
61 Masambanjati
62 Thuchila
63 Naminjiwa
64 Migowi
65 Mulanje
66 Chikwawa
67 Ngabu
68 Chiromo
69 Nsanje
70 Katuwo
71 Rumphi
72 Chikwina
73 Kamwanjiwa
74 Dwambadzi
75 Lisandwa
76 Mchinji
77 Lilongwe
78 Dedza
79 Chipoka
80 Mwalawayela
81 Lipinda
82 Chifumbe
83 Nasawa
84 Neno
85 Amalika
86 Kakoma
87 Chikonje
88 Senga
89 Hara
90 Rumphi
91 Limphasa
92 Salima
93 Rivirivi
94 Likangala
95 Mangulenje
96 Lunyangwa
97 Dwangwa
98 Chitedze
99 Bembeke
100 Tsangano
101 Bvumbwe
102 Thyolo
103 Swazi
104 Mimosa
105 Tomali
106 Makanga

KEY TO FORESTRY RESERVES (Chapter 39)

1 Matipa
2 Wilindi
3 Mugesse
4 Musissi
5 Vinthukutu
6 Nyika Plateau
7 Mzumara
8 Vwaza
9 Kaningina
10 Lunyangwa
11 Lusangadzi
12 Mtangatanga
13 Perekezi
14 Kalwe
15 Nkwadzi Hill
16 Chisasira
17 Ruvue
18 Kuwirwi
19 Chimalire
20 Kasungu
21 Mchinji
22 Nkhota Kota
23 Ntchisi
24 Mndilansadzu
25 Ngara
26 Kongwe
27 Nalikule
28 Lingadzi
29 Bunda
30 Dzalanyama
31 Tuma
32 Senga Hills
33 Maleri Islands
34 Dzenza
35 Mua Livulezi
36 Dedza Mountain
37 Chongoni
38 South Malawi Islands
39 Mua Tsanya
40 Bangwe
41 Pirilongwe
42 Mvai
43 Dzonze
44 Tsamba
45 Tambani
46 Majete
47 Lengwe
48 Mwabvi
49 Matandwe
50 Massenjere
51 Kalulu
52 Cholomwani
53 Thyolo Mountains
54 Mirale
55 Kanjedza & Soche
56 Chigumula
57 Chigwaja
58 Ndirande
59 Chiradzulu Mountains
60 Malabvi
61 Thuchila
62 Litchenya
63 Mulanje Mountain
64 Fort Lister
65 Michesi
66 Sambani
67 Zomba Mountain
68 Mulosa
69 Liwonde
70 Liwonde
71 Mangoche
72 Namizimu

ESTIMATED LANDINGS OF FISH (in short tons)
(Chapter 40)

Years	Lake Malawi	Lake Malombe & Upper Shire River	Lake Chilwa	Lake Chiuta	Lower Shire River	Totals
1963	8 100	2900	3600	100	400	15 100
1964	6 800	1300	5800	200	400	14 500
1965	7 100	1700	9800	200	2000	20 800
1966	6 400	3200	8000	200	1500	19 300
1967	5 900	4400	3600	200	1700	15 800
1968	8 600	8600	100 (1)	200	2300	19 800
1969	12 300 (2)	2600	3200	200	7200	25 500

(1) The fall in the amount of fish landed from Lake Chilwa in 1968 was due to continued drought and partial drying up of the lake. Many fishermen moved to Lake Malombe fisheries.

(2) The increase from Lake Malawi may be due to improved sampling methods.

OFFICIALLY DESIGNATED TRADING CENTRES BY PLANNING REGIONS,
(IN RELATION TO POPULATION AND OCCUPIED AREA), MID-1970. (Chapter 49)

	Lower Shire	Southern	South Central	Central	Central Lakeshore	North Central	Northern	Malawi
TCs of								
Grade A	2	4	2	2	1	—	—	11
Grade B	1	6	2	8	1	1	—	19
Grade C	5	28	12	22	5	6	2	80
Grade D	16	30	27	35	9	11	13	141
TCUs	100	518	175	361	69	70	49	1 342
Average estimated 1970 population per 'trading centre unit':								
	2 919	2 930	4 012	3 619	2 438	5 793	3 152	3 388
Average estimated 1970 population per trading centres of grade A, B and C:								
	36 500	37 900	43 900	39 600	57 900	24 000	77 200	41 333
Square miles of occupied land per 'trading centre unit':								
	5·5	2·9	6·6	6·7	5·3	20·3	6·7	5·8
Square miles of occupied land per trading centre of grade A, B and C:								
	68·2	37·7	72·2	73·4	202·9	51·8	165·0	70·4

TABLE 1 – IMPORTS CLASSIFIED BY END-USE*, 1967–9 (Chapter 58)

	1967 %	1967 £'000	1968 %	1968 £'000	1969 %	1969 £'000
Consumer goods	25	6 377	22	6 313	20	6 001
Non-durable goods	(21)	(5419)	(19)	(5422)	(17)	(5114)
Durable goods	(4)	(958)	(3)	(891)	(3)	(887)
Plant machinery and equipment	10	2 484	15	4 381	13	3 989
Operating machines	(6)	(1481)	(10)	(3042)		(2648)
Auxiliary equipment	(4)	(1003)	(5)	(1339)		(1341)
Transport means	14	3 611	16	4 536	15	4 720
Motor cars and bicycles	(4)	(1118)	(4)	(1024)	(3)	(1028)
Other	(10)	(2493)	(12)	(3512)	(12)	(3692)
Materials for building and construction	7	1 723	7	2 167	10	2 997
Basic and auxiliary materials for industry	26	6 667	23	6 674	26	7 880
Parts, tools and miscellaneous appliances	2	629	3	812	3	920
Commodities for intermediate and final consumption	13	3 343	12	3 548	11	
Fabric	(9)	(2215)	(7)	(1998)	(6)	(1885)
Oils, fuels and lubricants	(4)	(1114)	(5)	(1528)	(5)	(1637)
Other	(—)	(14)	(—)	(22)	(—)	(12)
Import transactions under £10	1	300	1	297	1	290
Miscellaneous transactions	1	292	1	363	1	408
TOTAL	100	25 426	100	29 090	100	30 739

* The end-use classification was revised at the beginning of 1967.

Source: *Annual Statement of External Trade*, 1969, Government Printer, Zomba.

TABLE 2: PRINCIPAL DOMESTIC EXPORT COMMODITIES

Description	1967 Quantity (LB'000)	1967 Value (£'000)	1968 Quantity (LB'000)	1968 Value (£'000)	1969 Quantity (LB'000)	1969 Value (£'000)
Tobacco, unmanufactured	32 614	4 226	35 506	5 285	32 144	6 323
Tea	37 126	4 491	34 815	4 850	38 024	4 763
Groundnuts	112 535	3 434	66 129	2 308	75 530	2 795
Cotton fibres	6 942	692	5 484	637	8 410	865
Beans, peas, etc., dried	60 327	764	22 909	431	34 945	511
Maize	201 600	1 639	191 744	1 504	104 288	1 066
Tung oil	3 882	205	2 072	123	2 515	153
Rice	3 346	79	1 967	47	3 699	137
Cassava	47 047	266	105 143	692	48 422	319
Coffee	371	51	435	56	397	50
Sisal fibres	677	18	249	7	—	1
Cattle-cake of oilseed	6 162	112	10 234	144	11 222	180
Wooden boxes	4 390	54	1 008	13	1 146	27
Hides and skins	745	84	740	83	717	91
Cement	4 552	34	13 240	89	—	—
Sunflower seeds	780	11	1 453	29	6 327	86
Other commodities	—	392	—	481	—	918
TOTAL domestic exports	—	16 552	—	16 779	—	18 285

Source: *Annual Statement of External Trade*, 1969, Government Printer, Zomba.